Pamela Nevills

Build the Brain for Reading
Grades 4–12

Foreword by
Patricia Wolfe

CORWIN
A SAGE Company

For information:

Corwin
A SAGE Company
2455 Teller Road
Thousand Oaks, California 91320
(800) 233-9936
Fax: (800) 417-2466
www.corwin.com

SAGE Ltd.
1 Oliver's Yard
55 City Road
London EC1Y 1SP
United Kingdom

SAGE India Pvt. Ltd.
B 1/I 1 Mohan Cooperative Industrial Area
Mathura Road, New Delhi 110 044
India

SAGE Asia-Pacific Pte. Ltd.
33 Pekin Street #02-01
Far East Square
Singapore 048763

Printed in the United States of America

Library of Congress Cataloging-in-Publication Data

Nevills, Pamela.
Build the brain for reading, grades 4-12 / Pamela Nevills; foreword by Patricia Wolfe.
    p. cm.
Includes bibliographical references and index.
ISBN 978-1-4129-6111-0

    1. Developmental reading. 2. Reading—Physiological aspects. 3. Reading, Psychology of. I. Title.

LB1573.8.N48 2011
372.41′6—dc22   2010031506

This book is printed on acid-free paper.

11   12   13   14   15   10   9   8   7   6   5   4   3   2   1

Acquisitions Editor:	Jessica Allan
Associate Editor:	Allison Scott
Editorial Assistant:	Lisa Whitney
Production Editor:	Amy Schroller
Copy Editor:	Adam Dunham
Typesetter:	C&M Digitals (P) Ltd.
Proofreader:	Joyce Li
Indexer:	Judy Hunt
Cover Designer:	Karine Hovsepian

Contents

Foreword

While nearly all of us read easily and with comprehension, most do not realize that, inherently, reading is an abnormal act. When we are born, there are no hardwired neural tracts for reading: We are not genetically predisposed to read. How then does the brain accomplish such a sophisticated task? This is a paradox whose answer has long eluded the best efforts of scientific and educational researchers. This is now changing.

Although much remains to be discovered, the advent of brain imaging has begun to unlock the black box of the brain, and a scientific understanding of the reading process is evolving.

Using some of the most current findings from neuroscience research, Nevills has written a sequel to the book, *Building the Reading Brain: PreK–3* (Nevills & Wolfe, 2009). This new publication focuses on older learners and readers, how their reading proficiency develops, how their brains differ from those of young learners, and how their unique needs can best be met. In this volume, Nevills deftly melds theory and practice. Sections of the book labeled Serious Brain Matters are dedicated to assisting the reader in understanding the brain structures and functions that underpin the learning process. These sections provide teachers with the foundational information they need to teach their students about their brains and how they learn. Following each of these technical pieces, Nevills then provides teachers with guidelines on how to explain the information to their students in nontechnical language.

Further enhancing the practicality of this book are chapters that suggest brain-compatible teaching strategies and resources for all subject areas generally using the standard curriculum materials teachers have on hand. Especially interesting and useful is the discussion of new technology, how it impacts the brains of today's learners, and how teachers can infuse this technology into their classroom instruction.

It is often stated that in the early years of schooling the focus is on learning to read, and from that point on the focus is on reading to learn. Given that this is probably an accurate statement, we are fortunate to have a book that gives classroom teachers the understanding and tools they need to help all their students enjoy the success that comes from reading to learn.

Patricia Wolfe, EdD
Napa, California

Preface

There are many reasons why a sequel to the popular *Building the Reading Brain, PreK–3* (Nevills & Wolfe, 2009) is necessary. Most obvious is the fact that the initial book culminates with third grade. Together, *Building the Reading Brain* and *Build the Brain for Reading* provide administrators, teachers, parents, and other professionals a composite look at the development of the brain for reading at each crucial stage. Children learn to read in the early elementary years and spend the remainder of their school years and their adult lives *reading to learn.*

Certain features of this book make it ideal for teachers and parents who work with older students and also make it unique. *What can you tell your students about . . .* sections provide a steady progression of what students can be told and what they can talk about to understand their own developing brains, encouraging them to become responsive and responsible learners. Students are empowered to partner with their teachers to learn and to know how to use their class and study time efficiently. Another helpful feature is the expanded use of tables and figures. Together with a talented friend, Herbert Higashi, the author was able to broaden information from the text through a variety of pictorial and chart related visuals. Their partnership illustrates the powerful thinking that comes from collaborative projects for adults as it does for children. Teachers can copy figures that provide pictures of the human brain to deepen understanding, or they can use tables to support learning, such as Table 8.2, Instruction for the Complex Nature of Reading Comprehension.

Is there a need for neuroscientists and educators to become partners? Is there a need for educators to know how their students learn and how they can orchestrate the learning environment to capture students' involvement and increase learning potential? With the world population advancing in knowledge, skills, and technology at exponential speed, working together is one sure way to obtain a greater understanding of our student population. A system of education that reflects how students learn can offer its students the best education possible to prepare them for a future with unpredictable demands on its future adult society.

Current, cutting-edge neurology is infused into every aspect of this book. Teachers and neurologists working together have identified a new field of study, neuroeducation. Although we are not completely adept at communicating and understanding how we each approach our work, there are some exciting outgrowths of the initial attempts to work together. Educators must exercise caution when they examine results from studies that use brain neuroimaging for classroom correlations or implications. When the same results are seen over and over again, researchers often conclude that one action causes the other. For example, recent discussion about teenagers and their behavior tends to identify the brain as the sole contributor to adolescents' good and unacceptable behavior. There is a correlation between how the brain is developing and how teens act; however, it is not proven that the developing brain causes all the behavior. Accordingly, there are neurologists who question the correlation altogether. There is a strong argument that the environment may also have a causal impact on adolescent behavior. This titillating discussion is featured in Chapter 6, Motivation and Ability to Learn Through the Grades: How Different Is an Adolescent's Brain?

An example of the numerous studies featured in this book is found in Chapter 9. A number of children received music training. At the end of the study, diffusion tensor imaging was used to map the brain's connective white matter. Strengthened connections among areas of the brain for auditory processing and motor skills were observed in the group that had music lessons. Some would take this information to mean music training could improve reading performance, because auditory processing, a major task of successful reading, was observed to have greater white matter connections. That response could be surmised, but it is not proven by a singular study. These results should be replicated for other visual and performing arts lessons. Increased connections in the auditory parts of the brain could be the result of any performing arts venue that has the potential to increase student attention, rehearsal, practice, and performance.

First and foremost in teachers' minds is the question, So what do I do about that in my classroom? There is a plethora of practical and easy to use teaching strategies, prompts, projects, and sample ideas for teaching units beginning in Chapter 3. All examples and suggestions feature efficient and effective teaching strategies reflective of neurologists' reports on the learning brain. Major research findings are abundant. An exhaustive reference section is provided for inquisitive readers to further their knowledge base. This combination of neurology and education helps educators grasp how and why students learn and realize that all students learn in personally unique ways that can be met in the regular classroom. Teaching suggestions are based on a standard curriculum with materials that are available in classrooms everywhere. Of crucial importance are the decisions teachers make for what to teach, how much depth or information and concepts to teach, how long to practice, and how to maximize learning through student engagement.

Four different assessments are available. The opening chapter invites teachers to do a self-assessment of classroom practices. The ideal classroom for a primary student differs greatly from the classroom needs of the upper elementary student. Add the pre-teen's needs based upon a developing brain, and specifications for the ideal classroom environment changes again. Finally, it is accepted that the adolescent's learning needs are closer to the needs of an adult than to that of a child. So, what are ideal characteristics of a classroom designed for the non-idyllic needs of high school students?

A student assessment in Chapter 7 helps them to understand overconfidence in what they think they have learned and how they can better develop a deep understanding of the topics they are studying. Research indicates that most students tend to think they know more than they actually do, which creates a problem for students when they take an exam. Neuroscience has an explanation for this situation and a solution for students to practice. Another assessment for students is found in the final chapter. The questionnaire looks at how students respond when they are exposed to ideal, brain-compatible teaching environments versus when the environment is not ideal. Students provide answers in focus groups at school or individually at home. The responses help all teachers understand how their teaching styles affect the learning attitudes of their students. Actual responses from students in the upper elementary and middle school grades are given for teachers to identify student comments that could represent the teaching environments they provide for their students. Teachers can also help students understand critical thinking, and lead them through an assessment of their skills in Chapter 7.

Teachers of all subject areas will find new and innovative teaching ideas. While initial chapters bring the brain into focus, subsequent chapters cover how the ability to read develops. As students become dependent on reading for learning, the impact reading has on each subject becomes clear. The last two chapters address all the content areas. Chapter 9 relates information from neurology to each subject area while the final chapter gives practical neurology-based classroom strategies and resources.

We are reaching and teaching the technogeneration. So, it is fitting that brain development is matched with teaching strategies that make innovative use of media and technology. Researchers are beginning to provide reports of technology's impact on youth. What is happening to the brains of students who are growing up in a world infused with technology? How can technology become a part of classrooms in a variety of ways and for a variety of subjects? And, to what extent is the use of technology compatible with how the human brain learns? These and a host of other questions are addressed as the fields of neurology, education, and technology are infused in Chapters 7, 9, and 10.

Acknowledgments

Corwin gratefully acknowledges the contributions of the following reviewers:

Diane Barone
Professor, Literacy
University of Nevada
Reno, NV

Dr. Heather Driscoll
Founder, Revolutionary Classrooms
New Castle, NH

Deborah C. Henry
Medical Physician/ Doctor of
    Neurology
Loma Linda Medical Center
Loma Linda, CA

Rosalind LaRocque, PhD
Professional Development for
    Educators
American Federation of Teachers
Washington, DC

Darron Laughland
Special Education/English Teacher
Kennett High School
Conway, NH

Karen J. Lehman, EdD
Assistant Professor, Special
    Education
New Mexico Highlands University
Farmington, NM

About the Author

 Primarily an educator, **Pamela Nevills** held various positions and leadership roles in education. She began as a teacher in grades one through eight and has managed and supervised programs for preschool through high school youth. Her expertise as a staff developer began with a county-level program; later, she managed a curriculum and instruction office. Additional activities include state-level leadership for teacher professional development and student-to-work programs, support for a mathematics research project spanning four states, and two-time participation on a state reading/language arts instructional materials selection panel. Pamela's other positions include supervision for student and intern teachers for the University of California, Riverside, a lecturer for multiple subjects' methodology classes, and she is coauthor with Dr. Patricia Wolfe of the book *Building the Reading Brain*. She is published through the state of California, the *Journal of Staff Development,* and she contributes to organizational newsletters. Of additional and very current interest is her new work emanating from neuroscience with a focus on mathematics.

As an instructor of children and adults, Dr. Nevills studies neurology, mind imaging, and research for education and neurology. By combining information about how the brain functions with learning, she provides insights for teachers to understand memory systems, to engage learners, to maintain attention and concentration, to access the best brain systems to help children become competent readers, and to organize learning for automatic and in depth recall. As a consultant and speaker, she has reached participants both nationally and internationally.

Pamela's website can be found at pamelanevills.com. She can be reached at 1619 Tecalote Drive, Fallbrook, CA 92028; phone (760) 723–8116; e-mail address: panevills@earthlink.net.

CORWIN
A SAGE Company

The Corwin logo—a raven striding across an open book—represents the union of courage and learning. Corwin is committed to improving education for all learners by publishing books and other professional development resources for those serving the field of PreK–12 education. By providing practical, hands-on materials, Corwin continues to carry out the promise of its motto: **"Helping Educators Do Their Work Better."**

1

Learning From Childhood to Adulthood

All learners are not alike. Learners at the same age do not have the same learning needs. Students from different age groups have unpredictable learning preferences that cannot be accommodated with a singular instructional approach. The system designed for education responds to this multifaceted learning crisis by varying instructional materials, curricula, classroom structure, and teaching strategies. Has the education system, however, done enough to respect and understand the learning requirements of each child or young adult? Realize that each learner possesses an unimaginably intricate human **brain** that is capable of modifying itself to respond to an ever-changing world. Each human brain is equipped with neurological richness through thoughts, plans, memories, and feelings. What is it that educators do not understand about student learning that could revolutionize schools into more effective learning environments? A place to begin is to study the learning organ, the human brain, beginning with an overview of its learning attributes.

In this chapter, issues of the brain are addressed, such as making a distinction between the terms *brain* and ***mind.*** Although the two words are frequently used as synonymous, each can be distinctly identified. The human brain is also described by an analysis of its physical attributes and its mental ability to remain open to learning throughout a human's lifetime. Mostly, it is known that the brain was designed for survival, but the attributes of learning through engagement and novelty are explored in many ways for their unique ability to incite and then to cement learning.

Learning itself can be somewhat mystifying. Most adult learners have not given much thought to how they learn. Children and young adults generally are untrained in practices that can help them to become better students. Specific sections of all but the last chapter address what students can be told about their brains and how they can take charge of how learning happens. The sections are identified by topic titles, such as, *What can you tell your students about* . . . Learners at any age have unique needs based on their physical and mental development. Characteristics of effective classrooms at primary through secondary schools are explored to discover how learning is maximized for the varying and unique needs of students in public, private, and charter schools.

ARE MIND AND BRAIN THE SAME?

Some people would say the terms *the mind* and *the brain* can be used interchangeably. For our purpose, which is to understand brain function and how students react and behave, they are not. The brain is referred to as part of the central nervous system, which is composed of the physiological structures in our heads and the spinal column with a system of nerves that spreads throughout the body. The brain is physically present. The mind differs in that it is consumed with thoughts, memories, feelings, and decisions that result from the chemical and electrical responses and connections within the brain. The workings of the mind are observed by the actions people take and the words they speak. While the brain allows an individual to speak, what is spoken can be attributed to the mind.

The mind as a complex structure is described by Steven Pinker (1997), a cognitive scientist who directs the Center for Cognitive Neuroscience at Massachusetts Institute of Technology.

> The mind is a system of organs of computation, designed by natural selection to solve the kinds of problems our ancestors faced in their foraging way of life, in particular, understanding and outmaneuvering objects, animals, plants, and other people. (p. 21)

Rita Carter (1998), writing during the same time, refers to a map of the mind that cannot tell us all of its secrets. She provides a word of caution as we go about the work of exploring the brain: "The current vision of the brain provided by neuroscience is most likely no more complete or accurate than a sixteenth century map of the world" (p. 8).

Noted author and professor Robert Sylwester (2005) in his book *How to Describe a Brain: An Educator's Handbook of Brain Terms and Cognitive Processes,* as well as other authors (Berninger & Richards, 2002; Doidge, 2008; Lyon & Krasnegor, 2001; Wolf, 2007), do not provide a definitive response to the question of the mind as different from the human brain. However, the issue remains and is powerful enough for Schwartz and Begley (2003), a research professor of psychiatry and a science columnist, to write a book titled *The Mind & the Brain: Neuroplasticity and the Power of Mental Force*. It is interesting to note how these authors approach the brain-mind connection.

> The explanatory gap has never been bridged. And the inescapable reason is this: a neural state is not a mental state. The mind is not the brain, though it depends on the material brain for its existence (as far as we know). (p. 29)

As the question of the use of mind and brain is far from being clear, another choice is to go to one who attempts to answer such sticky questions for children. In a book designed for inquisitive youngsters, *101 Questions Your Brain Couldn't Answer Until Now,* author Hickman Brynie (1998) responds to the question, "What's the difference between brain and mind?" Instead of a response from the author, Hickman Brynie searched writings from brain experts Restak, Crick, Pert, and Sir John Eccles and found no conclusive statement. Is the mind an illusion? Is it the responses and behaviors that result from the functioning of the physical structures within the brain? Possibly, it so closely aligned with the chemical and electrical happenings of this magnificent organ, the brain, that it cannot be separated (Hickman Brynie, 1998). The mind and the brain work together and need one another. They appear to be distinctly different in how they function. The brain is a collection of the physical structures for processing sensory input. The mind with its behaviors, emotional responses, memories, and phenomenon of new ideas continually reacts to the perceptual processes of the brain. One could say humans are identified by three distinct parts, the brain and the mind, which are unique from but jointly in control of the third part, the body.

WHAT CAN YOU TELL YOUR STUDENTS ABOUT THE MIND AND THE BRAIN?

Some people use the words brain *and* mind *like they are the same thing. However, we know the brain is a material thing (an organ), while the mind responds to what the brain is able to do (based upon chemical and electrical signals). You can see and touch the brain to know it exists, although you would need to have surgery to do so. You know the thoughts of the mind by listening to what you think and say and by looking at what you do.*

SERIOUS BRAIN MATTERS—LEARNING ATTRIBUTES OF STUDENTS' BRAINS

There are many approaches to studying the human brain. One way is to view the structures that constitute this elegant living organ, which is the focus of Chapter 2 (see Figure 2.3). Science has given a specific name to the study of the anatomy of the human brain, **neuroanatomy.** It includes revealing the structures of the **central nervous system** (the brain and the spinal cord) and the peripheral nervous system (the nerves in the **cranium** and spinal cord), which carries information throughout the body (Pence & Justice, 2008).

A second approach is the study of **neurophysiology,** which gives insights into the ways brain structures work together as a complex unit. This particular type of study examines brain activity when a specific task needs to be processed. Educators want to know how the physical structures interlace and bind the brain with the mind and the body. Neurophysiology provides an understanding of how students learn and process information when the brain reacts to incoming seemingly senseless data and makes sense of these experiences and environments throughout life.

Plasticity and the Human Brain

What would life be like if the human brain stopped changing at adulthood? People could not meet and remember new friends, keep in mind events from day to day, or even know who they are through age-related changes. The body's 30,000 genes are assigned the awesome responsibility of developing the human brain, beginning at conception, and to finish the job as work orders culminate at adulthood. However, the brain continues to be capable of learning and changing throughout life. Genetically controlled, time-sensitive periods occur during childhood and during the young adult years. Ongoing changes during adulthood at the **neuron** and **synapse** level allow humans to continue learning and responding to new information and changes from their environments.

Young children learn at an amazing rate as they literally grow their brains from an approximate one pound structure at birth to a three pound organ by the time of adolescence. All of the brain's structures and capabilities are present at birth. What is not in place is an extensive, dense wiring system among the neurons within the brain's parts and the development of pathways among cognitive systems. The wiring between neurons and the firing of the neurons actualize human learning potential.

Careful observation of a baby during waking hours validates that the main job of a young child is to figure out the environment, experiment with words, and express needs and wants. Growth and connections are occurring at the neuron level. Everything a very young child sees, touches, hears, tastes, or focuses on translates into electrical and chemical activity in the infinitesimally tiny nerve cells of the brain. A sorting process strengthens and speeds the connections that are frequented. Other intermittent connections, which are not reinforced, atrophy and are eliminated. This process, which is called *synaptic pruning,* occurs during childhood and is enormous. Eliot (1999) estimates that children lose as many as 20 billion connections during the preschool years. This neural and synaptic loss is a good thing, resulting in clear, efficient lines of communication and connections for the complex workings of the youngster's brain. Strengthened pathways provide an appropriate and necessary knowledge base and learning systems for children to survive and thrive in their environments.

This level of growth and pruning cannot continue. At the onset of adolescence, the human brain is basically organized and connected with the foundation and framework for learning for the rest of the human's life. From that time, the brain's plasticity is more limited as the brain's organization is mostly complete, but the organ continues to add depth of connections to enrich memory for life's experiences. People continue to respond to environmental changes through an elaborate sorting, filing, and categorization system. Adults learn new ideas, concepts, or skills with ease when they connect the new learning to something they have previously mastered. Although adult brains are less plastic than children's brains, they are certainly more efficient and every bit as purposeful.

The Physical Appearance of the Brain

The brain itself is a physical mass that weighs approximately three pounds (see Figure 1.1). It is similar to the size of a coconut, and its shape can best be imagined as a half of a shelled walnut. The brain's consistency is like Jell-O, and its overall color would resemble partially cooked liver. It is also referred to as the ***cerebral cortex.*** Contrary to what is frequently said about the color of the brain, it is not all **gray matter.** The living brain has a massive network of blood vessels on the surface which give it more of a pinkish color with other layers of neuron bodies and connections appearing as gray or white areas. The brain demands at least one-fifth of the blood pumped by the heart, and from the blood it extracts oxygen, carbon dioxide, and **glucose.** Other unhealthy substances that may be circulating from other parts of the body are stopped by a blood-brain barrier. Gray matter extends through six layers of the cortex and is made up of hundreds of millions of neurons forming wispy-like columns. An **axon** is a long extended arm emanating from each neuron that reaches out for connections to other neurons to form networks of **white matter.** Collectively, the white substance is composed of myelin sheaths that feed, cover, and protect the axons and form the blood-brain barrier (Berninger & Richards, 2002). Neurons, which are **microstructures** in the brain's structures and systems, are specifically defined in the next chapter.

Figure 1.1   An adult human brain is a physical mass with a weight of approximately three pounds. Its plasticity for responding to the environment allows it to learn throughout a human's lifetime

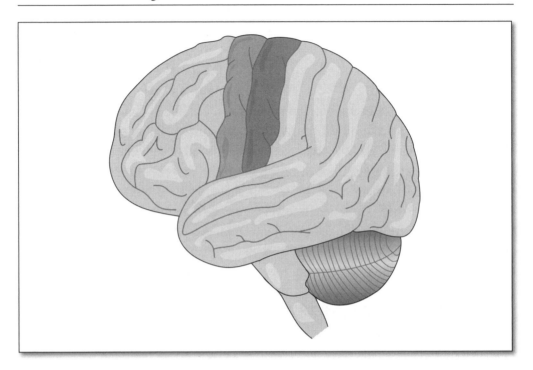

WHAT CAN YOU TELL YOUR STUDENTS ABOUT THEIR BRAINS?

Our marvelous brains are only one pound at birth and grow to become the three pound brain adults have. All brains are protected from bumps and jolts by a skull, called the cranium, *and brain fluid. A three-pound brain is about the size of a large coconut and looks like a half of a shelled walnut. Its color varies from gray to grayish pink to white. It is our hungriest organ and can demand as much as 20 to 25% of all the oxygen and food we have for our whole bodies. The brain is plastic, which means its connections can be changed, so you know how you should act and learn from what is happening around you. Even adult brains, although they are not growing in size, are able to change what they think and to learn new things.*

LEARNING AT ANY AGE

While this book focuses on how the human brain develops to read, readers are curious about themselves as learners, as well. Understanding adults as learners provides the foundation for what students aspire to achieve for their thinking brains. Adults are challenged to think about how new information is learned.

They face new situations, such as being a newcomer to a group of people who already have a shared knowledge base, teaching a different grade level, or developing a teaching plan for a new subject. An even bigger challenge for teachers is to teach a familiar curriculum with totally new teaching methods and materials. Adults who are parents face continual challenges while their child advances developmentally. They may have to learn about the Jurassic period when the child become fascinated with dinosaurs or learn names and describe functions of large machinery as little boys become infatuated with construction. Older children gravitate toward **technology,** which does not appear to be child's play to parents (or even more unlikely, to grandparents) from the nontechnology generation. Or, parents need to learn the rules and nuances of various team activities as students participate in youth sports. Active adults are not immune from and must be open to continuous learning or relearning as the children with whom they interact develop their interests and become cognitively sophisticated.

What Do Adults Do to Learn?

New and strange situations place demands on the adult brain. It is challenged to make new connections or to go to memory's storage places for previous knowledge that may or may not be well developed. How do adults do it? Do they engage in research on the topic? Do they practice and rehearse new names or information? Are they likely to head for the Internet and do a Google search for more information? Or, do they push forward and learn on the run? Most likely, the way mature learners respond to these questions is similar to the way they approached their last school experiences in high school, college, trade school, or post graduate work.

Because readers selected this book, they generally accept the challenge to learn more about the human brain. Using the human brain as a learning topic, adult study preferences can be analyzed. What if an adult needed to learn all of the brain structures that are addressed in this book? Additionally, the names of the structures, the correct spelling, and the location and function of each are required. If all this factual knowledge is tested by questions requiring fill-in, multiple-choice, or short-paragraph answers, how would adults study? When an incentive for attaining a score of 90% or higher is a check for $1,000, what are the ways adult learners would study?

People have a variety of approaches to this situation. Some of the most frequent responses are to make flash cards, use a model, make a tape recording, tape information on the bathroom mirror and refrigerator, study with a partner, teach someone else, distribute practice over specific time periods and days, do more reading, and develop a practice test. All of these study methods involve repetitive and elaborative rehearsal and practice to keep the information in **working memory.**

The more practice a person puts in and the more the information relates to what is already known, the more likely it is that an understanding of the brain structures will be stored in **long term memory** for automatic recall and application.

Adult learners give a rich variety of responses when questioned about the ways they learn. Study and learning preferences depend on how an individual's brain is organized and are based on how the adult learned successfully in the past. Most adults do not analyze how their best learning happens. They consciously or unconsciously select study practices and hope learning happens. Why is there a concern for adult learning issues? Dr. Russell Poldrack, faculty chair at the University of California, Los Angeles, explained the mystique surrounding how adults learn new facts, concepts, and skills during an interview with researcher Sue Buster (2008). It is accepted that adults are generally able to sustain a thought by using mature executive control and attention systems. Poldrack conducted studies using a functional magnetic resonance imaging machine (fMRI) to find out how much adults actually understand about their attempts to learn. According to this researcher, adults are not good at knowing how they learn, nor can they explain how they study to learn something well. They are not accomplished enough to understand how their brains operate. Oddly, they cannot accurately predict what they know or what they will be able to remember and recall (Buster, 2008). With this information, it makes sense to think about developing an understanding of brain parts and operations at a young age.

School-age children can be prompted to understand how to learn efficiently and how important their study choices can be. Imagine if fourth-grade children are exposed to information about their brain's structures and how they uniquely operate. Students could learn more efficiently at a young age; and with continual, advanced information from neuroanatomy and neurophysiology, they could potentially be successful learners for all their remaining school and adult years. It is important that teachers know what they can do to help students develop their learning potential and efficient study habits. Teachers are challenged to help students understand how their brains learn, so when students become young adults they are better equipped to learn the volumes of materials school systems require of them.

Issues for Teaching Primary Children Grades K–3)

Children come to school with a wide variety of expectations. First and foremost, they expect to learn how to read. Some children sense their parents' anxiety and apprehension as they enter school and know how important it is to be "ready for school." Others may hear parents speaking with relief that they will be in school and sense that parents are eager to leave them at a place called *school*. Whatever children think, they do not realize there is a tightly managed plan in place for them to learn. Adults, parents, teachers, administrators, curriculum advisers, textbook developers and publishers, state and federal governments, and the community at large are all consumers of the education system, and they have a plan for children to be in school and to be learning. School is everybody's business.

How School Is Organized for Learning

Society has demanded a comprehensive school curriculum that children must learn in order to become *productive citizens upon reaching adulthood.* Most children in the early years of schooling participate eagerly and are interested in the classroom (where things are and how it looks), management procedures (how they can do the things they want to do), and learning activities (what do they have to do to get the work done). It takes a while before young children become comfortable with school (see Table 1.1).

Table 1.1 Classroom Needs for Primary Students

- A good chance to be a successful student
- Clear rules and procedures developed by the teacher
- The same consistent rules and requirements for all students
- Continual student feedback on how the child is working and progressing in the classroom environment
- Opportunities for good work to be acknowledged or displayed

As the school years progress, their brains habituate, and they tend to become complacent, possibly even unmotivated by standard operating school practices. Teachers must continually strive to be innovative and novel in their teaching approaches to capture the attention and the engagement of their students' curious, yet easily satiated, brains (see Table 1.2). Students in the primary grades learn what their parents and teachers tell them they must learn. They expect it to be fun, interesting, predictable, and rewarding.

Table 1.2 Cognitively Challenging Teaching Practices for Students, Grades K–3

A Creative Classroom

- Is inviting, curious, and fun
- Features subjects and topics that relate to children's interests
- Gives children a chance to talk about what they know and have experienced
- Provides many different materials to read, use, and manipulate
- Requests children to speak clearly and requires accountable listening to others
- Features an environment to stimulate children's curious, insatiable brains
- Has stability and consistency
- Develops vocabulary and provides a wide range of background experiences

Learning Differences Between Boys and Girls

Recently, differences in learning and academic performance between boys and girls have caught media attention. A book published in 2001 by Michael Gurian, *Boys and Girls Learn Differently!,* encourages educators to respond to gender differences based on brain development, rate of behavioral development, and hormonal differences that transpire during the prenatal period, adolescence, and throughout life. The issue of learning differences is addressed by other educators as well (Eliot, 2009; Halpern et al., 2008). There are significant differences between the ways boys and girls learn, behave, talk, play, and relate to their worlds. One of the most notable differences between the genders is the developmental pace of language acquisition and their communication styles (Pence & Justice, 2008). Language development differences are attributed to maturation rates while communication preferences result from the different ways parents and care providers react to their boys and to their girls. During the toddler years, for example, conversations for boys tend to be more in play settings while girl conversations are more likely to be about objects and events that may be more perceptually complex. Boys experience conversation about what they are doing. Girls may be asked to respond to questions that use abstract language. It may be that boys are programmed in the preschool years to think and talk about concrete real objects while little girls are prompted to think in abstractions. These early experiences and the apparent way boys' brains are slower to develop for language skills can make an academic difference when reading is taught as if both genders are ready to learn at the same age and grade. Are there significant enough academic differences between boys and girls in the elementary years to warrant dramatically different classroom practices or placements?

Until recently, research has shown the differences to be less significant for gender than they are for other areas of discrepancy. Scientifically different school performance results were identified by Barnett and Rivers (2008) in an article presentation about single-sex schools. Rather than separating boys and girls for education purposes, they propose educators need to be more concerned about the significance of race, degree of poverty, population density, school type, and family characteristics. An additional study from Tel Aviv University (Schlosser, 2008) suggests that boys and girls need to be together in classrooms to achieve optimal learning. The researcher, Analia Schlosser, found that having boys and girls interact together in the classes at elementary, middle, and high school produced better academic achievement for both genders than sex-segregated classrooms.

While educators have accepted the challenge to level the playing field for children who are ethnically different and economically disadvantaged, another issue is emerging: Boys are not ready to read at the same age as girls (Whitmire, 2010). Just as school systems have braced themselves to provide intensive, direct instruction programs for reading beginning at kindergarten, statistics are pointing to alarming discrepancies between achievement levels of girls and boys. In the Kansas City school system class of 2008, 71% of Hispanic females and 52% of males graduate from the twelfth grade. A percentage of female and male students who tested as proficient in reading throughout the United States in 2008 showed females consistently more proficient; often by high school the gap reaches 10% or more (Center on Educational Policy, 2010).

Another study indicates that boys are not as confident about their learning abilities. Whitmire (2010) reports that while a higher percentage of high school students predict graduation from a four-year college in 2001 as compared to 1980 the greater shift is in the attitudes of girls. This study is also reported by the Center on Educational Policy (2010) and shows a full 62% of the study's population of females indicated they planned to graduate. Males had a 51% goal of college graduation. The confidence level of girls for school success appears to be greater than that of boys during high school. Initial reactions to these new data indicate that systematic reading programs are improving scores and attitudes overall, but boys are losing the educational advantage they had 20 years ago.

This trend is alarming and demands more study to look at when boys are ready for intensive reading instruction. It is interesting that educators acknowledge there are different issues that impact whether boys are successful learners for reading skills. Not prominently displayed, but listed, is brain research (Sloan, 2010). While all children need to develop the same reading systems to be successful readers, a percentage of boys are not ready for the intensive instruction that building readers demands. If they begin to feel incompetent during the early school years, it is difficult to rebuild an attitude for successful learning when boys are developmentally ready for reading instruction. Many educators have maintained that children are not developmentally ready for reading in kindergarten, while others have denied these claims. It just might be that the developmental issue is real for some students, mainly boys who just need a bit more time to be comfortable with school and successful with learning before they are placed into intensive reading instruction. While this information does not suggest gender segregation as the solution, education certainly could investigate readiness, not ability grouping. The days of three reading groups in a single regular classroom may return as a standard teaching practice.

Needs for Developing Learners, Grades Four Through Seven

Students need far more control of their learning than is traditionally found in schools for these grade levels (Tomlinson & McTighe, 2006). Students want to learn about things that interest them rather than relying on the structured, directive instruction of the primary years. The precise process of teaching skills necessary for students to become readers has all but ceased for students who are progressing at grade level. During the upper elementary years, there is a new urgency that reigns in classrooms. Students' brains require intensive support to organize information in ways that make sense. They accomplish this feat by providing meaning for words or ideas that are similar or different, putting small incidentals into big meanings, forming generalizations, and developing conceptual thinking to align with the way the brain is structured to learn. It is during these years that the brain is structured for learning and the learner is constructing a brain for life. In these later elementary years, students want to become active participants in their own educations.

Classrooms for Today's Preteens

An ideal classroom has a teacher who senses and values the self-worth of each child. All aspects of the child are considered. Children have physical and emotional needs as well as learning needs. When a teacher considers the partnership between home and school, all parts of the child's well-being are addressed through brain-compatible practices. Every day has the potential to be a successful learning day. In a productive classroom, the teacher will not allow differences in gender, race, past achievement, parental involvement, or any other factor to be an excuse for unacceptable, shoddy work that is less than what the child is capable of producing. A positive student attitude can be realized through definitive, predictable classroom characteristics (see Table 1.3). Preteens learn when their minds are engaged. A productive classroom environment attempts to deter their minds from straying during class time.

Table 1.3   Classroom Needs for Students, Grades Four Through Eight

o   High expectations for a smoothly functioning and organized classroom
o   Student developed rules based upon an understood rationale
o   Student opportunity to critique how well the classroom is operating
o   A clear sense of what is successful for classroom operation
o   Individual student contributions
o   Participation of all students to determine how the classroom works

Source: Tomlinson & McTihge, 2006.

Cognitively Challenging Teaching Practices

Teachers, realizing the impressive mental capabilities of these very young students, can organize teaching practices that look and sound very different from classes in the earlier grades. Upper elementary students need more classroom control through choices. They learn best when they are able to make a selection from several activities all of which lead to the same state-defined curriculum standards.

Students learn to interact with peers in cooperative groups or with study partners. They have choices as they select topics for research or project development. Students listen to and learn from each other. They depend upon teachers, classroom resources, and guests to extend oral communication and listening skills.

Children are exposed to a much greater world through television and Internet capabilities than early technology developers could have imagined. Schools can respond to our current culture, which exposes youngsters to more information, communication options, and sophisticated experiences. Technology as an active part of the classroom activities can be provided with safe and reasonable rules and regulations. The Internet provides an opportunity for students to seek information from research, communicate with other students, or access expert resources around the globe. Preteens can be engaged and excited about learning when school is a place where their curious brains are stimulated and organized with patterns, networks, categories, similarities, differences, and big ideas they need to learn. It is at this time the curriculum standards demand they remember more and more and more (see Table 1.4).

Table 1.4 Cognitively Challenging Teaching Practices for Students in Grades Four Through Eight

A Creative Classroom

- o Looks more cognitively advanced with each succeeding school year
- o Provides choices of what, how, when, and where
- o Organizes students into cooperative groups and study partners
- o Ensures resources are multifaceted
- o Exposes students to communication options and sophisticated experiences
- o Develops an environment to provide order and organization to students' curious and insatiable brains
- o Features patterns and big idea development

Learning Environments for Teens, Grade 8 Through Grade 12 and Beyond

Sometime between the end of grade school and the beginning of high school, students begin to find an adult emerging from within. There are periods of childish behavior and childlike decisions, and other times they think like, act like, and look very much like young adults. School systems are most successful when they thoughtfully work with students who have a quickly advancing physical appearance but a slowly maturing human brain. The curriculum can tackle the erratic needs of adolescence by respecting the person and being mindful of how the mandated curriculum can be managed as possible, popular, and potent.

Middle School Students

Students in middle school are in transition not only from elementary school to high school but also in transition between being a child and an adult. For the school system and its teachers, this is a powerful time to build relationships with students (Hinchman & Sheriday-Thomas, 2008). Time is well spent by discussing and researching social aspects for the teens themselves as well as social interactions or concerns for the population at large. Social and personal relationship issues consume students' attention at the early teen stage. Inside their heads, they are trying to make sense out of the social situations in which they find themselves as well as how they will fit into the bigger view of the adult world (see Table 1.5). The curriculum is most effective when it deals with topics that are motivating, interesting, and relevant to the concerns and changes the students are experiencing. This means using all the communication, reading, and writing skills built previously and expanding vocabulary, information, generalizations, and concept formation in ways that are very people related.

Table 1.5 Needs of Middle School Students

---

o **Transitions**—clear talk and conversation about changes in growth and development through life's stages
o **Relationships**—identification of all types of personal relationships, including immediate and extended family, friends, acquaintances, organization members, and authority figures
o **Curriculum**—how school subjects and issues have meaning and importance
o **Meaning**—learning what is important for school and personal success

---

High School Students

High school students continue to struggle with identity, and they also struggle with the person they will be. However, they are capable of taking challenges to resolve complex issues, dealing with abstractions, and forming their own opinions, often with vehement outspokenness. At this stage of students' cognitive and physical development, a teacher can provide new information, strategies, and resources—but becomes less of a teacher and more of a facilitator. Teachers are challenged to make information pertinent by using provocative ideas and greatly expanding resource options. When students are guided through experiential learning and encouraged to build self-generated concepts, the greatest learning outcomes can occur.

Students begin their school career as dependent learners (seekers) in highly controlled classroom structures. As they develop capabilities for independent thinking, they become selective learners, responding to information that will help them develop expertise in areas of requirements, needs, and interest (see Table 1.6). During the secondary years, they develop into connoisseurs of information who construct conceptual frameworks that are available to them throughout their adult lives. Self-confidence soars for most teens as they see themselves physically as young adults. Mentally, they are in possession of a human brain that is still under construction. Unfortunately, the very skills they need most—planning for the future, understanding facial expressions, interpreting body language, making decisions, having sound judgment, and being strong in times of group pressure—are areas that they are least capable of managing. Although the teen years is also a topic of a later chapter, a final suggestion is appropriate. It is wise for adults to understand the extreme responsibility they have to be good role models for developing youth. Young adults deserve to be treated with respect and to have their individual feelings and needs dealt with in an attentive and caring way.

Table 1.6 Learning Attributes of High School Students

High School Students

Accept challenges	Resolve complex issues
Deal with abstractions	Form strong opinions
Express vehement outspokenness	Think independently
Are connoisseurs of information	Construct conceptual frameworks
Show self-confidence	Are physically mature

Effective Learning Environments for Teens

High school students need even more choice and control in their learning environment than preteens do. School cannot be about lecture and teacher talk. Important findings have surfaced about the adolescent human brain. Students are capable of paying attention with their eyes focused on the teacher, but they may not be concentrating on a single thing that is being said. It is the adolescent look which says, "Ok, so I am listening to you, but I don't know a word you are saying." Neuroscience reveals that a person can only focus or concentrate on one thing at a time. So, if a student is not required to be engaged with learning and the topic is perceived to have little of no value, the student is most likely concentrating on something else. What teachers want to know is how to engage teens in the course content that is prescribed by district, state, and federal law.

Engagement is not simply paying attention with focused eyes. Outward appearance does not indicate what is going on in a teen's mind. Students are engaged with the selected learning when they talk about it, write about it, demonstrate understanding, or make a representative product. Motivation and engagement with learning are topics for Chapter 6. But, the point must be made that if high school teachers are doing the majority of the talking, they are the ones doing most of the learning about the topic.

Innovative High School Proposals

Current high school proposals call for new legislation that surpasses No Child Left Behind requirements. Exciting things are happening in high schools throughout the world. Major changes to the way high schools do the business of educating adolescents are evident as high schools are challenged to go beyond the 100-year-old high school system that was in place for most readers. The Association of Supervision and Curriculum Development (ASCD) has a promising proposal for high school reform. It includes multiple ways to assess student learning. Teachers are challenged to use instructional strategies that ensure success for every student. A system of personalized learning targets would extend beyond teacher accountability and request that students assume ownership for planning and meeting their educational goals (see Wise, 2008).

Another part of the plan recommends high schools use flexible school times and classroom structures. By the time a youngster becomes an adolescent, an individual time clock has been established. There are early risers, the larks; and there are people who perform better later in the day and into the evening, the owls. School systems and time schedules are often determined by the transportation system and adult perception of manageable, predictable classroom time periods, possibly without concern for when and where students could be optimally engaged in serious learning activities. A final element in the ASCD proposal requires high schools to collaborate and partner with businesses and the community (Wise, 2008). Students can learn about their worlds both inside and outside of the school institution. So we ask, *How are high schools being managed to be more representative of the world, and how can the world become more of a classroom? What proof do we have that students at any age do their best learning in a school classroom?*

Integrated into any reconstruction plan for high schools are professional learning and development. Hopefully, new proposals include what teachers need for professional support and are indicative of students' learning needs, developmental needs, and cognitive levels. Reform for all high schools could make a true difference for our young adults. They deserve school activities that allow them to build the best brains possible for a future that even the policy makers cannot define.

WHAT CAN YOU TELL YOUR STUDENTS ABOUT THEIR RESPONSIBILITIES AS LEARNERS?

First, it is important to understand your brain as the thinking organ in your body that receives input from the senses. Without information from the five senses, the mind would have nothing to think about. Your neurons, nerve cells, become active to make neural highways to connect useful thoughts. When you think real hard about something and keep rehearsing or practicing, there is a better chance you will remember the information. With some of the basic brain information, young and older learners can identify what they need to remember and how they learn best. Some want to learn by seeing words or pictures, or others may want to talk about it and play with words orally. Some students like to make their own drawings, diagrams, or charts. Each student uses different practices for different things they are attempting to remember. What works best for you?

[Children deserve to develop an understanding of how they learn at an early age. They need to know that terms like *smart, dumb,* and *knucklehead* do not belong in school. Students respond well to praise for their efforts, progress, improvement, and strategies—not for their innate intelligence. And, they need to think about their work as challenging and to know they have the potential to succeed.

High school students can learn the physiological parts of the brain.]

Different brain structures and systems help you do what you want to do and help you to become the person you want to be. Some of your brain functions are not completely developed, and for this reason sometimes you are faced with emotionally difficult decisions and situations. If you can identify when you are in a quandary and do not know how to respond, it is best to include an adult you trust to help you think through the situation. You did not choose to have a physical body that develops first while your brain is slow to catch up. Please know some aspects of your brain give you the potential to be a mental genius, but areas that control your emotions are still under construction. Knowing about your development will help you and your friends get through some painful parts of becoming adults.

The Learning Brain, Serious Structure Information

The next chapter is complex, as it could be a miniclass for brain physiology. The information is important as a backdrop for teaching decisions. When educators develop an understanding for what happens neurologically during even a simple behavior, thought, or response, they have insight into what needs to happen for students to learn and remember the complex curriculum designed for each grade. Although information about the brain's structures is scientific, it is approachable and manageable. Simplified messages are provided and can be modified by teachers to share with their students at all levels from upper elementary through high school. These sections explain the brain in practical and meaningful terms.

2

Brain Structures Accessed for Reading

How can a human brain be understood without a purposeful journey through the parts that make up this ever changing, complex unit? A search for meaning includes identification of brain parts for the chief executive officer (CEO), the mischievous emotional system that can override its executive boss, and all the other areas that instantaneously convert raw data from the senses into useful, enlightened wisdom. The human brain, designed for human survival, is a mastermind for communication and also for reading. A language pathway develops quite naturally in most children who have normally developing hearing, and it is a necessary foundation for the process of reading.

OVERALL APPEARANCE OF THE HUMAN BRAIN

The structures of the brain are complex and too numerous for a single chapter in a book about the process of reading. Here, information is limited to the brain's parts that do the majority of the work needed for students to read. Information that leads to understanding the structures of the human brain is exceptionally intriguing for some. Yet, it is not critical to remember or be able to recite these parts to understand how a student learns or develops a reading brain. For readers who do not need this level of specificity, summative sections, *What can you tell your students about the structures of the brain?* are provided at the end of each major section. Reader-friendly information that is available for students provides enough background about learning and brain physiology to understand the following chapters. Terms appearing in bold in the text are defined in the glossary located at the end of the book.

The global appearance of the human brain is defined by its shape and cumulative layers. The bony skull or cranium, which is a Greek word for bowl, provides the first layer of protection for the brain. But, the cranium itself is not enough protection for this vital organ. Between the skull and the tissues of the brain are three membranes. The ***dura mater,*** which is Latin for hard mother, the *middle **arachnoid layer,*** which is Greek for its resemblance to a spider's web, and the *inner **pia mater,*** which is Latin for soft mother. Additionally, a clear colorless fluid, the cerebral spinal fluid, CSF, circulates in the middle arachnoid layer and into the "belly" of the brain's four cavities. The CSF bathes and cleanses the brain by carrying away wastes and dropping them into the bloodstream. This fluid also cushions and protects the brain from abrasions and jolts (Berninger & Richards, 2002). The structures of the brain are beneath the hard shell and these protective layers. The secret world within this human organ defies understanding, but there is common knowledge that is agreed upon from the field of neurology.

HEMISPHERES AND STRUCTURES

The brain is activated through the central nervous system, CNS, with central and peripheral parts. The peripheral nervous system, PNS, is the branching spinal and cranial nerves that take messages from the brain to the rest of the body, while the CNS is the brain and the spinal cord. Three subdivisions, the cerebrum (the **forebrain**), the cerebellum (the **hindbrain**), and the brainstem (the **midbrain, pons,** and **medulla**), are identified in Figure 2.1.

The Cerebral Cortex

The human brain's outer layers comprise the cerebral cortex, while the entire brain is called the cerebrum. A description of the human cerebral cortex begins with two **hemispheres** and their lobes. The two sides are separated by a longitudinal fissure or very deep ridge. The hemispheres are distinguished by their names, the left hemisphere and the right hemisphere. They are two distinct parts of the same brain, and while some of the specific tasks of each will be defined in a later chapter, for now there is one brain with two parts. Our two hemispheres are always working together as they are joined by a thick fiber bundle the **corpus callosum.** Each side of the brain has lobes. At the front of the brain we identify the **frontal lobes;** one is in the

Figure 2.1   Diagrams of the Brain (Cerebrum)

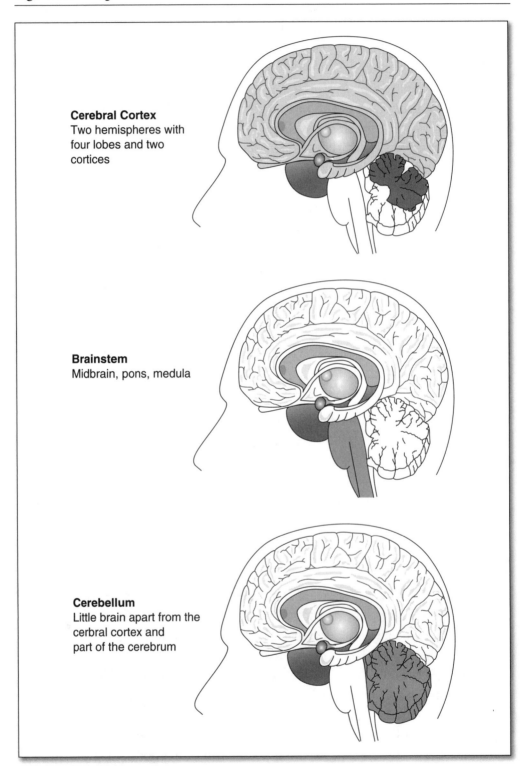

Cerebral Cortex
Two hemispheres with
four lobes and two
cortices

Brainstem
Midbrain, pons, medula

Cerebellum
Little brain apart from the
cerbral cortex and
part of the cerebrum

left hemisphere and one is in the right hemisphere. So, while there are four lobes, frontal, parietal, occipital, and temporal, it is important to note that there are matching lobes on each side of the brain. The lobes are defined from the front of the brain to the back and on the sides; two cortices, the motor and somatosensory cortex are also identified (see Figure 2.2). The lobes are gray matter structures 1.5 to 4.5 millimeters thick, consisting mainly of the cell bodies of the neurons and some of the branching **dendrites.** Because the cerebral cortex would be the size of a large dinner napkin if it were pressed flat, it is twisted and tucked to fit into a human-sized skull. The twists and tucks form gyri, folds above the surface, and sulci, shallow areas or valleys (Nolte, 2002). Singular terms for a fold and a valley are *gyrus* and *sulcus.*

Figure 2.2   The Brain's Main Lobes and Cortices

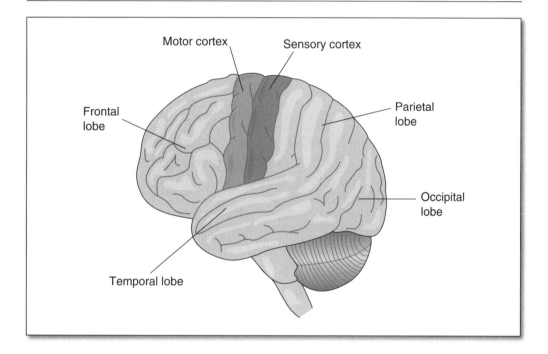

Frontal Lobes

The frontal lobes are located right above the eyes and cover the forehead area as they extend slightly more than halfway to the back of the head. The prefrontal part of these structures make our brain uniquely human, as they deal with the most integrated and highest order brain activities (Greenfield, 2000). Often thought of as the chief executive officer of the cerebral cortex, the frontal lobes are activated to deal with planning, problem solving, conceptualizing, integrating, and predicting. This frontal area is eloquently described for its executive function by G. Reid Lyon and Norman A. Krasnegor (2001), psychologists, developers, and researchers with the National Institute of Child Health and Human Development, as they identify the components of execution, self-regulation, maintenance, sustained mental productivity, and segmentation of space and time. It is no wonder you may catch a student with a hand covering this area, with eyes closed, and placing the weight of the brain's fore area on the elbow during deep thought. The highest order of conscious thinking occurs right there at the front of the head.

Motor Cortex

Toward the back of the frontal lobes and conveniently located to respond to executive thought is the **motor cortex.** It stretches across the top of the head like a headband and reaches to the area near the ears. This cortex directs nearly all of the conscious muscular activity that the brain initiates. Different areas of this strip direct the motor activity of distinct body parts. Beginning at the temple, near the ears, and moving upward are specific areas devoted to the face, lips, mouth, and tongue, which are the first to develop in a newborn. Moving up the motor strip, specific mid body locations have been identified by scientists that trigger movement for the shoulders, arms, and hands. Sensors for the legs and feet are located near the top of the head. Notice the assignments of body part movements are upside down, as the lower end of the strip controls the muscles in the head and face, while upper portions of the cortex work for the legs and feet (Eliot, 1999).

Somatosensory Cortex

Located next to the motor strip and at the fore section of the **parietal lobes** is the **somatosensory cortex.** As its name indicates, it is dedicated to touch sensations from various body parts. Again, the organization of the brain surprises us, as sensations from the right side of the body are received by the left side of the **sensory cortex** while left side feelings are received by the right side. And, remembering the motor cortex arrangement described above, the feet and leg feelings go to the top of the brain while feelings from the head and mouth are registered at the bottom of the motor strip, near the ears (Sylwester, 2005). There are more sensory receptors around the head, face, and mouth than there are at the leg and feet extremities. This overabundance of receptors allows a person to identify and respond quickly to sensory input that is emotionally pleasant or dangerous.

Parietal Lobes

Progressing from the front to the back, the parietal lobes fill the next portion of the brain. John Nolte (2002), author and professor of cell biology and anatomy at the

University of Arizona College of Medicine, describes the parietal lobes as a part of the cerebral lobe area, which identifies it as bound by the frontal, temporal, and **occipital lobes.** This neurologist includes the somatosensory cortex as the foremost area of the parietal lobes. The parietal lobes contribute to the comprehension of language as it interconnects with its neighbors the occipital and **temporal lobes** for speaking, reading, and writing.

In addition to their function for language, the parietal lobes participate in the recognition of danger and opportunities. The parietal lobes link with signals from our **limbic system,** a more primitive part of the brain, to keep us alert. Along with limbic structures buried deep and center in the brain for survival, these lobes provide a sense of being. People know how they feel, threatened, safe, comfortable, or even out-of-sorts, based on signals and messages from the parietal lobes. Rita Carter (1998), recognized for her achievements in medical journalism, identifies the additional functions of movement, orientation, calculation, and some forms of recognition in these lobes. Teachers know that if the body is at homeostasis, even, and at ease, a person is released from worry and lower order concerns so that mental effort can be directed to learning.

Occipital Lobes

Crowded into the posterior section of the cerebrum and nestled between the parietal lobes on the top side and the temporal lobes on the lower side are the occipital lobes. This set of lobes is ideally located to participate in language functions and particularly to be co-opted to work with the pathway that is developed for reading. *Occipital* translates into the seeing activities of the human brain. Most people remember the diagrams in elementary science books that show how the intake from the left visual field goes to the right side of the brain while the right visual field feeds the left hemisphere with images.

The occipital lobes are the smallest of the four lobes, estimated to occupy a mere 18% of the cerebral cortex, but their role in human sensory processing is critical (Sylwester, 2005). Nolte (2002) describes humans as a visually oriented species. That distinction coupled with the accessibility of the visual anatomy warrants the large amount of research available about the **visual system.** It is emphasized that the primary visual cortex within the occipital lobes sorts visual images from the eyes, associates them with known information from prior learning, and distributes their signals to other areas of the cortex for interpretation.

Temporal Lobes

The location, directly above the ears, gives an indication of one major function of the temporal lobes. They include the functions of receiving auditory input and associating sounds with what they represent. Activity in the temporal lobes determines if the sensation of sounds received are rhythmic pulsating music, a bird chirping, the clapping of thunder, the whisper of wind, or a human voice speaking.

The temporal lobes do not only process sounds. They function as a part of the language system with other lobes in the cerebral cortex. For language to make sense, associative activities from the visual, higher order thinking and olfactory sensory areas of the brain are united with input from the temporal lobes. As if language interpretation is not enough activity for the temporal lobes, according to Nolte (2002), the **amygdala** (the emotional alarm system) and the **hippocampus** (where working memory functions) are also within the working parameters of the temporal lobes. The amygdala and the hippocampus are located in the center area of the brain called the limbic system (the primitive brain). The emotional properties of the human brain and learning, as well as the temporal lobe activities for speaking, writing, and reading, are explored further in later chapters.

Other Lobes in the Brain

Neuroscientists have less information about another area that may be included as the brain's lobes are identified. John Nolte (2002) identifies a limbic lobe in his text. It is defined as a strip of cortex located between the corpus callosum and the frontal, parietal, and occipital lobes. It curves to occupy a surface area near the temporal lobe. The makeup of this lobe has the outward appearance of the brain's limbic, or more primitive, system identified earlier (Nolte, 2002). It is the limbic system that provides for our survival, including the flight or fight reaction felt during an emergency situation. Remembering the brain is designed to help humans move toward opportunities and away from danger helps with understanding the function of this brain area some neuroscientists describe as the brain's fifth lobe. Scientists also identify the insula, tucked under the temporal lobe, as one of the brain's lobes. The insula is fused during fetal development and then is concealed from view by the other lobes. Less is known about the insula, but most likely it has to do with food ingestion and automatic response systems (Nolte, 2002).

Cerebellum

A part of the cerebrum, yet apart from the cerebral cortex, is the cerebellum. It is often referred to as the "little brain." It is a convoluted subdivision of the brain's central nervous system, which is located at the back of the brain (Nolte, 2002). It is found below the back of the temporal lobe, next to and somewhat under the occipital lobes, and at the back bottom part of the skull (see Figures 2.1 and 2.3). The cerebellum is a servant in training. For reading, it patiently waits as children go through the skill development needed to learn to decode words. Once a series of reading skills (eye movement, accessing the reading pathway, knowing an extensive

Figure 2.3 The Cerebellum at the Back of the Brain

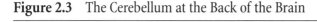

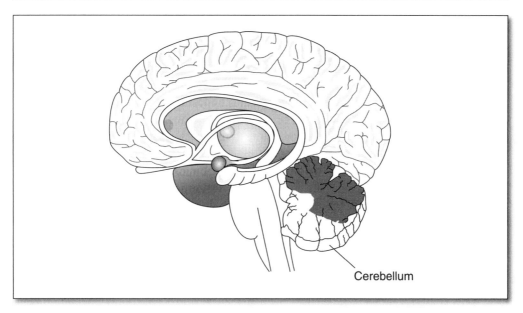

Cerebellum

volume of words) are learned with fluency and **automaticity,** the cerebellum is ready to take on the coordination of that task, freeing parts of the brain responsible for the conscious part of the reading process to focus on what the decoded words mean (Nevills & Wolfe, 2009). In general, the cerebellum receives inputs from the sensory system, which includes all five senses, and responds to the **vestibular system** function of perception for time and space.

Once thought to be primarily involved with coordinating movement, the duties of the cerebellum have been greatly expanded to include critical elements during the learning process. It connects with the cerebral cortex and coordinates activities for learning that happen at the unconscious level. During reading, for example, it controls somewhat sporadic eye movements across the page and movement down to the next line. Coupled with input from the frontal lobes, the cerebellum coordinates saccadic eye movements for words or phrases that require conscious thought during fluent silent or oral reading. Writing without thinking about the physical requirements to make markings on a paper and tooth brushing without needing conscious effort are attributed as some of the endless examples of the interplay of the cerebellum and the cerebral cortex. Other chores this brain structure assumes will be revealed in later chapters.

Brainstem

Described as the most ancient part of the brain, the brainstem could have existed in animals as long ago as 500 million years. The brainstem is a current day reptile's entire brain according to Carter (1998). Hence the term, *reptilian brain,* has been applied to the brainstem and its contributing parts. The brainstem, at the top of the spinal cord, has three distinct structures: the midbrain, the pons, and the medulla oblongata. Although it may be more than we need to understand, drawings of the brain may include the **vermis** without identifying it. So, interestingly, it can be described as the area that exists between the two hemispheres and occupies the zone adjacent to the cerebellum (Nolte, 2002). Its name, *vermis,* describes the curvy, winding turns that make up its delicate appearance (see Figures 2.1 and 2.3).

Unconscious body functions are regulated based on incoming signals from nerves connecting the brainstem to all parts of the body. We acknowledge the work of the brainstem as taking care of blood flow, keeping our hearts beating, controlling our breathing, signaling our glands for secretions, and other life sustaining assignments. All these critical activities continue 24 hours and day and seven days a week, so we can concentrate on learning and interpreting our environment—or rest with ease, knowing that our body cares for itself.

WHAT CAN YOU TELL YOUR STUDENTS ABOUT THE STRUCTURES OF THE BRAIN?

The brain has two hemispheres, or parts, a left part and a right part. Each of those parts has a partner on the other side. There are lobes for thinking, feeling, seeing, and hearing. There is a direct pathway for smelling. An area that helps you think about how you want to move is called the motor strip. Another area takes all the information you receive from touching and sensing. There is a little brain at the back of your head called the cerebellum *that helps you to do things like walking, riding a bike, and even reading and writing. When you have practiced an activity long enough, it becomes easy and automatic. The little brain lets you do many things without even thinking about it.*

WHAT WE KNOW ABOUT THE LEARNING BRAIN AND READINESS TO READ

The language system that allows us to hear and speak is simple to understand and develops quite naturally. Infants and young children, given an environment that we would determine to be relatively normal, will learn many if not most of the spoken complexities of our language during the preschool years. It is their major job to do so as the human brain demands to understand its environment. Words and language are the best system for accomplishing this feat. The **oral language system** operates within the temporal, parietal, and occipital lobes. It calls upon the motor strip to verbalize and the frontal lobes for comprehension and difficult thinking tasks.

The Oral Language System

A preschool child has an all encompassing task assigned by the developing brain: to figure out the environment in which the child lives. One close look at a child at six months, one year, or at three years of age helps us realize the importance of this work. The human brain completes its development based upon sensory input from the environment. How the brain organizes, what vocabulary is learned, what core knowledge is stored, and how the child reacts to varying situations is the result of what happens to the child and a human cerebral cortex that is eager to learn. At the end of the preschool years, each child has a unique system of connections for information storage and retrieval.

Thalamus, Auditory Cortex, and Heschl's Gyrus

To understand the oral language system, additional structures must be identified (see Figures 2.4 and 2.5). The pathway begins with sounds that are received by the ear and sent immediately to the thalamus, which is located in the center of the

Figure 2.4   The Oral Language Pathway in the Brain

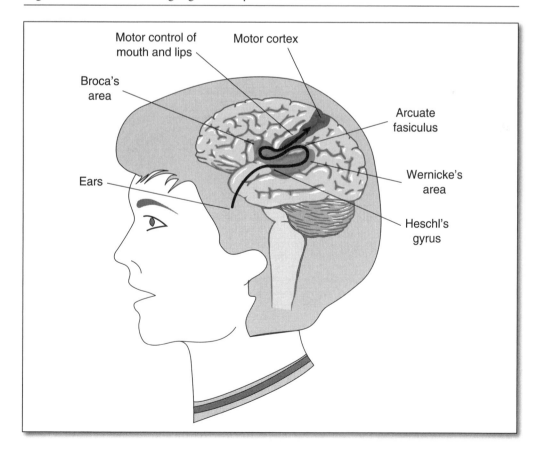

Figure 2.5   Flow Chart of the Oral Language Pathway

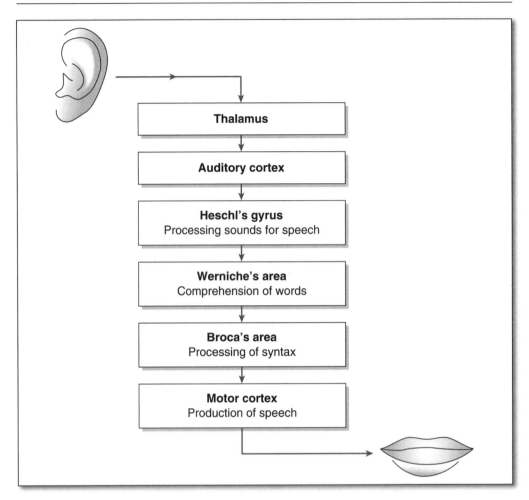

limbic system (see Figure 2.6). Its position in the middle of the brain allows it to be a sorting and sending station for all sensations received except the sense of smell. The purpose of this detour is to check the incoming signals for danger to survival, which could cause the thalamus and its associates, the amygdala and the **hypothalmus,** to override the executive thinking functions of the brain. Assuming the input is normal, the thalamus ships it back to the auditory cortex for processing. Once in the language processing area, the next station is Heschl's gyrus. The structure is named for Richard L. Heschl, an Austrian anatomist who defined this particular temporal area as being dedicated to sound analysis. Heschl's gyrus analyzes incoming stimulus to determine if it is some type of noise, music, random sounds, or actually language that needs to be recognized (Pence & Justice, 2008).

Although the left hemisphere is often acknowledged as the side for word identification, it appears that at least some aspects of processing sounds occurs bilaterally,

Figure 2.6 The Thalamus, a Way Station to Receive Input From the Senses

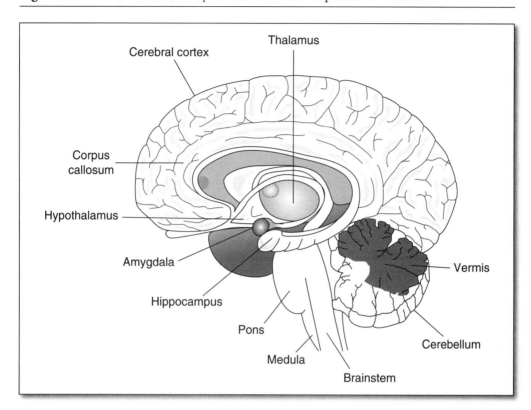

requiring communication between the two hemispheres. The rapid identification of sounds as language or words is more likely to occur in the left hemisphere while the overall characteristics of speech with its distinguishing qualities and appearance seem to be right hemisphere temporal activities (Pence & Justice, 2008). Therefore, while the left side of the brain may identify the sounds of *h-e-m-i-s-p-h-e-r-e* to be the word we say as *hemisphere,* the right side of the brain conjures a vision of a brain with two distinct parts and composed of matching pairs of structures.

Wernicke's Area

Once the sounds of a word or a phrase have been recognized as a part of the language system, Wernicke's area as the next step of the oral language system is enlisted to check semantics. Is the word or are the words comprehensible and meaningful? This area, also named after its discoverer, Karl Wernicke, a German neurologist and psychiatrist, is located at the junction of the left parietal and temporal lobes. Due to its function, it is not surprising that it is near the auditory cortex, as well (Nolte, 2002; Pence & Justice, 2008; Sylwester, 2005). Looking again at the word *hemisphere,* a reader of this book would likely be thinking of the two parts of the brain as a comprehensible word while other people may be picturing the hemispheres of our world, which is an equally appropriate response to the word's meaning.

Unless the pathway to identifying a word from the input of sounds crosses through Wernicke's area, words will not be understood. People who have damage to this area of their brains, called Wernicke's aphasia, can speak without difficulty, but much of their speech does not make sense to other people. Likewise, they are unable to understand what other people are saying to them.

Broca's Area and the Motor Cortex

Two remaining areas must be enlisted before a word, phrase, or sentence can be spoken. The oral language pathway next passes through Broca's area. The connecting neural fibers between Wernicke's area and Broca's area are identified as the arcuate fasciculus. This conductive pathway is significant, as the language pathway extends to the frontal regions of the cortex to include Broca's area and the motor cortex. Damage to this connector, the arcuate fasciculus, can result in conductive aphasia. In this instance, the person is unable to reproduce words said and received, as the incoming words from Wernicke's area cannot be transmitted to the frontal area for articulation (Nevills & Wolfe, 2009).

The name, *Broca's area,* is also named for its discoverer. The French neurologist Paul Broca discovered this area in the late 1800s. At this location, words are expressed as a code recognizable by the motor control area of the brain. The code directs muscle movements to control the jaw, larynx, tongue, and mouth for verbalization and production of speech. Aphasia at this point of the oral language pathway results in the inability to put words into phrases and sentences that make sense and are grammatically correct. Although the course of language from its input to speech production has many stops, the entire process happens in a mere fraction of a second once the oral language system has fully developed. Most likely, a child entering school has a fairly sophisticated system for communicating the language heard at home.

The oral language path and system is addressed again in Chapter 5 for its impact on the decoding reading pathway. Language is learned relatively naturally for children who have normal hearing and are exposed to a language rich environment prior to the start of formal instruction in school. However, a reading pathway is not naturally developed without direct, intensive instruction. For this purpose, the early primary grades focus on reconditioning the oral language pathway to function also as a reading pathway. It is an essential conversion for children to become effective readers in the upper elementary grades (Nevills & Wolfe, 2009).

**WHAT CAN YOU TELL YOUR STUDENTS ABOUT
HOW THEY TALK AND COMMUNICATE?**

[Most students do not realize that they learned to speak without anyone intentionally teaching them. As a young child, you were self-taught, highly motivated, and programmed to speak. Your most important job when you were a preschooler was to figure out your environment and to be able to talk with other people. There is a pathway in the brain that develops simply as you were exposed to sounds and having people around you who talked to you about what you were seeing, touching, tasting, smelling, and hearing. The pathway you developed uses many different parts of the brain that connect with an intricate, mandatory sequence. If there is a derailment along the path, you could have difficulty understanding others or communicating what you need or are thinking. Older students may be interested to know specific structures, their names, function, and locations.]

From Large Brain Sections to Infinitely Tiny Cells

The next chapter is where the action and the brain's brilliance really materialize. Although the large systems in the brain can be studied for their role in learning and behaving, nothing would happen in the structures without the neural chemical and electrical connections that light up the brain with activity.

3

Learning and Neuron Activity

Neurons, infinitely tiny nerve cells are the core of **neuroplasticity,** the brain's capacity to build itself during and following childhood for a lifetime of learning potential. The following account of neurons, their parts, chemical and electrical reactions, and their role in learning is detailed. It is provided for a thorough understanding of students' potential at the foundational level in the learning brain. Students learn when they are fully engaged, focused on the content, and motivated through interesting topics that encourage them to remember the information. The following account gives insight into how this is actually accomplished in the most finite parts of our human brain. A comprehensible, easy to understand summary of the technical aspects of learning follows the serious brain matters section. It can be found under the heading *What could you tell your students about their brain's cells and connections?* The second part of this chapter is steeped with practical classroom practices and strategies that result directly from how the brain works during learning.

SERIOUS BRAIN MATTERS—NEURONS AND NEUROPLASTICITY

A discernable focus reveals the minute details of the brain, the microstructures identified as neurons. Although neurons, the nerve cells in the brain, were first observed by a Czechoslovakian anatomist, Jan Purkinje (1787–1869) in the early 1800s, it was not until 1872 that an Italian physician, Camillo Golgi, developed a stain that made neurons stand out to be visible to inquisitive scientists under a magnification power of 1,500. With the **Golgi stain,** neurons appear to be black with an amber background. Fortunately, the stain shows only a random 10% or so of the neurons. If it stained all neurons, only a black blob would be observed due to the massive amount of neurons and their appendages located in each identified small section of the brain (Diamond & Hopson, 1998; Greenfield, 2000).

Neurons and Their Interactions

Neurons are varied in their appearance (see Figure 3.1). Some have short, fat, square, or rounded shapes with long thin branches while others may appear triangular in shape with short extensions. Neurons have two basic parts (see Figure 3.2). The first is the cell body, which does the important work of housekeeping, storing, and reacting to **genetic material,** genes and chromosomes. These tasks are much the same as the work

Figure 3.1   Neurons are varied in shape and size.

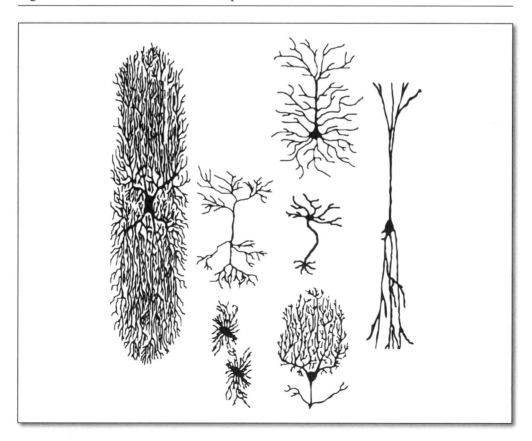

Figure 3.2 Neurons have two distinct parts, the cell body and the appendages.

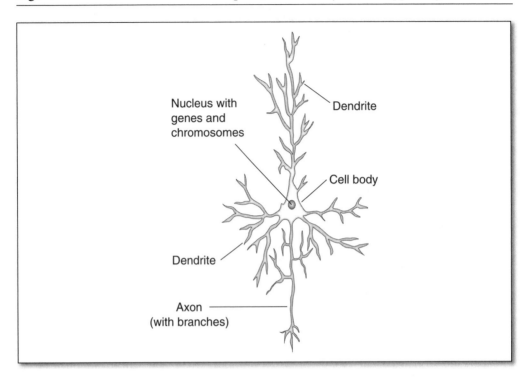

of other cells in the body. The housekeeping part of the cell makes proteins and molecules necessary for the cell's survival and guides the way neurons get wired together. The second part of the neuron is what makes nerve cells different from other human cells. **Nerve fibers** spread out from the neuron body as special appendages (LeDoux, 2002). The branches emanating from the cell body may be as tiny as the space between neurons, about a 200,00th of a millimeter across or as long as the dendrites responsible for connecting the entire length of the spinal column. The fibers, or appendages, consist of a multitude of dendrites and one axon (Greenfield, 2000; Nolte, 2002; Sylwester, 2005).

Dendrites branch out like tree limbs and seek connections with other neurons. A single neuron could have as few as 10 dendrites; or, as a dendrite develops and its surface is equipped with spines, there could be many thousands of areas on its numerous appendages for input (Diamond, 1998; Greenfield, 2000; Sylwester, 2005). While dendrites seek to draw in chemicals and connect with other neurons, their counterpart, the axon, is in a state of preparation to pass on a charge to the neighboring neuron (see Figure 3.2). Although each neuron has a single axon, each axon branches many times before its end with innumerable shipping terminals (LeDoux, 2002). Connection between neurons is accomplished as the neuron's internal positive charge becomes surrounded outside the cell wall by electrons with a negative charge. Positive ions inside the neuron are potassium. The ions outside the cell are negatively charged sodium. With positive ions inside and negative ions outside the cell wall, everything is in balance, but anticipatory. Scientists liken this state to a flood wall with pressure against it. If there is even the tiniest crack or break, the equalizing state is broken and water erupts. This resting state of a neuron is referred to as constantly generating a potential difference (learning potential). The potential difference is disturbed or broken when a neighboring neuron's axon shivers from an electrical charge created by an imbalance and spews a chemical into the tiny space between two neurons, which is the synapse (Greenfield, 2000; Pence & Justice, 2008; Schwartz & Begley, 2003). These chemicals are **neurotransmitters.**

Getting across the neural channel in the brain, the synapse, is accomplished in a nanosecond and at a speed up to 250 miles an hour (see Figure 3.3). Neurotransmitters diffuse across the miniscule space to neighboring dendrites and to waiting ion receptors,

Figure 3.3 Neurons communicate chemically across a synaptic channel and electrically within the neuron body.

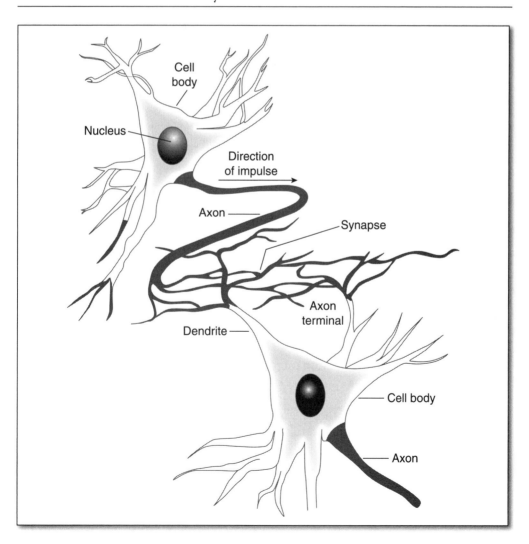

or docking stations. At this point, depending upon the strength of the reception at the stations, the neighboring neuron can receive a disruption of its resting state with an electrical charge itself, or it can be unresponsive. It is important to realize that a neuron is not limited to responding to single dendrite connection. One nerve cell could be receiving tens of thousands of inputs all over its dendritic branches (Greenfield, 2000). Additionally, hundreds or thousands of neurons could be involved with a single thought. Marian Diamond and Jane Hopson (1998) estimate 85 billion neurons with 1,000 trillion contact points are available to create electrical and chemical storms in each human brain.

Firing Neurons Determine Learning Potential

The strength and repetition of neural connections determine if the chemical and electrical sequence qualifies for permanence. If indeed it is a concentrated and elongated process, it will become permanent, and the pathway will continue to respond automatically. This amazing stellar activation process among neurons is the essence of what happens when learning occurs. An enduring chemical state is critical to learning. Depending upon the nature of the reception the neurotransmitters receive at their docking stations, an **excitatory postsynaptic potential,** could result, as described. Or, with a less than needed response an **inhibitory postsynaptic potential,** may shut down the action (Nolte, 2002). Strong signals support continued firing among neurons when learning is happening. Weak signals fail to excite neighboring neurons, connections are not continued, and the learner simply fails to notice.

Research Supports Learning Potential Proteins

Students can focus and force neurons to build connections by *concentrating,* reinforce the connections by *repeating,* and speed the processes of the neural firing along the routes by *practicing.* These concerted efforts force neurons to build automatic connections, and the demand on the circuits eventually becomes minimal according to Schwartz and Begley, 2003. These neuroscientists report that student concentration and willingness to sustain attention increases and amplifies blood flow activity in the particular brain circuits automatically selected for the task. Teachers cannot force students to learn; however, they can provide a setting and provocative information that encourages students to become consciously engaged with the learning process. Consider innovative practices, such as giving clues to identify a mystery guest, changing common games into vocabulary practice, writing a curious sentence to be proven or discredited, or playing hangman in reverse—earning a body part for each step toward a class surprise or a reduced homework assignment.

Active engagement of the chemicals within the brain's neurons leads to long term learning. Most likely, there are many proteins involved when students activate learning patterns. Recently, scientists gained important evidence of a particular protein's effect on learning and remembering. Researchers Whitlock, Heyman, Shuler, and Bear (2006) identified a protein, **PKM-zeta,** as the potential chemical for **long term potentiation,** LTP, for memory. To test their hypothesis, scientists trained rats to avoid a certain area of their cage where scientists had produced a mild shock zone. Next, the scientists tested for the effects of the LTP protein by giving the rodents a chemical injection to eliminate the protein from the neurons interacting in the hippocampus. The hippocampus is a structure in the primitive part of the brain where working memory originates. When the protein was removed, amnesia and loss of the learned behavior was observed. The animals returned to the area, forgetting that the area is where they would receive a shock. The protein elimination treatment did not have permanent effects, nor did it affect other proteins present in the hippocampus (Whitlock et al., 2006). The study is significant, as it provides further insight into one specific chemical the brain uses to excite neurons. Educators can use this information to consider how the instructional strategies they use will be likely to encourage students to become consciously engaged in learning. Without fierce chemical activity in the brain's hippocampus, students will not retain information or experiences that are important to recall.

Inhibitory Neurons Screen Sensory Input

Concentrated effort allows students to learn and remember, and it is important to realize that all sensory input cannot be remembered. The human brain is constantly blocking unnecessary, unimportant signals through a self-protective screening system. To understand the inhibitory system, researchers intentionally produced unimportant, irrelevant stimulation and noise. Then, they used brain imaging to determine what the participants' brains did to ignore unnecessary signals. Certain brain cells, called **inhibitory neurons,** were identified by Blankenburg and his colleagues (2003). These neurons screen out most of the unimportant signals from the sensory systems when they reach the **thalamus.** The thalamus is the structure in the primitive part of the brain that sorts potentially dangerous signals for action and relays normal type input to other parts of the brain for processing.

Researchers found another function of the thalamus. The majority of the signals were not only detained in the thalamus but dropped from memory as if they had never been received (Blankenburg et al., 2003). The process appears to unconsciously free the neocortex, the human thinking portions of the brain, to pay attention and concentrate on specific sensory information that is most relevant to the present task. In the classroom, teachers can observe the results of inhibitory neurons in the thalamus when students intentionally or unconsciously focus and concentrate on their work in spite of other noises and activities that could be distracters in most classrooms.

WHAT COULD YOU TELL YOUR STUDENTS ABOUT THEIR BRAIN'S CELLS AND CONNECTIONS FOR LEARNING?

To live and learn, people rely on the brain to talk to itself using all of its parts. Talk happens through connections among the brain's nerve cells, called neurons. *This elaborate communication system may be pictured as a forest of living trees. A walk through the woods reveals many different types, many sizes, and trees at many different stages of development. If we picture each tree having one trunk (an axon), a juncture where the main branching begins (the cell body), and many branches (dendrites), we begin to imagine a neuron (see Figure 3.2).*

Of course, a neuron is infinitely small and cannot be seen except with a dark stain, called a Golgi stain, and highly powered magnification. While a forest has hundreds, maybe hundreds of thousands of trees, your brain has over 85 billion neurons. Scientists estimate that you could have 1,000 trillion contact points in your brain. Check out what that number looks like. It is so large you could not count to that number in a lifetime. The forest has trees of many sizes and shapes. Some are short and squatty while others are tall and lanky. Neurons have many shapes as well (see Figure 3.1). Some are triangular shaped with short stubby dendrites and a pint-sized axon. Other neurons may be more square or rounded. Dendrites and axons may be several feet long if they are located in the spinal column. They may run all the way from your brain to your big toe to allow you to flex or point it. Axons are not rooted in the ground like trees: They may spread out from the cell body in any direction. And, some trees have not had a lot of light or may be crowded out by other trees. These trees have not grown. Similarly, some neurons have not been fed with chemicals and electrical charges, and they have not sprouted many dendrites. Their axons have not grown, either.

Neurons are different from other cells in a person's body. They are nerve cells, which means they have nerve fibers leading out from the cell body. The nerve cells are the dendrites, branches from the tree; and the axon, a trunk or single, different branch. In our brain, the dendrites are searching for messages to connect their neurons with other neurons. The axon is ready to send a message to a nearby neuron's dendrites.

When you think real hard about something you want to learn, you activate and excite your neurons. They become unstable and make a charge. The charge makes the axon excited to the point that it shivers and sends a chemical out one of its shipping stations. If you are really concentrating and practicing what you want to remember,

> *the charge is a whopping strong one. The chemical movement is intense and fast. The message is passed on to many other neurons, and you are very likely to remember the information. If you half-consciously look at the information and really do not concentrate and focus, the signal is wimpy and will not be passed on. The information will fade away like you never heard or saw it. So, when you really want to learn and remember something, you need to focus attention on it. You may need to write about it, draw a chart, practice saying it out loud, or quiz yourself over and over. What works for you when you want and need to remember information?*

Mirror Neurons

Over the course of the last 20 years, scientists have had one study after another validate the existence of another type of neuron called **mirror neurons** (Nevills & Wolfe, 2009). Mirror neurons are responsible when students remember something they watched someone else do. Mirror neurons have specifically been located in the somatosensory cortex. Researchers also expect to find mirror neuron activity in other parts of the brain. The specialized neurons are activated when people perform an activity and when they watch activity performed by others (Iacoboni, 2008; Society for Neuroscience, 2007, 2008). There are both social and learning implications from studies that stimulate mirror neurons. They allow us to simulate what other people do and to understand the emotions and feelings that are being expressed by the action. Imagine the implications of mirror neurons for sporting events. There are a small number of players at a football game, for example, and there may be many thousands of spectators. Imagine the electrical and chemical brain explosions throughout the stadium as each fan observes and simulates the players' physical actions throughout the game. Mirror neurons could very likely account for sporting events having such persuasive draw for spectator fans.

Another researcher, Iacoboni (2008), provides more neuron specificity by identifying **canonical neurons** capable of firing at the sight of objects. Mirror neurons, by contrast, fire at action or activity. The implications for learning are far reaching as neurons become known not simply as nerve cells in the central nervous system but are identified for specific tasks. Think about how people react to a tall glass of ice water on an exceptionally hot day or the sight of a loved one who returns from a long absence. The response is from canonical neurons at the miniscule level in the brain.

One of the outcomes from studies in neuroscience helps educators understand how students learn from watching others performing a task. Common classroom practice is for the teacher or for classmates to perform tasks, like a applying a complex formula to a mathematical equation, or model an activity, such as a scientific experiment. Could it be that neuroscience will some day identify the difference in neuron activity between watching an activity and performing it ourselves? School practices based on neural activity could help educators know what actions are most likely to form stronger neural pathways for recalling and remembering.

WHAT CAN YOU TELL YOUR STUDENTS ABOUT MIRROR NEURONS?

A number of years ago, neuroscientists discovered an interesting phenomenon. A study was being conducted with monkeys. For the experiment, the monkeys had electrodes pasted on their heads. During a break, one researcher reached for and began eating raisins. He glanced at the monitor and observed activity in the monkey's brain in the sensory and motor areas. He continued to eat, and the activity continued to happen in the monkey's brain. It was as if the monkey was reaching for the raisins and putting them in his own mouth. This accidental discovery led to a series of experiments over the last two decades to better understand specialized neurons, called mirror neurons. *Your mirror neurons ignite when you watch someone else who is actively doing something. We excite neurons and can learn from what other people are doing. You can learn when you watch a teacher model a problem on the board or another student conduct an experiment. The question, scientists will some day tell us, is what the difference is in how our neurons fire when we watch an activity or conduct it ourselves.*

TEACHING TO INCREASE LEARNING POTENTIAL

Students' ability to learn continues to become more complex and relatively pliable during childhood and early adolescence. Their ability to pay attention and concentrate increases as well. Teachers of any grade level are able to tell you how long their students can focus during teacher talk or lecture, silent reading, an experiment, or a cooperative group. For students to stay engaged with any project or sensory input, they must focus and participate.

Although some specialists attempt to put time limits on learning activities and preschedule learning breaks, there is no valid response to all situations. The answer to how long can students attend is, "It depends." The length of participation varies with the age of students and the complexity of the task. For one student in a particular grade a task may be highly challenging while for another child in the class it may not require much cognitive work. We do know that stopping an activity after an undetermined period of sustained focus, switching to something new, or taking a brain break are critical for learning to take place. During intense concentration, a student makes huge demands on the oxygen and brain fuel, glucose, which is available to the entire body. Although the brain may be a mere 3 to 5% of the entire body weight, it can demand 20 to 25% of all the available energy resources during periods when the student is engaged in intensive focus for learning and remembering.

Brain Breaks Validated

During a break or alternate activity, neurons and brain structures that were taxed during the focus period have a chance to quiet down and absorb, which creates a potential for remembering. Pushing students to stay on task for too long is counterproductive to remembering. Breaks from extended instructional time are beneficial. Teachers know intuitively from reading their students' behaviors and body language when a break is needed—whether it is in the lesson plan or not. A brain break can mean a shift in the mental state (drawing a picture of what you are thinking, getting up and talking with two other people about your ideas, moving to another part of the classroom, or doing a quick song with physical actions); likewise, it can be an all out physical activity (physical education, recess, lunch, going to the library, or taking a run around the playground).

Scientists validate giving breaks as good teaching practice. A current study involving 1,800 middle school students suggests that physical activities are as important as academic learning itself. This particular study showed a positive correlation between high scores for physical fitness tests and comparatively high achievement with academic testing (Parker-Pope, 2009). Physical fitness tests give an indication of the heightened state of activities students must do to attain high scores. Many recent studies validate the importance of recess, physical education, and active times for their positive impact on student learning. Research from neurology explains why human brains need to rest from active learning. Behavioral studies show positive correlation between physical exercise and student achievement.

WHAT COULD YOU TELL YOUR STUDENTS ABOUT HOW LONG THEY SHOULD STUDY?

The human brain is in charge of your entire body. As it is the central control station, it can decide without your knowledge where the body's fuel and energy can be used. When you are studying hard, practicing, rehearsing, or developing charts or diagrams to learn important information, your brain can commandeer a huge chunk of its resources for the work you have selected. However, it is important to realize that the brain fatigues easily, as well. When you feel yourself wavering from the task, take a break. Do something else. But, predetermine how long you will stop before you return to complete the work. It is simply too easy to stay away from and not return to difficult tasks.

The break you take or time out for another activity is actually an advantage for the brain. It helps the neural connections to quiet down and for learning to actualize or happen. When you start up again on the task, you are more likely to have strengthened your learning; it will be easier. So, be disciplined about your study—and your breaks.

Learning Application: Engaging Students With Learning

Teachers are neurosmart when they realize the focus in the classroom is not how they execute a perfect lesson. Teachers who have thought about the plethora of information from neuroscience know how important it is to understand how students learn. Student learning outcomes are of utmost importance. As we saw earlier in this chapter, students have the potential to learn when their brain cells are excessively excited, unbalanced, and wired together. This state does not happen when students are passively listening to the teacher tell them what they need to know. Remember, in a classroom where the teacher does most of the talking, the teacher is also doing most of the learning. Engaged learners learn.

How can a teacher teach to engage students the way students are able to learn? A classroom where students are actively engaged with learning is different. It is vibrant. It is moving. It is filled with conversation and a flurry of activities. The teacher is in control of what is to be presented and the flow of the lesson; the students are in control of the amount of learning that results.

Student Talk and Active Engagement

A classroom that demands student engagement does not allow any student to be disconnected from the lesson. Students remain in a continual state of readiness, for they are expected to think, to respond, and to learn. There is no time to think about anything else when a classroom is really cooking with learning potential. It is not a quiet, orderly, neatly managed environment. The teacher is in charge and has a plan for the lesson, but the responses, while anticipated, cannot be predicted. Students bring a wild range of information, a wide berth of needs, and a whimsical curiosity. The classroom can be anything but predictable when students are actively learning. They know it, and they savor the opportunity to be in happening, active classrooms.

Teaching brain compatible strategies look and sound very different from traditional practices that require students to *wait for teacher to call on me—or not.* The expectation is that students will be responsible to stay focused and at a continual state of readiness to contribute and respond out loud. This type of practice strengthens newly forming neural pathways to remain vital for learning and remembering. How does a teacher ensure student engagement? Opportunities are endless, but here are some suggestions.

Call out oral responses—the teacher stops talking and signals students to respond. There are many ways this engagement can happen. The most common strategy is to have all students answer a question out loud and in unison. If the expected response does not occur, the prompt is repeated. A variation is to request responses from the right or left side of the class, from boys or girls, from tables, or from rows. Students can also repeat the teacher's statements.

A more advanced strategy requires students to listen attentively to one another as if they are having a large group discussion. This technique requires individuals to keep track of answers given by others and wait for an opening to take a turn to talk. Note, the teacher's role is not to call on specific students; rather, it is to indicate attentiveness through a sign of approval, such as a nod, open hand, or step toward the self-initiated speaker. If responses are not accurate or moving away from the topic, the teacher intervenes and redirects the discussion. When the discussion is exhausted, the teacher moves on with the lesson. Students can also be asked to repeat someone else's answer or add to it. These more advanced call out strategies expect students to be attentive to what other students have to say. It requires some practice and enhances not only listening skills but also fosters respect among students.

Review of the previous day—at the start of class, the teacher asks for a paragraph that capitulates the prior day's information and learning. This can be developed in partner or table teams. The activity can also be conducted by having students give responses while the teacher types them into a computer to appear on a classroom screen. When the review is complete, students read their compositions aloud and identify and call out key phrases or concepts when they are prompted.

Talking with a partner—the teacher assigns or asks for students to partner up. Students are prompted to discuss the answer to a question, brainstorm a list, share an experience, develop a statement, or form another response that can be written or given orally to the rest of the class. Two or three partner teams can join together to form a group of four or six to extend the wealth of available ideas.

Jotting a note—students are directed to write their answers to a teacher prompt or a series of prompts. Next, they compare their responses with other students' answers. This could be done with students sitting near them or by walking around the classroom and getting a set number of responses to determine the correctness or expand upon an original response.

Listening for key words, team identify—teams of students are directed to listen for key words (or any other information important to the learning standard) during a listening or reading experience. The group collaborates for their responses. Next, a team representative goes to the board to write the team response. The team that finishes first and the one with the most correct responses are awarded points. This can also be an individual activity as students write responses and vie for the longest list.

Repeating and expanding upon teacher responses—the teacher pauses frequently to have a student, partner pair, or team recapture what the teacher said in their own words. "Can anyone add more?" and, "Does someone have a different answer?" and, "Repeat as closely as you can what the last answer was," or, "Do you agree with the answer, why or why not?" are key responses to encourage active dialogue and engagement.

Complete the sentence—the teacher says the opening prompt or places it on a screen or board. Students work in teams or with partners to complete the phrase. This can become more engaging if teams sign in when they are done for additional points to early responders. Incorrect answers are doubly subtracted from the team score.

Remember back to the first, second, or third point—the teacher announces there will be three (or another number) of key points the students need to remember. While teacher input is given, the teacher stops and asks the class to respond, "What was the first point (or second, or third)?" This questioning happens continually during the lesson to force students to hold important information or concepts in their working memory.

Split sentences—to provide a review of key information, statements are written in sentence (or paragraph) format. Each piece of information is separated into two parts. The parts are passed out, so each student has one. Students need to find a person who has the match to their own part to make their information make sense. The next step is for each team to explain, demonstrate, or draw a picture that will help others remember the important information they have pieced together. Some sentences (or paragraphs) may be duplicated, so there are enough written statements for every student to have one part.

Find the answer and post—the teacher provides questions on the screen or board that students need to answer by consulting research materials (the Internet, books, through interviewing others, or papers). Teams find responses and post answers for team points. This activity works well when there are a variety of answers possible for each question. The reverse activity—of the teacher providing the answer and having students develop questions—is also effective engagement.

Read or listen and make questions—the teacher selects material for the students to study. They review and then make questions that they feel represent the salient points. Student questions can be used as a class test to find out if they have mastered the information.

Provide a new heading—the students listen to a lecture or read a selection and then provide a new title for the session. They can work in partner or table teams. An additional task is to ask students to change topic sentences to better reflect paragraph content.

Find others who agree—the teacher selects controversial or multiple answer statements. Students respond individually, and then they walk around and talk about their ideas. They must find three (or any other number the teacher selects) other students who agree with each of their answers, or they must change their response.

Summarize, capitulate, diagram, or draw it out—at the end of the lesson, individuals or groups are responsible to summarize the key elements of the lesson by providing a written or acted-out product. This is a powerful strategy as students enter the summary or description in their daily journals, and they can use the information to prepare for an end-of-the-study assessment.

Special Classroom Setup and Materials

Classrooms where students are actively engaged in learning look different from those where the teacher is the main speaker. While the elements of active classrooms are diverse, some materials and setup ideas are listed.

Computer and screen, white board and markers, smart board, overhead projector, or a standard chalkboard

Chart board, paper, and wall space

Space for student movement and student projects

Notebooks or journals

Point system

Student learning incentives (going to lunch early; limiting homework; free, game, social, or computer time; bringing their music to class, free time to text message with others in the class, grade points, chewing gum or eating a snack in class)

Resource materials (include community experts to speak or be available for a call)

Internet access

Instructional use of cell phones (this option is addressed in Chapter 9)

Teacher Acknowledgment and Class Standards

For educators, providing activities and a classroom setup conducive and supporting of student maximum learning potential may be a challenge to standard operating practices in some present classrooms. Teacher acknowledgment that teaching is not about how teachers execute the ideal lesson is required. Instead, how teachers empower learners is imperative to this paradigm.

Class standards can be developed between the teacher and students at the start of the school year or class (see Table 3.1). Students select five (or any other number the teacher selects) to represent their learning preferences. The statements that are the best representation of the class are those posted as class standards. To have students truly identify with the class standards, students can talk about their preferences in groups and/or campaign for the ones they feel are most beneficial for

Table 3.1   Suggestions for Class Standards to Reflect Students' Learning and Developmental Needs

o All students come to school wanting and expecting to learn.
o Everyone is responsible for learning in this classroom.
o All students can earn A's in this subject.
o A productive class can be noisy and messy but totally in control.
o Classroom behavior standards are known and followed by every student, as there are more important things to do than to deal with classroom discipline issues.
o Classroom standards developed and maintained by students are most effective.
o No student is allowed to be lax in learning; everyone is responsible to encourage all learners.
o The responses and ideas of all students are considered and respected.
o Everyone is expected to be a responsible listener.
o Students work as they value learning and may also be rewarded with a point or incentive system.
o Students can count on the teacher to choose important concepts, facts, and important big ideas for students to learn.
o Students can show what they have learned in a variety of creative, innovative, and fun ways in addition to standard testing.
o Students cannot be forced to learn, but they can be encouraged and prompted to learn in dynamic classrooms that are built upon strong expectations for learning and important curricula that directs what is to be learned.
o Teachers understand, foster, and feed students' curious brains.
o Classrooms can be exciting places to learn and can extend beyond the classroom walls for a full, purposeful curriculum.

everyone in the class to be successful. Older students may add to or change a certain standard or provide a new one. The important thing, as teachers know, is to have total class buy in to the way the class will be managed.

Safe Learning Environments

The human brain is designed with an overarching need for safety and survival. These features are built into the primitive part of the cerebral cortex and are located centrally in the brain in the limbic system. The need for self-preservation is so prominent in the brains of students—and all animals, as well—that the thalamus (the way station of the brain), the amygdala (the emotional response center), and the hypothalamus (the automatic body function regulator), can override the frontal lobes (the executive director of the brain). If the executive director is shut out of thinking, learning may occur about safety issues, but it will not occur about the classroom subject (see Figure 3.4). Any figure or drawing as a representation of the brain is severely limited and not adequate to capture the chemical and electrical storm that is raging in a threatened individual's brain. This figure does, however, give a simple

Figure 3.4   The thalamus and the amygdala located in the limbic system can override the frontal lobes when students feel unsafe in the classroom.

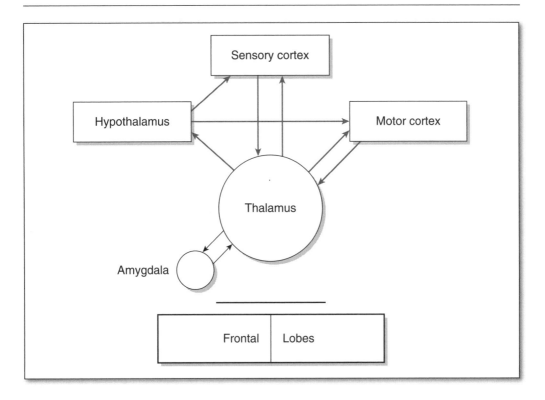

view of some basic structures that are involved with an emotional response to a threatening environment.

The response to dangers can happen momentarily or be ever present. For example, if a reluctant, slow reader is asked to read a paragraph out loud, fear may be temporary until the reading is finished. If, however, the struggling student is continually required to read material that is too difficult, both orally and silently to be successful in the classroom, the limbic system is constantly on alert. Neural activity to learn the subject matter is consistently annulled by negative learning about the student as a threatened individual and a poor learner. Being asked to read is only one example of a situation that creates high negative emotions. Other situations, such as bullying, having a fight with a boyfriend, a challenging home environment, or even a bad hair day, can upset the emotional balance needed for subject matter content to be learned. Teachers respond to these situations by enlisting class standards from the previous section, creating an environment that assures students are safe from ridicule, and providing work projects that allow every student the potential for success. Additionally, when teachers attempt to develop a personal interest in every student, they are sensitive to the safety needs of each one.

**WHAT COULD YOU TELL YOUR STUDENTS ABOUT
BEING RESPONSIBLE LEARNERS?**

We are all in this school situation together. It is the best place for us to be, because teachers choose to teach, and students inherently have a lot to learn. The school environment can be dynamic, exciting, pertinent, and engaging. Classrooms are active laboratories of learners. Teachers expect students to focus, concentrate, and practice the important concepts from the curriculum. Students expect teachers to make learning meaningful, engaging, and possible for success. All learners need to feel safe to try out new ideas, as we listen attentively to each other. We need to work together to set up classroom practices that work for learning and a classroom physical setup that allows movement and activities. As students and a teacher, we need to work together to maximize our time, to complete the course, and for everyone to experience successful learning outcomes.

Learning Relies on Memory Systems

We can have the best intent possible to be responsible learners, but the brain must cooperate and allow us to recall what we hoped to remember. The next chapter reveals the memory systems. Sensory memory, working memory, and long term memory work together and separately to allow learners to remember, recall, and recount what they want to know.

4

Memory Systems and Learning

Much of what we know about the brain's intricate memory systems we owe to a man with a brain insult of tragic proportions. The world knows Henry Molaison as H.M. He did not know his contributions to neurology, even though he worked with a plethora of scientists and psychologists for the last 55 years of his life. According to an article in the *New York Times* (Carey, 2008), written upon his death, it is estimated that H.M. participated in hundreds of studies. Through his tragic brain injury, significant understandings were revealed in the biology of learning, memory, physical dexterity, as well as the very nature of human identity. We learn first of the memory systems from H.M.'s participation with researchers and then move into other areas and structures of the human brain that help students engage in memory and learning. This chapter culminates with ways to activate each of the memory systems, sensory, working, and long term.

WHAT IS KNOWN ABOUT THE BRAIN AND MEMORY

When H.M. was nine years old, he was hit by a bicycle rider and sustained a significant jolt to his head. Following the accident, the young boy had severe seizures, but scientists had no way of observing what effects the accident had on his brain.

Imaging machines had not been invented in the 1930s. Eighteen years later, H.M. was suffering from blackouts and devastating convulsions, which debilitated him and kept him from his work repairing engines. When all other known treatments failed, his neurosurgeon decided to remove two finger-sized slivers of tissue from H.M's brain. The seizures stopped, but Henry Molaison was forever changed. At the time of the surgery, it was not known that the hippocampus, buried in the center of the brain, was the place all declarative long term memories originate. H.M. had lost the function of the hippocampus and his ability to form new memories from the major memory system in the human brain.

Through painstaking exercises, which he could not remember from one session to the next, H.M. proved to neuroscientists that there were two systems for long term memory. The one based upon words, language, semantics, and images had been destroyed. It depends upon the medial temporal areas and particularly the hippocampus. The other system of long term memory was intact for H.M. He was able to remember procedural tasks. He learned to do a complex drawing task by looking through a mirror to see his own hand movements. Although he had no memory for doing the task, he continued to become more proficient with each drawing session. The memory system discovered through his patient efforts is subconscious and depends on memory and learned skills from systems other than the hippocampus. This alternate system, which often relies on the cerebellum, is responsible when we ski, for example, even if we have not done it for a number of years and we still are able to perform with precision.

Henry Molaison passed away in December 2008. His life was changed by surgery that quelled his seizure disorder but tragically limited his ability to form new memories. Although he never knew the significance of his patient participation in one study after another during his long life, and he never remembered the researchers who consistently worked with him, he is a hero for his major contributions to neuroscience and its implications for learning and remembering (Carey, 2008; Doidge, 2007; Hilts, 2009). More information is provided about H.M. at http://www.pbs.org/wgbh/nova/sciencenow/0407/02.html, a Nova, *ScienceNow* website.

Sensory Memory System

Neuroscience actively pursues understanding of the memory systems, although scientists are the first to admit the field is still far from unraveling all the secrets of brain function during memory formation. The memory model used by educators is defined by a schema with three hypothetical boxes, **sensory memory, working memory,** and **long term memory.** Access to the memory systems begins when information is received from the environment. Almost any first-grade student can name the senses, but do we realize that input from the five senses is the only way we know anything? If various notifications, visuals, or stimuli do not come to us through the sensory system, there is no process for communication from the environment outside the human body. Either the senses receive it or it is not known. The school system gives special considerations for children who do not receive information, or have limited reception, from one or more of the senses. Their view of the world is dependent upon input from the senses that are active. Educators attempt to fill in needed experiences, replicating the limited or nonexistent sensory input. Children with limits to sensory input learn to maneuver and interpret their environment with minimum or extensive challenges depending upon the severity of the sensory loss.

Certain neurons of the thalamus act without conscious thought (see Chapter 3), and the **basal ganglia** with concentrated effort protects learners by filtering out unimportant information (see Chapter 5 for information about the basal ganglia's inhibitory system). Memories begin from sensory input. Although sensory memories are the first in a series of stops to create long term memories, well over 90% of all the sensory stimuli is dropped without as much as an afterthought (see Figure 4.1). What does filter through to working memory is significant—for a limited time. Limited, that is, unless it is consciously selected for practice and engaged thought.

Figure 4.1   Input from the senses lasts only a second or two, and it is either dropped from the system or sent to working memory for further thought.

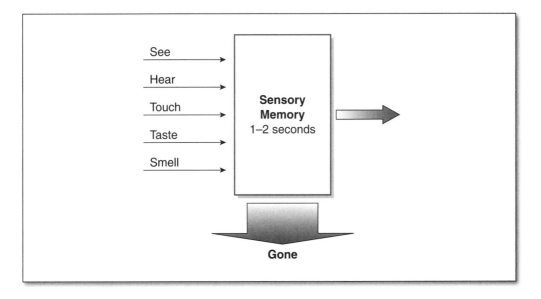

Working Memory—Where the Action Is

Attributes of working memory are not only interesting to know, for all people own and use a brain, but also are significantly important for strategic teaching. A student in the upper elementary through high school years can hold from three to nine unrelated chunks of information that are available to be manipulated in the hippocampus, where working memory functions, for about 24 hours, or one full day. The number of projects a human mind can manage using working memory continues to expand until about age 15. At that age, the capacity for using working memory is fixed at seven plus or minus two chunks of unrelated information. For something to initially be held in working memory, there must be conscious realization that the information is important or interesting. Without some form of rehearsal or concentrated thought, the information is dropped from the sensory memory system after 10 to 30 seconds depending upon the intensity of the initial input. This information is thrown out and never reaches the working memory system for manipulation and maintenance.

Where is working memory in the human brain? Scientists have located the hippocampus as the origin of working memory from studies with participants, such as H.M. With the availability of brain imaging techniques, activity, thought processing, and brain systems can be mapped and locations identified. Information is held, manipulated, and associated with previously known information in the hippocampus. Eventually, it is either moved for permanent storage to another part of the brain, or it is dropped for lack of interest and concentrated effort. Working memory activates other parts of the brain as learners attempt to associate and make sense of the new information. For example, someone who wants to get a new dog will do a quick mental search for information as each breed of dog is considered. The mental search might go to the visual area of the brain for size, color, and overall appearance. The temporal area may be accessed as the potential owner attempts to remember the breed's tendency to bark and the sound of the barking. Parietal lobes and limbic system may be active as comfort with the type of dog is considered. A quick survey may include questions such as, "Is this breed likely to be a watch dog?" or, "Do these dogs jump on people?" or, "Are they barkers?" or, "Are they likely to seek constant attention or provide companionship?" All these thoughts are processed sequentially or consecutively and instantaneously as a feeling is developed about the type of dog. This working memory action extends from the hippocampus to various association areas of the brain where previous knowledge is stored (see Figure 4.2). The brain doesn't find a single response; rather, an undeniable stream of knowledge spews forth. The richness of the association loop depends upon the depth of information already stored (Wolf, 2007).

Figure 4.2   Information in working memory located in the hippocampus may stay for 10 to 30 seconds if it is not reinforced with concentrated effort. With practice, rehearsal, and association activities, the information can stay for about 24 hours.

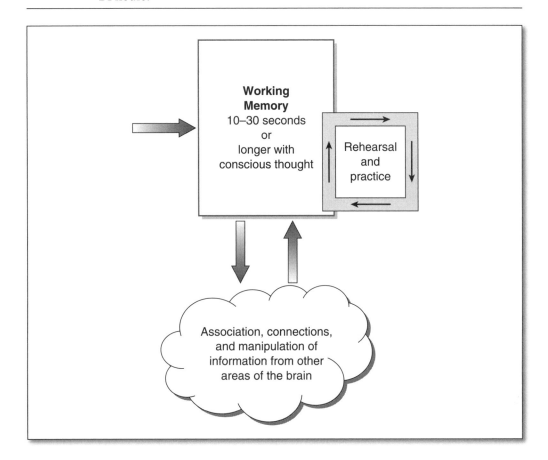

Another perspective for working memory is provided by Anita Woolfolk, a professor at The Ohio State University. She provides a model with a slightly different perspective. This model is designed with three discernable parts of working memory, a central executive system, a recycling loop, and a visuospatial sketchpad. The central executive system engages a pool of mental resources to determine if the thought is comprehensible, and if it is about sustainable information (Woolfolk, 2008). Central to this process are questions: "Does this information have any relationship to what I am doing?" "Do these words mean anything to me?" or "Is there anything I already know that I can use to make sense of this information?" and "Is this important enough to practice it can be recalled it later?" A short term buffer helps the executive resources, which are most likely the work of the frontal lobes and the basal ganglia by recycling items over and over in what Woolfolk identifies as a phonological loop. This loop uses words for rehearsal and repetitive subvocalization to keep the potential learning active in the working memory system. The third aspect of the model Woolfolk identifies is the visuospatial sketchpad. This process reasonably would occur in the hippocampus to allow the information to be viewed, manipulated, and held (see Figure 4.3). Regardless of the working memory model used by teachers, knowing the complex nature of the brain as it attempts to learn is implicit to knowing how to select and plan teaching practice.

Figure 4.3   An alternate model for working memory based upon thoughts from the frontal cortex, with a recycling loop and the hippocampus acting as a sketch pad. A stream of visual and spatial thoughts and ideas are received.

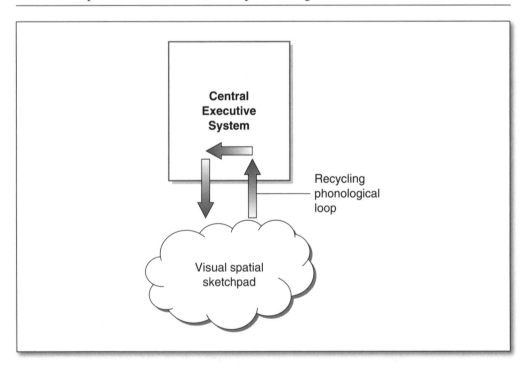

Neuroscience's Fascination With Working Memory

Neuroscientists are intrigued with the attributes of working memory, particularly the degree to which only relevant information is selected. One study using functional magnetic resonance imaging, fMRI, directed participants to focus on relevant information, which was identified as three red circles. Scientists wanted to identify activity individuals use to prepare to filter out irrelevant information. Through a series of practices, some with distractors (triangles and different colored circles) and some with only the target stimuli, individuals made conscious effort to select the target circles. Areas of the frontal lobes and basal ganglia were identified to search for relevant information. The researchers found these two areas to have control over access to working memory (McNab & Klingberg, 2008). Significant to educators from this study is that students' capacity for working memory is not happening in the hippocampus itself; rather, the frontal lobes working with the basal ganglia determine what information is important to the task at hand (refer to Chapter 5).

Implications for instruction are not directly eminent. But, the importance of instruction that emphasizes and focuses student attention on sorting processes is indicated. Students can be directed and taught to determine the relevance of instructional content and to eliminate what is simply inconsequential information. Control over what information deserves attention and focus can make studying time efficient and specific for students. Teachers can teach students a process to consciously seek meaningful information and inherently force the basal ganglia and the frontal cortex to sort and recommend important information for memory storage. There are five steps, and they all begin with the letter R.

1. Recognize important information.

2. Reduce it to a meaningful amount of content.

3. Record it through practice, rehearsal, and elaboration.

4. Remember it upon demand.

5. Recall it by writing or speech or by making a product.

To employ the sequence, let's suppose a student selects to learn about the agricultural economy of their state or country. First, the important products and their financial impact are identified. Next, the information that is really important to the agricultural story is identified, such as what equipment is needed, where are farms located, or what percentage of the population is employed by the industry. The most important information is targeted to learn and remember. Aspects of the agricultural picture are recorded in the brain through practice by writing, listing, visualizing, or some other means that is successful for the individual student. When the student can remember the important elements, recall them consistently at a later time, and apply the information to written work or infuse it into a project it has been moved into long term memory.

Long Term Memory

The ability to find information, put it into understandable language, and demonstrate it through speaking, writing, or creating a product is the essence of learning. All of what is done in the school system operates around the assumption that students can gather, sort, file, recover, identify, and communicate what they know from a common human knowledge base and specific educational standards. Neuroscience provides understanding of how a human brain is equipped to do this work. The education system undertakes the awesome task of working with the minds of students to assure the knowledge base is embedded in each student's memory. At the end of the school years, young adults graduate with the assumption they know how to approach and learn new information, and they can demonstrate their learning skills and levels of comprehension in any field of knowledge.

Declarative Memory

Students must make a deliberate choice to engage with the information to remember and recall it at a later time. Facts, concepts, or processes are moved from working memory to long term storage through elaboration, rehearsal, or attaching the information to a previous knowledge base. The actions can be done singly, doubly, or using multiple processes. A student who is attempting to memorize the names of the United States' presidents in order may begin with the current president's name and something humorous that is known about this man. Then as additional presidents are added in reverse order, the student keeps looping back to recall and practice the ones already studied. This study method uses elaboration through humor, attaching prior knowledge by starting with the current president, and has a continual articulatory loop for rehearsal.

Long term memory has two systems. One system is obvious and deliberate while the other happens unconsciously (see Figure 4.4). **Declarative memory** is accessed with conscious effort. It is voiced, written, or demonstrated and continually shows what learners know and can access readily from long term memory. The other type of long term memory, procedural memory, is less obvious but critical nevertheless. Studies of individuals who have lost the ability to form new long term declarative memories, such as H.M., demonstrate how radically life is impaired if no new memories can be formed. How procedural memories are secured and stored is less well understood, but it may be every bit as important to learning and developing during the school years.

Figure 4.4   Long term memory has two distinct systems, declarative and procedural

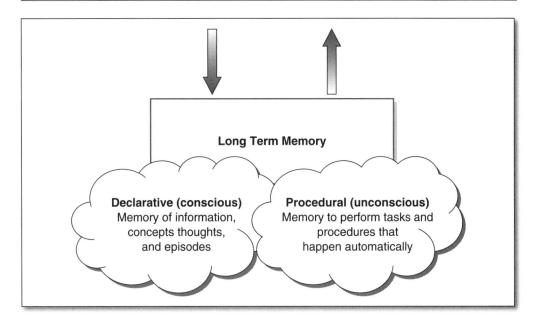

Procedural Memory

In the early years of life, babies demonstrate the wonder of the procedural memory system. They learn to reach and grasp, pull themselves up and balance, turn faltering baby steps into seemingly effortless running, or raise a cup with specific ineptness to their mouths. All this happens through encouragement and modeling. A baby does not learn how to crawl through an adult coaching model. There are a series of steps to be mastered, but they are not learned through teaching. It is not possible for an adult or even another young child to talk through and teach a youngster to crawl. This feat is learned by watching, trying, getting stronger, practicing, and developing the procedural memory for the motor activity identified as crawling.

Youngsters become developmentally ready and learn procedural memory tasks as different parts of their brains mature or neurons become myelinated (coated by glial cells). They become adept at something they have practiced with determined effort over an undetermined period of time. Procedural memory tasks develop unconsciously. A baby is unable to tell the steps they took to be able to sit up once they can talk. It just happens. Likewise, school-age children learn to grasp a thin pencil, put the point of the pencil to a specific line on a page, and move the writing object to produce letters or numbers. Older students can text message using letters in unpredictable formations to communicate a message with speed and automaticity. While the writing example does happen with deliberate school instruction, the process eventually happens with automaticity, without the student thinking or talking about the physical process that emerges. It is available through procedural memory.

Much of what is expected in school through the declarative memory system could not happen without the quiet, underlying attributes of procedural memory. For reading, it is as if the cerebellum, the small brain at the back of the cerebral cortex, and its companion the motor cortex are in training during the primary grades. The cerebellum, as was described earlier, is primed by all those years of phonemic awareness activities, phonics instruction, decoding words, sight vocabulary, and silent and oral reading practice to take over the task of word calling and identification. Action processing by the procedural memory system, greatly facilitated by the cerebellum, frees memory space in the working memory to deal with comprehension and analysis of text—not identification of words. In the instance of reading, the reading pathway must be automatically accessed and activated with fluency and efficiency. If any word is not known, the process stalls and the task is redirected to focus on what the word might be rather than what the word means to the passage.

Procedural memory is so prominent in everything humans do that it is impossible to mention all of its attributes. At the start of the school day, for example, a student automatically responds to the warning bell and moves toward a classroom to take a seat. Procedural memory was responsible for the student moving as a response to the bell, being able to walk to class, identifying the right classroom, maneuvering into the classroom without bumping into the doorframe, having the ability to judge the distance between the chair and the standing position, and even the ability to set down the textbook on the top of the desk. So, as elated as neuroscientists were to discover procedural memory during their work with patients like H.M., once identified, educators cannot imagine human activity or learning without it.

Procedural Tasks Follow a Developmental Timeline

Some students are unable to develop procedural memory for commonly learned tasks. There are relative time periods when procedural tasks are expected to be mastered. When children fail to develop according to generally accepted time frames, they are identified for individualized help with special education programs at school age or earlier. In simple terms, when children have developmental delays, the limitation occurs in either or both declarative and procedural memory abilities. Depending on the severity of the delay, the child may receive services in a less or more restrictive educational setting.

A child who lacks ability for procedural tasks is difficult to teach. The whole concept of task analysis, breaking down learning jobs into miniscule proportions, must be determined. Students who are delayed in unconscious procedural memory tasks must undertake a deliberate, concentrated learning path. Direct, explicit, sequential reading instruction is a teaching response that has proven to yield positive student outcomes when a child experiences developmental procedural delays in reading. Programmed reading instruction teaches children who do not learn how to break the code for reading words during regular classroom reading instruction. Struggling readers are unable to move the process of reading from rote word-to-word reading into fluid, smooth, effortless identification and comprehension of words. Readers who struggle with the very process of reading is the focus of Chapter 8.

WHAT CAN YOU TELL YOUR STUDENTS ABOUT MEMORY SYSTEMS?

To learn is to remember and recall what you have studied. Your memory systems are the foundation of all that you know. The three memory systems are sensory memory (information that you gather through your senses), working memory (information that is retained for thinking, reviewing, associating, and analyzing), and long term memory (information that you can find, recall, and reproduce). Sensory memory receives all information that comes into your brain, but it keeps very little of it. Most of what you take from the environment is useless information that your brain drops as unimportant. If you had to remember every sound, visual image, and touch to your skin, your brain would be filled with meaningless data.

In working memory, you can practice, rehearse, and replay information that you want to learn. Much data that enter working memory are also dropped if you decide it is not important to you or if you already have too much information in working memory. While information is floating around in working memory, you are consciously sub-vocalizing it, searching for other knowledge you have that connects to it, and trying to make sense out of it in your schema of understanding. You may call some information from your long term memory into working memory to mesh the new and known information into a sensible version for new understandings. This process is so very important to activate and strengthen neuron passages. That is how new information and concepts are consolidated into your long term memory system. You can see how the three aspects of the memory system work together in Figure 4.5.

You own and control information when it is cemented into long term memory. A series of steps happens as you move information from working memory to long term memory. Each step begins with an R. To do this, you have to recognize what is important, reduce information to what is meaningful, record the information through easily accessed neuron networks, remember how to activate the neuron memory trail, and be able to recall the information. Our awesome brain is able to work to bring the information we want to mind.

Figure 4.5 A complete traditional model of the memory systems beginning with input from the sensory system with a small amount of important information transferring into working memory where information is manipulated until it moves to permanent storage through the conscious declarative system or the unconscious procedural system.

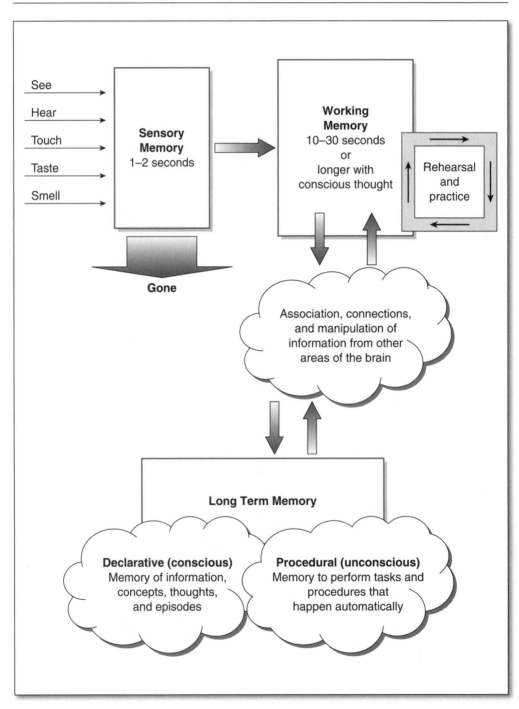

Human Capacity for Memory

Concentration, focus, and engagement are key to learning and remembering. What surprised researchers is that people are capable of remembering thousands of items and details from those items with remarkable accuracy. A study funded by several national science foundations and reported by Clara Moskowitz (2008), a *LiveScience* writer, found that over an extended time period even minute visual details can be remembered. Participants in this study ranged from age 18 to 40. For a task of picking out a previously viewed object from a pair of two different objects, participants were 92% accurate. When objects were the same category of item but a different model, scores averaged 88%. And, picking the specific item from a pair of the same objects with a slight variation, such as a drawer open rather than closed, the score was 87%. Researchers were surprised at the accuracy with which the study participants could respond. What motivation did the participants have to remember details with such accuracy? First, they were looking at items that were familiar to them from their everyday lives. Additionally, they were primed with a bit of competition: The person with the highest score was given a cash prize of an unknown amount (Moskowitz, 2008).

A study like this has implications for teaching. We can surmise the visual system is adept at concentrating on and remembering even minute details. A corresponding study could be of benefit to educational process if it could focus on minute details in auditory format rather than strictly by visual cues. Could subjects remember a high percentage of details they heard and had to visualize on their own? Also of interest to teachers is the motivation of the participants. Individuals are most interested in information that is somewhat familiar to them. The objects selected to be remembered were common, everyday items. For students to remember, they must have background knowledge to link to the new information. Teachers are validated for selecting a lesson plan format that provides an introduction or anticipatory set to excite neural pathways to familiar, already known information.

Finally, the very act of creating competition can be an incentive to learn. While there is caution against bribing children to learn and get good grades, there is something to be said for competition. It is a part of the real world for which students are being prepared. As the human brain completes its organization sometime between ages 15 to 25, the ultimate position is for students to set their own competitive goals and to intrinsically set timelines for completion. Chapter 6 delves into maturation and the adolescent brain.

SERIOUS BRAIN MATTERS—MEMORY IS MORE THAN NEURONS

Neurons are the building blocks for all learning. Certainly, they are the foundation of all connections and lead to the development of the communication patterns and pathways we use for talking, responding, behaving, and remembering (Nevills & Wolfe, 2009). Neurons, as miniscule as they are, can be broken down further into identifiable chromosomes, genes, proteins, and chemical changes occurring within the nucleus. Neuroscientists can spend entire careers peering into highly powered microscopes, injecting laboratory animals with chemicals, and altering the way genes are able to be expressed. This focused intensity frames the backdrop for Marco Iacoboni's (2008) statements: "In modern science, specialization is the order of the day, and then specialization within specialization. Most scientists focus on a single research issue, using just one modality of investigation" (p. 20).

When Efforts to Learn Fail

The field of **epigenetics** studies changes in DNA located within a neuron's nucleus without permanently altering its genetic construction. Scientists in this area of neurology look at genes and their ability to produce learning proteins. They are finding that when chromosomes are tightly wrapped around proteins called **histones** genes cannot be expressed, and learning that produces remembering cannot happen (Levine, 2008). Think of a very tightly wrapped roll of plastic wrap. The end must be found to unravel the sheet; but if it is so tight and the end is invisible, the roll is impregnable. Likewise, a bag of tightly, heat sealed chips can be impossible to open even by the strongest male in the house. Often, we resort to opening the bag with a knife or scissors to release the contents. These visuals help us to understand what happens within our DNA when learning does not occur. Certain neurons that are designated for the learning task simply are impregnable, and do not respond even under ideal learning circumstances.

In Chapter 3, LPT was introduced with its impact on learning outcomes. Teachers know that if students do not have interest in what is studied, do not practice, or do not space practice over time, learning new information may not be successful or may happen minimally. Amir Levine (2008), a psychiatrist and neuroscientist at Columbia University, studies memory to unlock further mysteries of our minds. He predicts that when there is damage to certain neurons that should be doing the job, other healthy neurons take over to complete the task. How does that play out for learning? Some students focus and engage, are motivated, practice over extended periods of time, and still are not successful learners. It just could be that students who have a harder time learning and remembering certain areas of the educational curriculum need to develop alternative routes among neurons to learn. We know that finding alternate neuron paths and stimulating their growth is harder work than taking the roadways that are designed for the task, but it is possible.

Levine's review of animal studies allows him to speculate about learning environments. A rich, stimulating classroom captivates students' attention and cements learning. This act increases the number of protein groups. Histones, small, basic proteins commonly associated with the DNA of genetic makeup are increased while the genes expression is revved up to influence memory. This type of study from neuroscience again encourages educators to create learning environments that are invigorating, interesting, and challenging to students.

WHAT COULD YOU TELL YOUR STUDENTS ABOUT MINISCULE PARTS OF THEIR BRAINS THAT HELP THEM TO DEVELOP THEIR MEMORY?

We know that all brains are not alike. Actually, each brain is distinctively unique. No two brains are connected in the same way. Sometimes, one of our classmates learns things exceptionally quickly with what appears to be very little study time. Other times, this same student may struggle with certain subjects. Some students always learn slowly. We are all so different in the ways we think and the amount of stimulation we need. Isn't it interesting to know we can decide to put forth effort and to learn, but the amount of effort and time it takes to remember is different for each student? And, isn't it even more interesting to know that we do not have any control over the amount of effort it takes? All of the cementing of learning happens within the tiny neurons in our brains. In each brain cell body, our genetic makeup, our chromosomes and genes, are really in control. Sometimes, the chromosomes are so tightly woven around proteins that the genes cannot express themselves as they need to for the learning process to fire and wire lines of communication. When this happens and we find ourselves struggling to remember, we need to spend more time on the learning task. The brain essentially says, "Ok, I can see this is really important to you, so let's take another pathway. You'll have to rehearse and repeat purposefully and mightily to develop this new road." It is more work, but you can learn.

The Visual System Signals Other Areas for Learning

Educators and scientists agree that it is stimulus from the outside world coming into the brain through the senses that allows children to complete the building of a brain that can continually learn. However, it was only recently that one of the mysteries of critical times for learning unraveled. What triggers the brain's ability to learn? Why are young children so curious and persistent in their attempt to make sense of their world? And, how can that sponge-like intensity to soak up new information be maintained throughout a lifetime? A protein called **Otx 2** has been identified by a team of neuroscientists led by Takao Hensch (2008) from Children's Hospital in Boston. What Hensch and his investigative team built upon is the generally accepted idea that the visual area of the brain develops from environmental input. They discovered that when the visual area is mature enough to build understanding it sends the Otx 2 protein to other parts of the brain. Essentially, the message is that signals are on their way that will allow the brain to make more sense out of what is being seen. Previously, it was thought the brain somehow developed on its own timeline.

This study indicates when the eyes are ready the learning protein is produced in the retina and sent to signal other areas of the brain. This protein announces that the visual system is intact. It can begin to receive signals to support the child to learn with even more depth and intensity. The visual area is the easiest one of the senses to study and is the first sensory area to yield this insight. It is speculated that further investigation would yield similar results. The auditory, olfactory, and other sensory areas may also act as triggers for **learning potentiation** (Hensch, 2008).

WHAT COULD YOU TELL STUDENTS ABOUT HOW THEIR BRAIN PREPARES THEM TO LEARN?

When a baby is born, only the sense of smell is completely developed. All other senses develop based on the information they receive. The first years are all about completing the development of the senses and stimulating other parts of the brain to begin the lifelong process of remembering.

We can watch a small child and find out a lot about how everyone learns. The youngster observes and ponders everything as the child's eyes dart around the area. Things are picked up to look at and put in the mouth. Any noise, especially a new sound, draws attention. These activities happen naturally. A child's curious brain is determined to understand the place where it lives.

Scientists who study the brain are called neurologists. Until recently, they did not know how the brain responded to its developmental clock. For example, a baby is not born being able to talk. When the time is right, the child begins to form words and to communicate. Neurologists wanted to know how the brain decides that the time is right for learning at different stages of childhood. They identified a special protein that is made in the retina of the eye that is sent to other areas of the brain when the time is right. So, you developed your senses first, so you could learn and develop your brain based on signals received from your senses about your family, home, and living conditions. Scientists speculate that when your senses completed their development, they sent a special learning protein to other parts of your brain to let those parts know more complex learning could take place. As an infant, you learned to form and understand words; now, you can read those words, write your own words to form ideas, and remember important information and concepts. You are able to learn more and more difficult concepts as your brain continues to develop.

HOW TEACHERS ENGAGE STUDENTS WITH EXCEPTIONAL LEARNING—BEING NEUROSMART

An understanding of the memory systems, sensory memory, working memory, and long term memory has implications for classroom practice. Teachers can focus on desired outcomes for their students and determine what memory activities are likely to activate long term learning. While we do not teach to a specific memory system, knowing the memory systems and the sequence that moves critical learning into remembering and recalling from long term memory is useful.

Stimulate the Sensory Memory System

What are some classroom characteristics that reflect what is known about sensory memory? A classroom setting can be designed to acknowledge and deal with noises, images, and feelings that bombard students and may enhance or distract from learning.

Insist on quiet times for reflective thinking or test taking.

Help students to focus on classroom learning by identifying what lesson objectives are and providing varying learning conditions (independent work, partner activities, small-group and large-group activities and discussion).

Provide innovative approaches to new learning (include bright colors, varied ways of introducing information, find and provide appropriate music, allow students to make or sample food, or bring "smelly" items that intensify what is being learned).

Differentiate how information is available for students with different needs for learning. Provide more persistent, intensive stimuli for students who are struggling learners.

Prime Working Memory for Action

We know working memory is where students can focus on critical learning attributes. A classroom or any other learning environment can be staged to entice and encourage students to choose to give concentrated focus on the selected curriculum content. Educators identify this teaching practice as building on background information to learn something new.

Draw attention to something students have already learned or experienced and associate new ideas and information. For example, assume a preassessment tells what students understand about Alaska. Their understanding appears to be limited to topics of cold weather, igloos, and Eskimos' clothing. A unit of study is planned about the economy, weather, and land forms in this state. Students need to be prepared to learn new information. In this case, they need background information to link and to connect new information. One strategy would be to show a video that illustrates modern-day living in Alaskan cities and the country. Students can imagine how their lives would be different if they lived in Alaska. They are directed to draw parallels between the state where they live and the state that is at the far north before the study unit begins.

Find similarities and connections between what is known and what needs to be learned. Information and resources challenge students to search for answers. For example, if the class knows how an automobile accelerates, what do they need to know to find out how a space shuttle explodes through space? When students know about the Earth's atmosphere, how can they learn about Mars and the elements that surround the planet? Additionally, they can determine if life is possible on that planet.

Help students to focus and concentrate on important ideas by telling them the educational objectives that will be learned over the next several weeks. The facts students need are given to them, and the teacher explains how they can lead to generalization and concept formation. Students engage in conversation to form and validate the concepts identified for the study unit. Next, they rehearse and practice the big ideas until they are in long term memory to recall them when they are needed.

Identify what has already been learned. Concepts are taken to a higher level and associated with something entirely new. An example from science or biology is when students understand how seeds, bulbs, and roots can be planted to start a new plant, then they can explore other methods to propagate new plant life. An extended study would be to search for methods that develop new species or varieties from known plants.

Long Term Memory for Problem Solving and Abstraction

Sometimes, problems occur, things do not behave in an expected way, or thoughts that once made sense are now challenged with new information. Drawing upon long term memory for solid concepts, generalities, and validation of conclusions offers higher level thinking opportunities for students. Challenging educational strategies from this level of thinking yield rewarding outcomes and encourage students to accept assignments that once may have seemed unattainable. Teachers who understand the rich thinking that is available to their students can turn any lesson from a boring recapture of incidentals and facts into an exciting, stimulating, learning laboratory—as these three situations exemplify.

1. Take known concepts and turn thinking upside down with new information. Students can be given information and then challenged with a unique outcome. An example is from history and social studies. Since its inception, the population of the United States has been predominately of European descent. Until about 20 years ago, most pictures of people in our country for advertising have been White or Caucasian. Now, an honest vision of our country through all aspects of media reflects a rich heritage reflecting a melting pot of people from many cultures. What is responsible for this change?

2. Create a situation where students accept the identity of a different person with a challenging situation. Teachers anchor a situation with solid facts. What if you are a California legislator representing the state's Central Valley. The state of California is famous for its rich history in the film industry, its lush farmlands, its contributions to **technology,** its draw for tourism, and its moderate weather. It is a state that is considered one of the wealthiest in the nation. But in 2009, California was on the verge of economic collapse. Assign a county to each student or to groups of students. Ask students to analyze the conditions in the area you represent and around other parts of the state to determine what could cause such a powerful state to experience deep financial crisis. Plan how you will explain the situation to your constituents back at home as they request relief from their business and personal financial problems.

3. To understand a culture or another country, students benefit by understanding the social context of the people. Show a video clip, that has emotional value and strong facial expressions, of people from the society. Play it without sound. Have students delineate what is happening in the scene and tell how they interpret the situation. Share scenarios in groups or with the entire class. Then, view the scene again with the sound. Explore the differences and similarities of student assumptions and the actual situation. Ask students what they learned about the people from the country that is different than what they expected.

Students who are privileged to have teachers who respect their ability to think and problem solve never forget the episodic experience or the lessons learned from this type of educational environment. When adults remember teachers from their school days, they are generally educators who facilitated learning activities that are not traditional teaching practices. Exceptional teachers intentionally challenge students and prepare them for life as they access and develop all their memory systems, learn new approaches to thinking, and prepare to face life's issues that are sometimes riddled with absurdities.

5

Reading With Comprehension, Automaticity, and Fluency

Scientific studies using **neuroimaging** are numerous, and educators can easily be overwhelmed with the possible implications for classroom practices. To be neurosmart without being overwhelmed is the goal of this chapter and the ones that follow. A quick review of the development of the reading decoding pathway acknowledges the value of explicit and direct teaching instruction. The education system is geared for children to learn to read; however, not as much is known about teaching students to use reading to learn. The focus of this chapter is to look at teaching strategies that will help students who know how to read to know how to approach reading for comprehension. Teaching strategies from cognitive science and classroom best practices such as the importance of connecting reading, writing, and spelling, identifying word form areas for vocabulary development, and analytical word analysis are given. Another look at the brain's way of protecting students from overload of information is uncovered as a conscious filtering system. Finally, teachers are asked to consider visualization strategies. Classroom discussions about what students picture when they read can greatly enhance the possibility that students will record, remember, and recall information at a later time. Practical classroom examples help make research relevant. Advanced reading strategies are most constructive when students have developed into natural, competent readers.

LEARNING AND GOOD READERS

Encouraging and supporting students to be successful learners is difficult to achieve in upper grades if children have not learned to read in the primary grades. Successful reading beyond the primary years can only happen if children have become automatic decoders and readers. This feat happens through adjustments to the oral language pathway. Building a decoding pathway in a child's brain is the major work of the early school years. However, if students come to school in the upper elementary or secondary school years without automatic, fluent reading skills, this deficit must be addressed and remediated.

How the Brain's Pathway for Speaking Becomes a Pathway for Reading

During the primary years, practice with **phonemes,** the smallest individual sounds in words, along with study of phonics rules, develops a few permanent detours from the oral language pathway in the brain. For most students, a revised version of the oral language pathway becomes a reading decoding pathway as they are taught through a classroom implemented reading program (Nevills & Wolfe, 2009). Other children need extended practice and review to convert an established speaking route in the brain into a reading super speedway. A small number of students need intensive intervention to force their brains to develop an automatic reading path. What is the difference between the speaking and listening oral pathway and the route used to read and identify words?

Reading Begins in the Brain's Visual Center

To speak, neurons excite a pathway from the ears through the temporal, parietal, and frontal lobes with some effort from the visual association area to bring visions of the spoken topic. Reading, however, begins with the visual center as images are received, recorded, and rerouted for identification. Once again, activation occurs in the temporal, parietal, and frontal lobes, but the initial input originates from the eyes, not the ears. A reader must be able to connect written symbols to sounds and combine sounds that form words. Once it is determined that the sounds are words, the reader wants to ascertain that the words are sensible. The words need to give meaning to others before and after them.

Angular Gyrus—Matching Letters to Sounds

The silent reading pathway that develops includes a structure, the **angular gyrus,** which has not previously been described (see Figure 5.1). This brain structure is located

Figure 5.1 The Silent Reading Pathway in the Brain

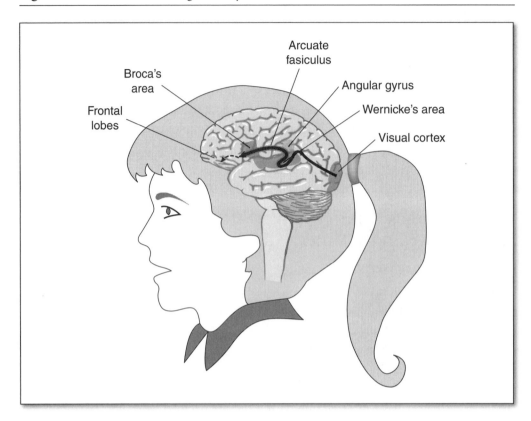

at the junction of the occipital, parietal, and temporal lobes toward the back of the cerebral cortex. This location perfectly situates the angular gyrus to be a bridge between the visual word recognition system and the rest of the language processing system (Nevills & Wolfe, 2009). Additionally, it snuggles close to Heschl's gyrus, a part of the oral pathway. As letters are interpreted in the angular gyrus, they become sounds, which we identify as the phonemes of spoken language. Realize this process begins by hearing sounds without attaching letters to them. During preschool and the early elementary years, children engage in many activities that help them play with the sounds of language. They sing songs, listen to nursery rhymes, and play games with words. "If I say *bake* and ask you to change the *b* sound to the *m* sound what word do you hear?" Or, "How many new words can you think of that end like the word *dog?*" And, "What sound do you hear in the middle of the word *swim,* and what other words do you know that have the same *I* sound in the middle?" Children engage with oral language activities, games, and whimsical playing with words during their preschool years. Then, they are generally ready for instruction that helps them to develop a pathway including and through the angular gyrus to formulate a new loop. Activation of this structure makes decoding of actual words and matching letters to sounds become an attainable task.

WHAT CAN YOU TELL YOUR STUDENTS ABOUT THE SOUNDS OF LANGUAGE?

To become a good reader, it is important to be able to hear and play with sounds. These sounds are called phonemes. Interestingly, phonemes are sounds students learn without knowing what letters make the sounds. For example, you know your brain has two hemispheres. Let's think about how the word hemisphere sounds, not how it looks with letters. Count the number of unique, individual sounds you hear when you say hemisphere. When you carefully break down the sounds into their smallest sounds, phonemes, you will most likely hear and identify eight unique sounds (h-e-m-i-s-f-e-r). And, take the word brain. Drop the B and replace it with TR. Now, you have train. Replace the ending with PS, and you have traipse, which means to prod or walk through. Using traipse, and changing the long A to short A and dropping the S ending, you have trap. Being able to do these sound manipulations in your head without seeing written letters forces your brain to build a new thinking pathway to prepare you to read. Playing with word sounds is challenging for you and necessary for the brain to understand words you read.

Spelling and Writing Ignite for Reading

The connection between spelling and writing words correctly is obvious, but the connection of spelling instruction to reading success has been less clearly defined. Authors and researchers, Malatesha Joshi, Rebecca Treiman, Suzanne Carreker, and Louisa Moats (2009) provide convincing conclusions about the importance of explicit instruction for the rules and nuances of spelling. These clinicians assert that helping children to acquire an awareness of sounds and representative letters that make up words has a direct correlation to reading comprehension. This proficiency with language is actualized through correct spelling and writing. Children take the plunge from thinking about sounds to writing letters. Accordingly, they can appropriately use words in their own writing and put meaning to words they read. These authors propose coordination of a comprehensive spelling system with any reading program (Joshi et al., 2009).

A look at spelling instruction will bring us closer to understanding how students use their brains to wrap around spelling instruction, writing, and reading as a neat productive package. To many people, spelling instruction means to memorize words and to write them repetitively until they can be retrieved from rote **nondeclarative memory.** Many poor spellers in the world today are the causalities of spelling instruction based upon the premise that spelling could best be taught by using visual memory skills through drill and repetition.

The English language is predictable enough for comprehensive spelling instruction. Only a very small percentage of words cannot be taught by sound-symbol relationship, understanding the origin of the word (Anglo-Saxon, Greek, or Latin), or identification of single sounds in words that do not follow orthographic rules. This small amount, about 4% of English words needs to be taught through the brain's visual memory system. Repetitive learning activities hold words lacking conventional spelling in working memory until they are remembered by rote recall. The remaining majority of words in the English language, however, can be taught sequentially and in tandem with words introduced for decoding in reading instruction.

A proposed educational sequence to combine instruction for decoding words and spelling begins in kindergarten (see Table 5.1). During the first year of school, children learn letters that make only one phonemic sound while they also learn names for the corresponding letters. They begin also to memorize sight vocabulary. First-grade students learn regular consonant and vowel sounds and their letter correspondences. They learn common patterns for sounds that allow them to read fully decodable text selections. A few exceptions to rules for phonics are also learned. By second grade, students are ready for more complex letter patterns and common patterns for word endings. Multisyllabic words, unstressed vowels, and common prefixes and suffixes are learned in third grade. Students in the fourth grade learn Latin-based prefixes, suffixes, and roots. Greek combining forms can be introduced during fifth through seventh grade (Joshi et al., 2009). As a child's brain builds upon the spoken language pathway, developing a spelling system to express language through writing is a critical attribute to the **reading system** that develops and expands simultaneously.

Table 5.1   An Educational Sequence for Combined Word Decoding and Spelling Programs

---

Kindergarten: Phonetic sounds produced by one letter and the corresponding letter name and some sight vocabulary

First Grade: Consonant and vowel sounds and the letters that make them, more decodable words, some exceptions, and an expanded sight vocabulary

Second Grade: More complex letter patterns and common patterns for word endings are identified and applied to spelling and writing

Third Grade: Multisyllabic words, unstressed vowels, and common prefixes and suffixes are found in reading and spelling instruction

Fourth Grade: Latin-based prefixes, suffixes, and roots add to a growing vocabulary for reading, writing, listening, and speaking

Fifth Through Eighth Grade: Words based upon the Greek language and other words found in content level texts and reading selections (Joshi, Treiman, Carreker, & Moats, 2009)

WHAT CAN YOU TELL YOUR STUDENTS ABOUT THE IMPORTANCE OF WRITING AND SPELLING?

Words are funny. They can be spoken, listened to, read, and written. In the brain, there are a series of pathways connecting different senses and thinking systems for the purpose of transporting words. It is quite like an interchange in a very large city. Cars, like neurons, move in every direction coming from various locations as their drivers are determined to arrive at a variety of locations. So it is with words in the brain. Reading starts with the eyes seeing letters representing words. Speaking begins with a thought or vision to be described from a memory system and is produced through the motor cortex as understandable sounds. Writing is initiated much like speaking but is carried out through motor control of the hands as they direct a writing instrument. Listening originates in the ears and records in a memory system. No one else knows what you hear, unless you write or repeat it. Think about this flurry of activity all around words and how it helps us to understand why we use four different types of vocabulary: reading, speaking, writing, and listening. They are all interrelated and important to us as learners. Think and talk about which types of vocabulary might be readily accessed and have a larger volume. Can you read and understand a larger variety of complex words than you are able to use in conversation? Why do you think that happens?

[Students are directed to realize that we have a much larger reading and writing vocabulary than what we are able to use when speaking. This happens because during reading and writing the brain is in an automatic-pilot mode. It is able to access an extensive vocabulary that is stored in long term memory. When we speak, we can access words that are not only known but also must be available to be pronounced. The very act of speaking and interpreting feedback from the listener or audience limits the brain's capacity to find more advanced words.]

The Brain's Silent Reading (Decoding) Pathway

A blending of reading instruction, including deep understanding of how words are identified for their sounds, letters, and spelling sequence, reinforces and reconfigures the oral language pathway to form a silent reading pathway (see Figure 5.2). If you attempt to identify when you became a reader, most likely it will be difficult for you to think of a day or even an approximate age that you could celebrate as your *day or age of reading independence.* At some point during your elementary years, you just knew you could pick up a book and read without someone else's help. Brain development that allows a person to read is nothing less than spectacular. Neuroscience tells us that when the **myelination** of the axons in specific systems occurs, the system is able to operate with efficiency. The reading decoding pathway becomes mature when glial cells on the axons of the pathway are developed. The system is said to be myelinated

Figure 5.2 Flow Chart of the Silent Reading Pathway

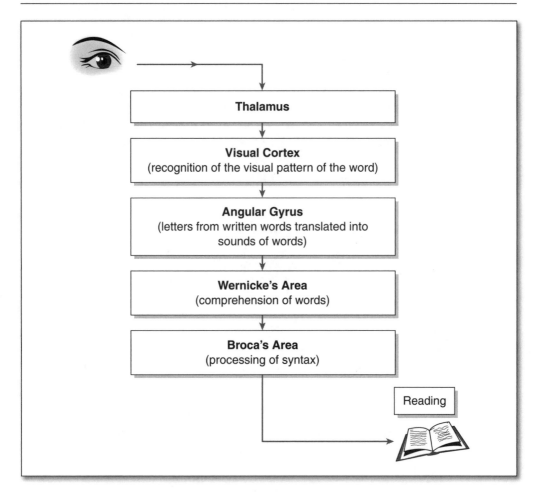

and the process of building for reading is complete. When the reading decoding pathway has axons that are coated with glial cells, reading becomes automatic. The dividend of spending time practicing reading out loud and silently, drilling the rules of orthographic language through a phonics and spelling program, applying rules and exceptions to words and phrases, and rehearsing sight vocabulary through visual memory comes to fruition. The system is fully operational, and the elementary aged child no longer needs to focus on learning to read; the reading system is ready (though still needing to be advanced and tweaked) to be used to learn.

COMPREHENSIBLE READING

Educators in the primary grades know the "science" of teaching reading. During the last 10 to 15 years, textbook publishers and educators have diligently reviewed research, learned new programs and approaches to teaching, and have persistently applied new reading procedures to their teaching toolkits. Neuroscience is now rapidly validating successful outcomes from systematic instruction by producing brain scans of reading structures from students who have undergone clinical reading remediation. There is evidence of increased myelination in the word identification areas of the brain. This increase means the area is developed and accessed during word identification tasks (Keller & Just, 2009). Scientific teaching with direct, systematic instruction can potentially permeate every necessary skill students need to become accurate, rapid word decoders. Students practice lists of sight words and commit them to memory. Simultaneously, readers build skills for lower level comprehension as they answer questions of *who, what, when, where,* and *why.* This portion of reading instruction and skill attainment is known and in place in most, if not all, schools. Basically, we know how students learn to read, and when they do not succeed we know what to do to help them overcome their struggles.

These bold statements could not have been written in the early 1990s. But since then, the country is focused on being a nation of readers. Word calling and word decoding are not the end of the story for reading teachers. Advanced instructional techniques are necessary for upper elementary and secondary school students. Moving beyond initial skill development, teachers find students' curious brains and advanced learning capabilities demand more stringent instruction. Reading becomes increasingly complex for older students.

Beyond Building a Reading Brain

Teaching children to read is the most studied process in the reading and language arts process, and it is the easiest to teach. It can be quite a prescriptive although detailed process. The more brain challenging task of reading to learn and understand content for upper elementary grades and into high school is multidimensional, but it is underacknowledged by research and instructional planners. Students must grow extensive word networks for complex vocabulary, develop deep comprehension for words in increasingly long sentences, and become empowered with neuron connections to various areas of the brain to be able to answer questions that involve analysis and synthesis. How can reading with this level of intensity be taught?

Reading with automaticity, fluency, and understanding is developed during the upper elementary grades. A series of higher order thinking skills necessary for expert reading constitutes an impressive list.

Advanced vocabulary development

Rapid thought processing

Deep understanding of phrases and collective sentences

Familiarity of word conventions and networks

Evaluation and analysis of published works

Organized thinking and problem solving

Synthesis of thoughts for writing and speaking

Development of research reports accessing a variety of resources

Communication of thoughts and concepts stimulated by reading

Utilization of technology as an information and communication system

The reading curriculum must utilize the benefits technology can bring to encourage the type of brain power needed for these reading abilities. Fortunately, neurologists with educators as their partners are beginning to see this as a viable area for study.

Development of Word Form Areas

For students to develop advanced reading skills, we look again at how their brains have organized themselves, quite unconsciously, for reading. Sally Shaywitz (2003) reports that word form systems are used to analyze words for their model (word form), spelling, pronunciation, and meaning. The occipital and temporal lobe junction is the site of storage for these **ganglion,** which constitute congregations of related neurons. A word envisioned sets off a string of neural activation about that word and all the information stored to relate to the word. During silent reading, a skilled reader can speed through text fully engaging, exciting, and igniting chemical and electrical reactions among word form areas as one word is identified and another added to create meaningful interpretations. The most successful readers are identified not only by their word calling ability but also by the unconscious act of creating stormlike activity in the word form areas in the occipital and temporal regions of the brain.

Teachers help students establish extensive word form areas during instruction and reflective conversation. Yes, it is still important to learn and study vocabulary in Grades 4 through 12. Janet Allen (2009), teacher and author, during a presentation at the Illinois Reading Council Conference, provided the following technique to build connections among word networks. Word networks are commonly known by educators as *background information.* The teacher selects critical words, proper nouns, and meaningful phrases from the reading passage. Fifteen to 20 items are appropriate. Students are asked to work with a partner and to write a sentence for each of the words or phrases. Each sentence cannot have more than two of the vocabulary terms. Next, a classroom set of sentences is generated and recorded for all to see. The sentences are recorded as they are given by students, and they are not changed if vocabulary is incorrectly used. Note, the incorrect predictions are not copied by the students or rehearsed, they are just listed. It is not recommended educational or cognitive practice to have students focus and attend to erroneous thinking that requires replacement learning.

Each day when the students finish reading, they go back to the sentences to determine if they are true or false based on what they read. After the students have read about one-third of the selection, or three chapters of a book, they return to the sentences as a class. Students rearrange the words or revise the sentences to reflect what has been read. This type of rich, interactive vocabulary experience allows students to interact among peers, build background information, and fortify word networks for future recall. This teaching strategy can be used with any content area, according to Allen. In a biology class, the words selected for study could be the teacher's choice, the textbook author's predetermined list, or the words in the textbook printed in bold (Allen, 2009).

WHAT CAN YOU TELL YOUR STUDENTS ABOUT THE COMPLEXITIES OF READING?

Knowing how to pronounce and define words is work for the early years of school. Schoolwork becomes increasingly complex, and the number of pages students are expected to read become large as students advance through the grades. Sometimes, college students are expected to read hundreds of pages between the time their class meets on Monday and the next class meeting on Wednesday. How do students in the middle school and high school years prepare to become ferocious readers ready to take on the demands of advanced schooling or, as adults, jobs that demand they are familiar with technical journals or company procedures? To be able to read heavy volumes of printed materials requires lots and lots of reading of many different types of reading materials. While you build vocabulary for reading, word form clusters build in your brain. Soon, you are able to identify words and their multiple meanings depending upon the contents of the passage you are reading.

You would know from a previous example that the word hemispheres *is referring to our planet earth and not to your brain in this sentence. The northern and southern hemispheres are divided by an imaginary line called the* equator. *As you read, your neurons are igniting in various areas of your brain. The temporal lobes are identifying the sounds. Feelings you have about the words are exciting the parietal lobes. Visual pictures of the words are being created in the occipital lobes. During the nanosecond that all of this action is happening, the frontal lobes are putting it all together to help you understand what you are reading. As pathways cross and connect throughout your brain, you identify what the words mean and how much of what you read you will remember. It is not simple to explain, but your brain does all these things instantaneously, automatically, and unconsciously when you are a skilled, fluent reader.*

Analytical and Anchored Word Analysis

Reading with a fluent, sophisticated activation pattern differs from initial reading that relies on the silent or oral reading decoding pathway. The reading decoding pathway is activated by advanced readers only when a word is unknown and needs to be analyzed. Research by Juel and Deffes (2004) tells about successful word identification techniques for advanced readers. Contrary to reading practices used in many classrooms today, research does not support word identification through *contextual clues*. This strategy relies solely on reader background and experience. It does not strengthen the possibility that the word will be recognized when it is encountered again. Interestingly, research by these two specialists supports what we know about how the reading brain works.

A student can be directed to **analyze** a word by seeking the distinguishing characteristics of the word and to involve the senses. Determining how the word looks, sounds, feels, and applies to the reader's unique interests allows the word to be held in an association loop in working memory. This intense analysis increases the likelihood the student will remember the word the next time it appears in oral or written language. The process also fortifies possibilities that the word will move into long term memory storage with other similar words.

A second approach supported by the same research is the **anchored** condition. This strategy also exemplifies how the brain is most effective by focusing on properties of the word, its beginning, ending, root, and sounds. The student looks closely at the word to search for other words with the same or different meanings (Juel & Duffes, 2004). For example, in the following sentence, *The distinguished scientist tripped on his way to the platform where he was to receive an award,* the word *distinguished* is very similar to *disgruntled, disgusted, disturbed,* or *distraught.* Looking specifically at the beginning and ending of the word could lead to an incorrect choice, but including the middle of the word separates it from the rest of the choices. Combining an analytical and anchored approach, students could be asked to think of other words that have the same or similar meanings. Identifying the words *respected, honorable,* and *admired,* for example helps to cement the word in the word form area for the next time it appears. An anchored or analytical approach to word analysis for expert readers increases the opportunity for words to be moved to the semantic, declarative memory system and to be remembered.

SERIOUS BRAIN MATTERS—MORE ABOUT THE BRAIN'S FILTERING SYSTEMS

The previous chapter explained that unnecessary sensory stimuli—a cough, a plane flying overhead, the hum of the air-conditioning motor, or numerous other distractions—are simply dropped from memory as if they never happened. Inhibitory neurons exist in the thalamus, the brain's central control center for incoming data. These special neurons offer protection. The brain does not have to think about every input from the sensory system. Most are no more than annoying disruptions to what is important in the environment. The system our brains use for protection from overload is even more complex, as neuroscience has identified another inhibitory system.

Filtering Unnecessary Information

Researchers uncovered evidence that the basal ganglia, an area involved with important movement and other tasks, and the prefrontal cortex, the rational, thinking, problem-solving part of the brain, are particularly active during filtering trials. Cognitive specialists identify the basal ganglia's function. The basal ganglia are described as a group of subcortical nuclei located under the motor cortex and are involved with modulating the frontal cortex (Nolte, 2002). They regulate and inhibit automatic movement (Carter, 1998; Sylwester, 2005). Nolte provides a broader sweep at the multivariate role of the basal ganglia and the strategic structures included in its area of the brain:

> Although the precise function of most of these connections is unknown, there has been enough recent progress that we can not only consider the consequences of damage to some of these connections, but also begin to speculate about their normal function. (Nolte, 2002, p. 469)

The connections referred to by Nolte (2002) are multiple circuits or loops among the structures of the frontal lobes, parietal and temporal lobes, as well as most other cortical areas, the somatosensory and motor cortices, the thalamus, and the basal ganglia. These loops are possible as neurotransmitters excite or inhibit the connections between neurons. The conclusion is that the basal ganglia, in addition to its known role of influencing motor activities, has been identified as active during the very act of strengthening connections for learning or inhibiting actions to interrupt or weaken the strength of action.

Research Support for This Second Filtering System

In 2004, Russell Poldrack and Paul Rodriguez from the University of California, Los Angeles, were interested in classification learning. By using functional neuroimaging, they looked for interactions between the basal ganglia and the medial temporal lobes. They were particularly interested in how medial temporal lobe activation and deactivation happens during learning. They attempted to link learner attention and engagement with the brain's memory systems. Their work suggests that different memory systems compete for the brain's attention based upon the demands of the task and the behavioral success experienced by the learner. These researchers found the **prefrontal lobes,** interacting with the basal ganglia, to be moderators of which competing memory system would be energized. Filtering or interference created by these brain structures formed negative signals to modulate activity in the hippocampus, which is known for its important role in holding and manipulating the brain's working or short term memories.

Studies from Poldrack and Rodriguez (2004) are far from conclusive about the complex interactive nature of the brain's structures during learning. McCollough and Vogel (2008), from the Department of Psychology at the University of Oregon, are also attuned to learning and learner responsiveness. They analyzed and reported on research conducted by McNab and Kingberg. The selected study looked at visual working memory and attention of participants. McNab and Kingberg required study subjects to consciously select visual stimuli for their focus. Participants were asked to select objects of certain colors and to ignore other colors. Predisposed concentration required an inhibitory brain system, which is different from the unconscious filtering of unneeded information by the thalamus.

Imaging techniques used by the neuroscientists showed an additional system. There was increased activity in the prefrontal cortex, including the area of the basal ganglia. The structures of the basal ganglia were identified as they acted with the prefrontal cortex to excite or inhibit information. The task described required study subjects to control the flow of information into working memory. Rather than being limited to controlling movements of the human body, the newly identified actions of the basal ganglia affect *conscious decisions needed for learning.* This recent study adds to our understanding of the brain's ability to limit incoming stimulus and to allow a student select what is important to learn.

Classroom Implications

Implications from this study are exciting for educators. Outcomes from studies by neuroscientists are beginning to show educators how students are cognitively equipped to select and become engaged with content educators present during lessons. For successful learning, students must want to learn. Figure 5.3 shows the brain as it halts unneeded information first at the thalamus then at the basal ganglia and prefrontal cortex. The basal ganglia system acts as a police system to protect the brain by allowing the learner to make conscious decisions that stop unnecessary

Figure 5.3   Diagram of the Brain's Systems for Filtering Information With the Thalamus
(Unconscious) and Basal Ganglia Systems

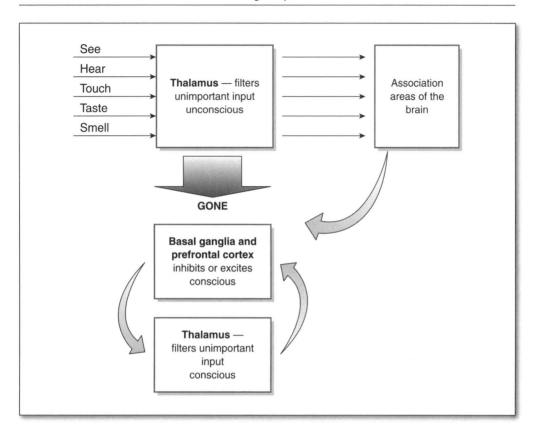

noise or distracting input data. Notice that information selected to be worthy of more consideration flows through connecting fibers back to the thalamus. From there, it is distributed for interpretation in the association areas of the brain. Working memory is dependent upon a constant rehearsal of information and a loop that continues to associate new information with what is already known.

Students consciously select what is worthy of their concentrated efforts. Teachers cannot make students decide to engage with information from their lessons, but they can make the learning environment appeal to the curious and personal nature of the human brain. Giving students information about how their brains respond to new information and helping students to gage how much time they personally need for rehearsal and revisiting is inherently an effective teaching strategy. Students need to be aware that it is an individual choice to practice and study. Information students select to learn ultimately is transferred into long term memory for recording, remembering, and recalling.

WHAT CAN YOU TELL YOUR STUDENTS ABOUT THE CHOICES THEY MAKE FOR LEARNING?

Earlier, we talked about how you can own and control information to cement it into long term memory. The steps you take are represented by words beginning with the letter R. They are recognizing, reducing, recording, remembering, *and* recalling. *Tell your partner how these steps happen by talking about how your brain works to access long term memory.*

Now, we will add a new piece of information. You realize that most of the input you receive from your senses is not acknowledged by your memory systems. Most information is forgotten, and you do not have to even think about it. There is another system that filters information and allows you to decide if you want to think about it enough to remember it. This area of your brain is in the prefrontal lobes at the forehead area of your brain. It joins with small structures called the basal ganglia. *The basal ganglion system was identified by neuroscience as controlling unconscious physical movement. New research studies show that the basal ganglia also allows you to decide if you are interested enough to rehearse and try to remember something you have received from your senses. For example, let's say your study in science has to do with genetics, the study of biological processes to transmit unique characteristics of a living organism to its offspring. You have a choice. You can jump into the study by thinking about how this information can be exciting and important for you to know. Or, you can think it is boring and decide to expend as little cognitive energy as possible to just get by during the study. If you choose to engage with the information, you will practice and manipulate it through a series of steps as you recognize, reduce, record, remember, and recall information that has meaning and is interesting to you. If you choose to slack off with this topic, chances are you will not make a good grade, nor will you remember the slightest bit of information when you need it later in your school years or in your adult life.*

Visualizing Words and Comprehending Meaning

Students need to understand what they read, but the task is not a simple one. This critical aspect of competent reading requires activation of the occipital lobes and the brain's visual system. Again, neuroscience provides insight into what is happening in the brain. Interestingly, the visual system is critical to young children as their sight matures. Young children see objects, tag a name on the object, and learn to pronounce the word. The visual association system allows children to learn to speak. When children learn to read, the visual system is challenged to adapt to receive and interpret arbitrary shapes in the form of letters and combinations of letters. The input in symbols needs to be matched to images stored in long term memory to comprehend what is conveyed on a page of written letters and words. The reading process starts with the oral language pathway, which developed from pictures provided by the occipital lobes. Reading switches the direction as the proficient reader turns words back to the visual association center of the brain to interpret in pictures what is being read. It is not quite that simple, as sometimes what is being read not only creates pictures or images but also emotions and feelings. It is easily seen that comprehension requires much more of the brain's physical structures and capacity and is a much more advanced reading action than merely identifying words through the reading decoding pathway.

Teaching strategies to take advantage of the visual aspects of comprehension were identified by Nanci Bell as early as 1986. Her teaching tool, *Visualizing and Verbalizing for Language Comprehension and Thinking* (Bell, 1991), created a flurry of interest in the education field. Not much was known about the reading brain and its complex pathway. Now, it is more common knowledge that the brain initially uses the visual system to learn words and then reverses the system to understand the words it read. Bell's teaching techniques helped children who read well, but it could not answer comprehension questions. The author and researcher discovered a direct relationship between making visual images, comprehending text, and thinking about what was read. Readers can be encouraged to make pictures when they read. Students are asked to imagine and describe what they read. Vocabulary selected to describe what a child envisioned reveals that all students conjure similar, but not identical, images from the same passage. Connoisseurs of neuroscience know that different images are created by each student due to personal unique memories stored in long term memory systems. Activated word form clusters allow individually invented pictures of thought. Here are examples of prompts to stimulate visualizing and picture forming.

Think about how the people looked. Describe the characteristics of the people in this region of the world.

Picture the mama grizzly and her cub. What words would you use to tell inherent characteristics between these two animals?

Picture the historical figure you read about, and think of how you would describe him or her to your reading group.

Make a mind image of William. Choose some words that tell how William felt when he was discovered hiding the money.

What does the word *majestic* mean in this sentence? Describe a scene you remember that was majestic.

There are no right or wrong answers to these prompts. Rich conversation is likely to result. Deeper thinking is required as students are requested to infer, deduce, or predict based upon visual images they create in their minds after reading a section or passage.

Neurosmart Strategies—What Is Next?

Neuroscience helps educators and parents understand older students as they view themselves. As they mature, teens learn they can be competent yet unpredictable learners. Teachers of secondary schools can look at adult learning preferences to find that they closely align with high school students' learning preferences. Yet, classrooms may be more closely associated with learning practices that appeal to younger children. Preteen and teen years are laden with developmental and neurological changes. The next chapter answers questions about brain maturation and poses a new question about developing young adults: Is unacceptable adolescent behavior a result of brain underdevelopment, or could environmental issues have an equal or greater impact on teen behavior?

6

Motivation and Ability to Learn Through the Grades

How Different Is an Adolescent's Brain?

Parents and educators have been exposed to media reports of the many neurological changes happening to children as they gain adult bodies and mature minds. But, reports from experts may focus too much on the problems of adolescence. As a people, we are doing better for our youth. An article from *Time* and CNN (Cloud, 2007) tells parents to relax. Statistics tell us young adults in the United States are getting smarter and making decisions that are better than teens did in the 1990s. Also, there is less drug, tobacco, and alcohol use. Teen pregnancy and suicide rates have decreased, and teen crime is lower (Cloud, 2007). Scientific studies tell us that adolescents have better reaction times, although neurology tells us their ability to calculate and perceive distance is far from trustworthy for driving purposes. These young adults also have better access to memories than their parents and often are quick to correct the adults around them. Society has teens who are striving to be treated as adults, but who need to be nurtured and taught. The challenge is to prepare them to be contributing individuals for a world that has not yet revealed what it will be like during their lives.

This chapter is packed with important information for those who work or live with children who are approaching or who have reached the teen years. The preteen and teen years are complex and dynamic. Certainly, these important years are fertile ground for researchers from neuroscience and behavioral psychology. Educators and parents are advised to look for correlations, not causal issues, between neuroscience and parenting or classroom practices. The brain is not solely responsible for adolescent behavior. It cannot be blamed for what is happening during the physical, hormonal, and emotional transition from childhood to adulthood. While the brain controls the automatic functions of the body, the environment influences the behaviors resulting from the workings of the mind.

HOW ADULTS LEARN

Students advancing through the grades almost unknowingly aspire to prepare their brains for their adult lives. Sometime during the middle and high school years, these learners become more like adult learners than the children we educate in the primary grades. To understand these advancing learners, it is beneficial to look first at the theoretical aspects of adult learners. Adults have three distinguishing behavioral characteristics as learners.

1. Adults learn most effectively when they have input into what they will be learning.

2. Mature learners want to apply what they are learning to what they currently need in their personal, career, or professional lives.

3. Active engagement with learning results from internal motivation and not through prompting.

These three characteristics are evident to each adult with consideration to learning that is occurring right now. Readers most likely selected this book for its application to personal, family, or work situations. The parts of the book that are meaningful are read without being assigned by someone in authority. Consider the young adults present in schools today. Do they appear to have the same adult learning characteristics? Do they have options for their learning situations, as adults would? Studies of brain development reveal that the older students are, the more like an adult learner they have become.

Adult Learning Cycle

Adult learning theory has been available for decades. Its concepts are generally reserved for higher education, but they are valuable to understand development of the adolescent learning brain. A cycle developed by Claxton and Murrell (1987) is an outgrowth of classic work from John Dewey and Jean Piaget. The **learning cycle** begins with a *concrete experience* (see Figure 6.1). For adults, this could mean

Figure 6.1   The adult learning cycle begins with an experience and may end with active practice of a new skill or application of new learning.

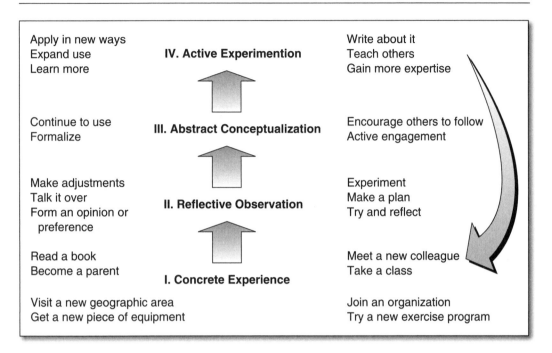

becoming a parent, starting a new job, experiencing a seminar, going on a vacation, having an accident, meeting a unique person, or reading a book, for example. Following this personal concrete experience, there is a time for *reflective observation.* Reflection and observation can take many forms individually or with others. It is a time for talk, experimenting with new information, fitting it into what is already known, and experiencing the "something new" within the context of one's own life.

Each individual comes with what Mary Jane Even (1987) calls *baggage barriers.* Adults carry baggage collected along life's pathway that results from history, values, finances, philosophies, physical abilities, beliefs, and education, to name a few. All this background baggage affects how a new idea, concept, or skill will fit into the adult's life. This is the stage where the new learning is rejected, accepted, or could be put on hold. Assuming it complements current needs in life and is not rejected because of previous experience, it is *conceptualized in abstract terms.* This means, for example, when teachers know how helpful it is for students to understand what kind of learner they are, they fit the newly conceived ideas into future lessons. They look for opportunities to tell students how to maximize learning. At the abstract conceptualization stage, adults consciously weave new information into action.

The fourth and final stage completes the cycle, as the new learning becomes a part of the way things are done. Through *active experimentation,* an adult takes the information, conceptual learning, or skills developed and uses them in many other places and many other ways within and outside the classroom. The learning curve for an adult has come full term.

To move from this theoretical, highly synthetic model of learning to what is really happening in the classroom, it is important to acknowledge that the human brain did not develop for "sit and get" instruction. Step-by-step, sequential, linear, and even cyclical methods are used to teach children to read, write, and compute. However, these direct teaching strategies used during the primary years do not work for many other aspects of the curriculum. At all ages, the human brain was designed for survival and is forced to survive in the school environment. The brain's operational mode for learning prefers to use discovery, risk taking, and exploration. Through these methods, a student attempts to make sense out of each experience and out of each class. The degree of engagement is the degree to which learning occurs. Additional information is needed about the brains preteens and adolescents are using for learning.

Middle and High School Students as Thinkers

Society has overpublicized the teen years as traumatic and problematic. When adults think about their adolescent children and students, they may beget a feeling of uncertainty or even inadequacy. Teens look like adults. Their bodies have matured in advance of the completion of the connections in their brains.

Often, they are asked, "What were you thinking?" Teens are unpredictable. At times, adults can be comfortable with a teen's maturity, and then the teen does something completely out of character or simply thoughtless. Although many have blamed the teen brain for adolescent turmoil, it is not entirely the fault of the developmental maturity of the teen brain.

Two of the major frontal lobe areas have not completed their development. These areas are responsible for foresight and insight functions, according to Robert Sylwester (2005). Sylwester defines foresight as logical, rational thought process on how to do something. As adolescents physically mature, so do their cognitive abilities for foresight. They can be stunning at following through with a very complex project, requiring abstract, independent, or selective thinking. Other areas of cognitive brilliance include the teen's insatiable curiosity, enormous appetite for new information, superior memory, and potential for unquestionable intelligence. Young adults are capable of taking in interesting information, placing it in their sphere of interest, forming a conceptual basis, and using the information (the adult learning cycle) with such rapidity it is as if they never lacked the knowledge previously.

When it comes to insight, however, preteens and teens fall short. Insight requires mental processing based on environment and experience. Social skills need to be developed for empathy and decision making. Neuroscientists identify the areas of the adolescent brain for insight as not completely developed. Also, the executive, adultlike thinking area is not effectively wired. These two areas need to be speaking to each other to counteract swings of emotion. Developmentally, the human brain completes and fortifies these connections in this stage of pre-adulthood, and the environment plays an important role on how it develops. Parents know if their teen has ever selected an inappropriate activity or behaved poorly when they "should have known better." During the time connections for parts of the brain to exercise judgment are still maturing, adult insight and role modeling are of ultimate importance.

WHAT CAN YOU TELL YOUR STUDENTS ABOUT AREAS OF THEIR BRAINS THAT ARE DEVELOPING?

What is happening in your brain right now is very natural and expected. You are potentially brilliant in your ability to work on very complex projects. You have an awesome ability to understand abstract issues and to voice your individual preferences. Added to these advantages, as a young adult, you are capable of unending curiosity and can take new information and form it into exciting and creative concepts and products. Your mind is quick and capable.

There is one area, however, that may not be complete in adolescent brains. Connections between the frontal lobes and your emotional areas of the limbic system may not be as efficient as they will be. Psychologists like to call thinking between the brain's executive area, the frontal lobes, and the emotional areas insight. Teens sometimes behave as if they do not care what happens and as if they are running their lives based upon emotions. It is important for you to know that myelination of the neuron's axons is happening in this area. And, more importantly, you are basing your decisions and insights on information coming to you from your environment. What kind of environment do you have? What parts of the input and signals that come to your brain from your environment do you have control over? Where do you choose to go and be? With whom do you spend time? Remember, everything that comes into your mind from your senses has the potential to determine what kind of person you are and will become.

SERIOUS BRAIN MATTERS—PARTICULAR CHANGES DURING ADOLESCENCE

Young adult brains have been literally on fire under the avid scrutiny of neuroscience. Due to the advantages of imaging processes, such as functional magnetic resonance imaging (fMRI), researchers are able to set up situations and record what is happening in the brain as adolescent subjects react and respond. Other imaging equipment allows neuroscientists to establish volume of areas and even the amount of glial coating, or myelination, that has happened for different age groups of students.

Three Major Changes Occur During the Preteen and Teen Years

Three particular events continue to capture scientists' attention. They are plasticity, myelination, and synaptic pruning. During the preteen and teen years, there is a strong, beneficial influence of childhood synaptic plasticity (Patoine, 2007).

Plasticity

Plasticity, the ability of a brain to rewire its connections as a response to the environment, is more possible during the young adult years than at any other future time. As a result, young adults are at the pinnacle of learning, a time period for learning that is only equaled during the preschool years. The rapid changes apparently happen at the synapse where axons and dendrites exchange neurotransmitters. Adolescents are so ready and able to learn due to the effectiveness of the second major change that speeds the transition of neural signals.

Myelination

This second event, *myelination* of critical thinking systems, complements the brain's plasticity. What is the myelination process? In Chapter 3, neurons and their learning potentiation were described. Each neuron has a cell body, an undetermined number of dendrites, and one axon with many sprouts. Upon examining the axon closely, it is observed to be coated with what scientists describe as a myelin sheath. This fatty substance coating the axon is made of glial cells. Glial cells are developed and recruited for this process during times of learning. **Oligodendrocytes** wrap around the axon to speed electrical conductivity between nerve cells. Certain areas of the brain, mainly the prefrontal lobes and areas of the limbic system, may be only 80% myelinated in adolescents, according to neurologist Frances Jensen (2007) at an annual meeting of the Society for Neuroscience. When a brain region or system is myelinated, there is increased signal transmission speed along the axon as it seeks to connect with the dendritic appendages of a neighboring neuron's axon. This activity happens as literal mind storms during engaged learning or problem solving.

Synaptic Pruning

The third brain type occurrence is *synaptic pruning,* or the elimination of connections between neurons in the cortex, particularly in the gray matter where the cell bodies and connective dendrites are located. As many as 30,000 synapses are estimated to be eliminated in one second (Price, 2005). It is as if the neurons have an *on* or *off* opportunity. They must be involved with a major network intricately reinforced by experience, or they are eliminated. Another member of the glia family, **astrocytes,** busily work to clean up debris, which includes dead or ineffective neurons. If left unattended, this neural rubbish could form roadblocks to efficient transfer signals. The removal of synapses that are not reinforced allows the human brain to respond to important stimuli more rapidly and efficiently. With this increased ability to respond to environmental influences, risk taking impulses can be moderated by exercising judgment, which is determined by the frontal section of the brain. With age, brain development allows more adultlike responses to curb inappropriate adolescent behavior.

From Near to Distant Brain Connections

Recent information from neuroscience provides rich validation for the self-pruning activities of the brain. Cortical thickness is reported to decline during the teen years. Science writer Andrea Thompson (2009) reveals an accompanying finding to validate the lessening of teens' cortices. Youngsters and teens prior to age 16 use physiologically close brain regions for mental processing. When young brains complete the process of cleaning up unneeded synapses and connections, they are more likely to have links among brain regions that are distant from one another. Lengthier neural pathways allow more comprehensive, richer thinking. Following synaptic pruning, the teen brain functions more like an adult brain, selecting connections for difficult tasks that are based on the mental function and not on proximity of neural networks. This recent information would imply that children in the

---

WHAT CAN YOU TELL YOUR STUDENTS ABOUT SPECIFIC BRAIN DEVELOPMENT DURING THE PRETEEN AND TEEN YEARS?

There are three interesting changes that happen between the years of approximately 11 and 20. First, there is a period of superb neural plasticity. That means the brain is ready and extremely able to learn new things. Connections among neurons happens easily, and new information can be learned at rapid rates, comparable to the time when you were a very young child and the whole world was waiting to be explored. Neural plasticity allows you to learn easily, remember more, access your memory quicker than most adults, and form strong informational highways you will be able to count on for your adult life.

(Continued)

(Continued)

Myelination is the second important brain activity. You learned earlier that some sections of your brain responsible for insight and decision making are not as efficient as they will be. And, you know how important your environment is to the development and order in your brain. To complement new connective routes in your brain, neurons become myelinated. As you remember, that means the axons on the neurons become coated with a fatty substance, myelin, which is composed of glial cells. The coating allows chemicals and electrical reactions to happen with rapidity and efficiency. A problem some adolescents experience of an apparent lack of insight is aided with new, efficient connections among brain systems for executive function and emotions. You become more able to think through issues and make more informed choices based on insight and consideration of past experiences and outcomes.

The third fascinating brain activity occurring during adolescence is that your brain has engaged a cleanup crew. This crew of specialized nerve cells made up of astrocytes. They are a special form of glial cells that are able to sort out and eliminate synapses among neurons that have not been used. This process is called synaptic pruning. *It is essential to fast, efficient neural networking during thinking and learning. Your brain is being prepared to be an effective, efficient machine for all of your adult life. The most amazing thing about the brain altering that is happening now is that you do not have to do anything consciously to direct the activities. This is a normal developmental process. Your genes and chromosomes are directing all the work crews. It is preprogrammed to happen now, just before you have to assume adult responsibilities.*

primary grades learn the complexities of reading using the decoding reading pathway, which is located in a relatively cohesive area of the brain. As they approach adulthood, they are more able to draw in resources stored in various memory areas of the brain for comprehensive insight into reading.

Normal Brain Developmental

It may be more important to realize that the brain is in a continual state of growth and development from conception than it is to highlight certain developmental processes occurring specifically during adolescence and early adulthood (see Table 6.1). Certain areas peak in their volume and activity as early as 11 or 12, while other areas, such as the corpus callosum, which connects the two hemispheres, continue to gain volume until close to age 40 (Epstein, 2007).

Table 6.1 Normal brain development happens at different times during the preteen and teen and adult years (Epstein, 2007; Giedd, 2004; Valeo, 2007).

| | Average Ages in Years | |
	Girls	Boys
Frontal lobes gray matter	11.0	12.1
Temporal lobes gray matter	16.7	16.2
Impulse control (dorsolateral prefrontal cortex)	early 20s for both	
Connecting two hemispheres (Corpus Callosum)	30s for both	

A study conducted by Giedd (2004) used magnetic resonance imaging to get accurate anatomical brain images without the use of ionizing radiation needed, for example, with positron emission tomography imaging. This study followed adolescent brain development and changes throughout adolescence. White matter, a dense layer of axon connections coated with the fatty myelin sheath, was reported to increase in a roughly linear pattern. Gray matter is equated to assemblies of cell bodies of neurons, their dendrites, and their connecting blood capillaries. Gray matter in the frontal lobes peaks at 11.0 years in girls and 12.1 years in boys. The temporal lobes see peak volume in gray matter for girls at 16.7 and for boys at 16.2. The **dorsolateral prefrontal cortices,** with a propensity for controlling impulses and the superior temporal gyrus, are reported to be last to complete their development, which may not happen until the early 20s (see Table 6.1). Giedd reports anatomical changes during adolescence but encourages ongoing investigations to understand how this information from neuroscience can be used to explain behavior (Giedd, 2004; see also Valeo, 2007).

The Brain, the Body, and Hormones

A complex interplay of body chemistry, brain development, and cognitive growth affects teenage behavior. At the very time the brain is busily pruning connections, synapses, and unnecessary connective dendrites, the body is under assault by raging hormones during puberty (Wallis, 2004). Researchers report the two are not necessarily occurring simultaneously. Brain development happens on schedule, while some young adults experience early or late puberty. At puberty, estrogen for girls and testosterone for boys is poured into the blood stream. These sex-related hormones are extremely active in the brain as well, and have an immediate effect on **serotonin** and other neurochemicals that regulate or deregulate mood and emotions (Wallis, 2004). It is further reported that boys who mature early experience more popularity and possess higher self-esteem. Girls, however, who reach puberty at an early age are more likely to engage in risk-taking behavior. These findings suggest that pubertal maturation, rather than hormonal influence, may at least cause some of the behaviors seen as erratic, intense, or dramatic (Price, 2005).

Environment, Emotions, and Behaviors

The environment of the Western world is different for teens than it is in many other cultures. What is the environment in which Western world teens live? Adolescence in this society is identified by Epstein (2007) as "the result of what I call 'artificial extension of childhood' past the onset of puberty" (p. 59). Furthermore, he describes high school environments, which group and isolate teens from adults and subject them to more school laws and restrictions than are imposed upon incarcerated felons. Adolescents react to any environment imposed on them, and the brain responds as well. Considerable studies show that a person's emotions and also behavior continue to change the brain and its connections. Teens in tumultuous environments experience a greater impact from chemical and electrical responses that change the brain. Virtually all activities a young adult experiences will alter the brain. The way society treats its teens has at least as much or more influence on their physical behavioral and cognitive responses as the continued development of the brain's connections and maturation of its physical regions.

Neuroscience confirms the brain is a vulnerable system. The brain system experiences many stresses and challenges in current times. It is more difficult for adolescents to exercise control during times of high emotion than it is for adults. The fact that the human brain functions as it does during adolescence may be a good thing. The slow, steady maturation of the brain allows the teen to mature consistently with the ever changing environment. Teen brains are different, but not radically different, from adult brains. The differences represent a stage of development on a continuum of brain maturation (Sabbagh, 2006).

Neuroscientists caution society. Adults seem to be eager to take information from the laboratory and apply it to real-life situations. They warn that it is dangerous to assume a snapshot image of furious activity in certain regions of the brain implies causal relationships with behavior. Relationships of correlation are noteworthy; for example, the activated brain region can be identified while a behavior is observed. But, saying that brain activity occurring in one region and lacking in another caused a behavior is simply not proven. Development of the brain or its rate of maturity cannot be blamed for teen behavior. What can be implicated when teens are overly emotional and make unpredictable behavioral responses? The answer may well be the environment in which our teens live and learn (Epstein, 2007).

Teens have superb mental abilities, and most have no trauma related to their age. It is reported by Dahl (2004) that up to 80% of adolescents have few or no major problems during their teen years. Some adults would like to promote adolescence as problematic. "Trouble and the Teen Brain" is the heading on a Life and Health section of the *Santa Rosa, California, Press Democrat* (Hesman, 2006). The subtitle is even more indicative of what is being promoted. It reads, "Research Shows Mental Health Problems Begin in Adolescence, a Fact With Broad Implications for Just About Everyone." The article cites many changes that take adorable children and make them into somewhat moody adults. It simply is not so for most teens. While some mental health conditions surface during the teen years, it does not mean that all young adults are susceptible to mental illness because they are teens (Hesman, 2006).

Learning to Drive a Car

An ad by a leading insurance company is titled, "Why do most 16-year-olds drive like they're missing a part of their brain?" (Allstate, 2007). An accompanying picture shows a brain of a 16-year-old with a car-shaped image missing from an area in the back of the frontal lobe on the right side. The ad further states, "But when it happens it is not their fault. It's because their brain hasn't finished developing." Another statement reports that the part not developed "plays a critical role in decision making, problem solving and understanding future consequences." All of these behaviors relate to decisions teens make about how fast to drive, when to drive, and with whom they drive. Another key problem for 16-year-olds is their lack of experience in estimating distance and maneuverability of a machine the size of a car. Again, the problem is not the underdeveloped brain but rather with the environment and lack of exposure and experience. What is it about our society that allows teens to drive cars? The expectation that a youngster in their mid-teens is able to handle the responsibilities of driving may be out of sync with their mental and emotional readiness. Driving requires skills that are too complex for many teens at age 16. Early drivers lack experience and have not developed skills to estimate distance and size. Statistics from the insurance company in this ad suggests 300,000 people are injured and 6,000 killed in the United States by 16-year-olds each year. The number decreases significantly for those aged 17 and 18 (Allstate, 2007). Furthermore, it is known most car rental agencies refuse to rent cars to those under age 25 due to the increased accident rates for drivers under 25 years.

WHAT CAN YOU TELL YOUR STUDENTS ABOUT THEIR MENTAL READINESS TO DRIVE?

Insurance companies, car rental agencies, and parents are right. Driving a car is serious and dangerous business. As exciting as it is to have control over where you can go and to get places quickly, students in the middle teen years are better able to maneuver bicycles. Sorry, but the statistics tell us that 16-year-olds are risky drivers. It is often not something you consciously did, and you may not think you are being careless. That is, unless you show poor judgment by doing something like text messaging while you are driving. Most teens approach driving with the serious attention it deserves. But, even the most careful teens can have an accident. First, adults are quick to blame adolescents for their impulsiveness. And rightfully so—some teens decide to drive too fast, take friends along illegally, answer their cell phones while driving, engage in text messaging, or decide to drive when they are sleepy or have been drinking. These are poor judgment decisions. Other teens may be as cautious as they can be and still become involved with an accident.

An equally dangerous situation is that driving takes a lot of experience. The two areas where the brain is not ready for driving are estimating distance and maneuvering a large machine—a car. It is important to have driver's training and lots of time behind the wheel with a responsible adult driver. Adults can judge distance, determine approximately how soon an oncoming car will be passed, and know how long it takes for the car to stop when the brakes are applied at a certain pressure. These things happen with automaticity for experienced drivers. They have learned through exposure and experience how to judge and estimate. You remember the work of the cerebellum. It learns to take over tasks once you have trained it through experience. This training takes time and repetition. Adults can drive to work and maneuver the car in and out of traffic. They can make turns and stops without even thinking about what they are doing, unless something unexpected happens. Teens are not ready to drive with automaticity until they have had lots of practice behind the wheel.

The second issue is one of size. Yes, you know just how much to lean to get a bicycle to turn and just how much space you need to cut ahead of a runner when you are bicycle riding. But, it is another issue for the brain to calculate how much space a large machine, like a car or truck, will need. This problem occurs when we pass vehicles, change lanes, and when we attempt to park. Again, it takes time to train the brain to increase the personal space to include the individual space needed between cars. If two volumes of mass, cars, attempt to occupy the same space at the same time, an accident occurs.

So, if you are a driver, learning to drive, or preparing to drive, remember, it is not that simple. Your brain is capable, but is able, only through lots of exposure and experience, to drive a car safely.

Sleep Issues

Generally, it is safe to assume teens are sleep deprived. They report getting six to seven hours sleep a night during the school week. Nine hours or more would be ideal for this age student, respective of their body growth, mind alterations, and emotional needs. Fallone (2010) identifies the affect of melatonin during the adolescent years. Melatonin is a chemical that signals the body to shut down and go to sleep. It affects the amount of time people sleep. This substance is produced by the **pineal gland** located at the base of the brain. Adolescent brains take longer to respond to darkness and produce melatonin than brains of adults or young children (Fallone, 2007). Teens are slower to get tired. After a night of minimal sleep, efficiency of thought during waking hours is also compromised. Serotonin levels are higher. Serotonin is produced to compensate for a lack of sleep by calming teens down when they are awake.

Schedules for teens change frequently and regular sleep patterns are simply not built into their personal schedule. In 1995, Bonnet and Arand reported that a loss of one to one-and-a-half hours of sleep can reduce daytime alertness by one-third. When adolescents get a small amount of sleep, behavior variations occur and include missed school, irritability, low tolerance, poor judgment, slow reaction time, hypersexuality, and increased mishaps and accidents. The outward appearance of sleep deprivation does not account for all that the teen brain misses. Sleep experts tell us hormones critical to growth and sexual maturity are mostly released during sleep.

Decreased Rapid Eye Movement During Sleep

Earlier in this chapter, the topic of teen synaptic pruning gave insight into the massive changes the brain undergoes to become more efficient during adulthood. Scientists Campbell and Feinberg (2009) conducted a longitudinal study with 59 children. Some of the children entered the study as nine-year-olds while others were twelve. The study was conducted over a five-year period. The purpose was to measure the amount of rapid eye movement (REM) during sleep. The neurologists were surprised to find they were more likely to account for non–rapid eye movement than they were for REM. They found there was a decrease of 66% of the time the brain was in deep slumber with slow rhythmic brain waves between the ages of 11 and 16. The researchers predict that the decrease in eye movement and rhythmic sleep is most likely reflective of the synaptic pruning that is happening (Campbell & Feinberg, 2009).

Memory consolidation necessary for learning happens during REM sleep. Performance of a new task improves following sleep, according to researchers Stickgold and Wehrwein (2009). Sleep provides the extra practice time the hippocampus and the neocortex need for uninterrupted talk. While the hippocampus allows us to hold information in memory, the work of the neocortex is undeniably important for long term memories. It is in this frontal area where new and old information is woven together to make a cohesive, meaningful memory. Calamai (2006) explains the work of researcher, Jan Born from the University of Luebeck in Germany. Born identifies five stages of sleep and specifically seeks their effects on declarative memory. It is expected that straightforward facts are recalled during sleep stages three and four. By infusing an artificial current in a natural frequency to mimic delta waves, this researcher was able to improve word memory tasks of the control group of university students by 8%. He believes natural or imposed oscillations affect the hippocampus where unimportant information is filtered out, and important details are retained (Calamai, 2006).

Conflicting Sleep Issues

The sleep studies reported are somewhat conflicting. Teens are reported to have greatly reduced REM sleep, but they have increased memory consolidation abilities. Most researchers agree that many of the brain's consolidation activities happen during deep REM sleep. It is further suggested that for every two hours a person is awake an hour of sleep is needed for synapses to be strengthened and important memories to be stored. Well-rested individuals reportedly have improved working memory, planning ability, pattern recognition, and inhibition of impulsive behaviors. It can assuredly be stated that some of the stages of sleep produce enhanced cognitive abilities (Patoine, 2008).

Teens get less sleep, and when they are sleeping they have decreased REM sleep. Yet, they are reported to experience powerful memory abilities. They also possess a brain that demonstrates extreme plasticity for learning. These contradictions about sleep requirements and adolescent sleep patterns continue to keep researchers fascinated with the topic of adolescence and sleep needs.

WHAT COULD YOU TELL YOUR STUDENTS ABOUT SLEEP AND SCHOOL SUCCESS?

There is no compromise for the amount of sleep you need. Either you get your eight hours of sleep or more a night, or you will experience the consequences. What do you think happens to you when you don't get enough sleep? The list is staggering and varied. What are the results of how you feel when you are sleepy? This is such an interesting topic that researchers have spent significant time and financial resources to learn what happens during sleep and why it is so important. They report that all people—children, adolescents, and adults alike—need minimal amounts of sleep based on their stage of life. Obviously, young children and very old people need a lot of sleep, but you may be surprised to learn that teens need more sleep than children in upper elementary school. There are more unusual things happening in your brain and with your bodies than at younger ages. Your brain is more open to learning, which is called neuroplasticity. It is pruning away and cleaning up learning pathways that are not useful and unused with nerve cells called astrocytes. *And, it is busy streamlining your neuron pathways with a fatty substance called a* myelin sheath, *composed of glial cells called* oligodendrocytes. *If that is not enough confusion, you add to your brain's burden by continuing to learn new information and skills that have to be consolidated into memory. Consolidation happens in a big way during your sleeping hours. On top of all that brain activity, we haven't even considered what is happening with hormones as your body changes and matures. You will feel better, respond better, and do better with more sleep. Do you get enough sleep? If not, how can you do something about your schedule to build in enough sleep time?*

Social Implications

Educators acknowledge the importance of teenagers' social lives. Entire days and weeks of school can be lost when some dramatic situation is bothering a student. Emotional and safety issues can override learning. Another cerebral area that remains underdeveloped, according to researchers, is recognition of facial expressions. Young adults may not be equipped to make good decisions about how others are responding to them based on facial expressions or body language.

For many years, studies have revealed that humans make instantaneous judgments about others based on facial expressions. Opinions are formed within milliseconds and teens draw dramatically on appearance. A person may be feared or trusted based on facial appearances. McLean Hospital, Belmont, Massachusetts, neuropsychologist Deborah Yurgelun-Todd (2002) conducted emotional tests based on pictures of faces. Teens under 14 tended to mistake photos of fear to be anger, sadness, or they found them unclear, according to images showing an activated amygdala. In the study, the same subjects were tested as they aged. Their brain activity patterns changed as they used areas of the frontal lobe to respond, which became more similar to adult responses. Fear was the emotion identified as most likely to be misinterpreted. Being able to understand fear on a peer's face is important among friends. It is questionable, however, to imply from this study that older teenagers are not able to provide appropriate responses to facial expressions. More study is needed before these results can be generalized to the entire teen population at all ages.

Two issues can be gleaned from the study's neuroimages. First, some adolescents do rely more on the emotional regions of their brains when interpreting facial expressions. Also, younger teens are more likely to access emotional regions of the brain, while older teens are likely to also use the frontal cortex, more like adults. Use of the frontal, executive area of the brain while interpreting emotions allows individuals to draw upon past experience and rationally decide how to react to the other person. A preteen may misinterpret a teacher's expression of seriousness about the topic to mean, "The teacher does not like me because I did not complete my homework."

However, the teacher may not even realize the student's homework is not finished. Interpretation of facial expressions depends upon so many complex human responses; we can not draw conclusions based solely on studies of brain images.

STUDENT CONCERN FOR LEARNING

A common complaint from school personnel is that many students really do not care about school and are disinterested in the school curriculum. A study conducted by Mihaly Csikszentmihalyi and reported by Scherer (2002) revealed how students viewed different aspects of the school day. Rather than observing reactions of students during school, this researcher identified 1,000 students from sixth through twelfth grade from different school districts in Florida and California. The selected participants represented a cross section of cognitive and behavioral abilities. Each carried a pager, which went off eight times a day. When the alarm sounded, students would take out a notebook and record what they were doing and thinking, their concentration level, how happy they were, and how creative they felt. The study generated 30,000 reports that allowed the researchers to understand what students thought was school work, what was more like play, and what school activities were neutral. Surprisingly, their responses broke down into percentage categories of 30, 30, 30, and 10. Students felt they were working 30% of the time. The next 30% was considered to be playtime. Students could not identify whether they felt like they were working or playing another 30% of the time; and finally, 10% of the time, they felt they were working and playing (Scherer, 2002).

What Students Want and Need

Student responses to the previous study favored curriculum activities with computers used as instructional tools. They reported positive feelings about school work that engaged them with individual work, group work, and even quizzes. They felt less engaged when they were listening to the teacher talk and watching audiovisuals. Realizing that young adults are emotionally charged to seek stimulating activities, which appeal to the emotional parts, often the thrill-seeking areas of their young brains, it makes sense that school work needs to invite engagement. Csikszentmihalyi concluded the report with bold ideas for the education system. He proposes, for example, that schools offer advanced study topics, particularly for upper-grade students. Students, however, do not have a right to attend, rather they would have to earn admittance based on their interest and curiosity.

Researcher Nancy Hill of Harvard University examined 50 studies with more than 50,000 students to pull information about parental involvement with middle school youth. The results gleaned from a review of studies spanning 25 years indicate the single most important advantage parents can give to their student is not to help with their homework but rather to be involved with goal setting. When parents have conversations with their children during the times they make important decisions about classes to take or a career to seek, parental guidance is particularly powerful (American Psychological Association, 2009). A teacher's most effective role is to have enormous volumes of information available and to utilize technology with our technologically savvy students. Csikszentmihalyi (see Scherer, 2002) identified that student motivation to learn is ultimately dependent on interest and relevance to the student's world, which is a common characteristic of adult learners. The human brain continually seeks to make sense out of the environment. When neural networks build upon previously successful study topics that are immersed in a solid cognitive base, students will garner more attentive energy to ignite neurons, which ultimately leads to expanded learning.

WHAT ADDITIONAL INSIGHTS CAN YOU GIVE YOUR STUDENTS ABOUT LEARNING?

We talked earlier about your responsibilities as a learner. Now, let's go a bit further and talk about your needs as a learner, emotionally, socially, and procedurally.

Adults and teens alike know you are more like an adult with your learning needs and your learning abilities once you approach the middle school years. What about the conditions of school make you feel like an adult learner? What conditions in school make you feel like a child? Referring to the things you listed for the second list, what suggestions could you give that would make you feel more responsible and respected as a student? What other parts of your life make you feel mature? Identify times you feel you are treated like a child.

Encourage Learning

> I would give wings to children, but I would leave the child alone, so that he could learn how to fly on his own.
>
> —Gabriel García Márquez, 2009

An easy-to-remember set of principles can be used to engage students and hold their attention. Six summative insights are (1) to address student humanness, (2) appeal to personal interests, (3) build on background knowledge, (4) make success attainable, (5) make rewards for assignment completion possible, and (6) appeal to social needs through group activities. Adolescence is a critical time for brain development; however, brain development is not the sole cause of positive or questionable student behavior. The environment in which teens live has a dynamic impact on how they respond and behave. The next chapter is filled with neural-positive classroom practices to create a learning environment in all curriculum areas for these cognitively powerful, emerging adults.

7

Neurology and Technology for All Aspects of the Curriculum

Neurological aspects of learning efficiency for the preteen and teen years can be found in this chapter. Students beginning at the fourth grade, through the senior year of high school, are different from when they were primary students. Teachers at all grade levels report behaviors that make teaching them different. Parents know childhood experiences have shaped memories in their offspring that are dissimilar from the experiences they had. Neurosmart teaching with the same curriculum and standards but with an emphasis on quick and effective learning may mean taking a diverse approach to lesson design and student engagement. Deep thinking and critical thinking can be typical learning outcomes. Smart decisions by teachers and infusion of technology in a variety of ways can ignite cognitive responses in our reticent or often reluctant tween and teen students.

NEUROSMART TEACHING

Those who study neuroscience report that children have brains that have developed with different ways for learning. Yet, visits to classrooms at various grades and throughout the Western world would reveal mostly classrooms and teaching strategies that are very similar to those of the past. What is it about most education system that resists change? Is it that the buildings are so rigid and so present? Are the people who make decisions and teach the youngsters so steeped in "the way we do things"? Does the education system understand our population of students well enough to know what to do to teach them? Our system of teaching based on frameworks, standards, and assessments simply does not reflect nor respect what is going on in a student's head during learning.

Instructional Materials Do Not Solve the Problem

It is amazing that educators often do not get the idea that something different is needed. Working harder and developing more complex systems and materials for teaching is not producing the changes that are needed. For example, a recent brochure (WestEd, 2009) states, "Students often seem to understand a concept in class, but then on assessments their understanding easily caves into pitfalls." It further states the intervention curriculum being featured helps teachers "tackle tough concepts and common pitfalls head-on, so that learning is robust and stands up to rigorous assessment." The ad goes on to tell how the format, lessons, and teaching guide provide an easy to follow process (WestEd, 2009). The intent is not to focus on this particular publisher; rather, it is to give an example of what is available for educational decision makers as they tackle hard learning problems. Unacceptable numbers of students are not progressing according to expectations. It is not about the materials. There are superb teaching materials in most schools across the nation and in many other countries.

Knowledgeable Teachers Know How Students Learn

Education systems and the people who educate youth generally do not understand how students learn. Educators of older students are well advised to know what is going on in the brain as it organizes itself for learning. This organization begins during the early elementary years and culminates prior to adulthood. Perfectly, strategically, systematically designed instructional materials will not work unless they are presented by teachers who are knowledgeable and can make good instructional decisions. Timely and instantaneous decisions must be made during instructional time. These rapid responses are based on how the class is responding to learning at that time and in that place. There are no instructional materials available that can account for and prompt teachers for all the possible scenarios that could occur during each lesson with a particular mix of learners. It takes an accomplished teacher.

Neurology and technology are combined in the next sections to follow a standards-based curriculum across the grades and content areas. It is important to keep the center of attention on students, their age-related needs, interests, and concerns, and of most importance is how learning can happen effectively.

THE BASICS—CAPTURE ATTENTION TO CREATE LEARNING

Teachers can influence even hard-to-reach students to pay attention, engage, and learn. Some instructional strategies can be richly rewarding for all learners. Specific characteristics of good teaching practices are strength of the stimuli, novelty, associations, task, and level of difficulty.

Strength of sensory stimulation: Vivid pictures, colorful labels, a variety of fonts, soft or loud verbal input, rhythmic speaking, chanting, innovative technology, and students' demonstration and teaching all provide strong stimulation.

Novelty and curiosity problem solving: Uncovering a secret, giving students an unusual set of directions, having them find the answer to an unusual problem, following clues, solving the puzzles, finding the missing parts, responding to a conundrum, and talking about a controversial issues will introduce novelty and pique students' curiosity.

Associations: Activating background experience and positive feelings, discovering commonalities or differences, trust building activities, engaging personal interest through questioning, and bringing in items from outside school or guest speakers are all ways to engage students through the interest inherent in association.

Task demands: Purposeful, beneficial, interesting, sensible, age-related, or thought-expanding tasks are neurosmart teaching tools.

Level of difficulty: With the right level of difficulty, assignments, projects, and tasks that are challenging, possible to attain, rewarding, and create pride in accomplishment and the achievement of a new level of understanding will engage students.

An engaging classroom environment invites students to attend to the task. Schwartz and Begley (2003) describe the chemically affected and activated brain during engaged learning. Brain circuits become amplified. When students are willing to sustain concentration over a period of time, with many reinforcing repetitions, learning happens. The student is able to produce information, recall concepts, and perform procedures from long term declarative or procedural memory. With enough practice, information and concepts are no longer new, and the demand on neural circuits in the brain is minimized. Working and thinking becomes automatic, habitual, and easy. At this point during the learning process, the brain has developed new and stronger connections for more specificity and depth of learning. The obvious outcome is a student with positive feelings about the learning that is going on in this classroom. Additionally, there is pride in the accomplishment and a feeling that learning can be rewarding and fun.

WHAT CAN YOU TELL YOUR STUDENTS ABOUT TAKING THE SCHOOL CHALLENGE?

Sometimes, we learn just enough to get by. Then, that topic comes up again, and we realize how sketchy our learning actually was and that we have to go back and build the basics for that topic. When a new unit or topic is introduced, students are fortunate if it is presented in a way that is interesting, novel, and challenging, yet possible to be completed successfully. What new units or subjects can you think of that appealed to you because of the way they were introduced, and what appealed to you about the presentation?

At other times, it is "school as usual," and there is nothing to grab your attention, but you still have to do the assignment and learn the process or information. What can you do to make each new school challenge meaningful and possible? Some suggestions may be to challenge yourself to earn a couple more points on the assignment or to maintain a previous level of success, to promise yourself a reward at the end of the task, or to keep a chart of what you need to do and get the satisfaction of checking it off when it is complete.

Confidence in Learning

Cognitive psychology professor Daniel T. Willingham (2008–2009) encourages his college students to talk about devising their own unique system for studying. All students develop their personalized learning system during the middle and senior high school years—with or without thinking or planning it. By the time they become young adults, learning style and preferences for studying are well established. Most likely, the learning habits will remain for the rest of the adult life. Because the years addressed here are those where students are generating their own learning patterns, it makes cognitive sense to help them identify what works best.

This professor and author discovered adults generally think they know more than they are actually able to remember. In studies where adults were asked if they knew answers to some common knowledge questions, they frequently responded affirmatively. But, when asked to give actual responses, their answers were only partially correct. This type of over confidence can get students into trouble as it leads them to study just enough to think they are ready to tell or demonstrate their learning. This is particularly painful if they need to take an exam. They may have simply spent as much time as they had available to them to review the material. Willingham (2008–2009) provides a solution to the "not studying enough" dilemma. He suggests students add 20% more time to studying than they had planned to develop a deep understanding of the material. Both young adults and adult learners could be more efficient if they understood how desperately the brain needs the rehearsal loop to strengthen neural networks necessary for deep learning.

WHAT CAN YOU TELL YOUR STUDENTS ABOUT OVERCONFIDENCE AND DEVELOPING A DEEP UNDERSTANDING?

There is a difference between spending the amount of time you have available to study and studying for the amount of time needed to develop a deep understanding of the topic. Have you ever studied for a test, and felt good about how much you knew and understood, only to find you were totally unprepared for the actual test? There is an answer to this dilemma. A psychologist who studies how people learn, named Daniel Willingham (2008–2009), developed an activity to test out a hunch he had. We can try it now. I am going to give you some questions. You will not have time to give the answers, but rather you need to respond "yes" or "no" regarding whether you think you know the answer or not. Remember, you will not have enough time to actually write the answer. All you need to do is decide if you can answer correctly and respond "yes" or cannot and respond "no."

[Teachers are encouraged to select questions that are not too easy or too difficult for their students. The information can relate to a current unit that is being taught, or it can be general knowledge questions. Some of the listed sample questions are from Willingham (2008–2009, p. 25) while others are representative of general domain knowledge.

1. Can you give the names of the seven dwarfs from *Snow White*? (Sleepy, Dopey, Bashful, Grumpy, Sneezy, Happy, and Doc)

2. Can you write the names of the continents of the world? (North America, South America, Africa, Europe, Asia, Australia, Antarctica, and the Arctic)

3. Can you name six of the most recent presidents of the United States? (B. Obama, G. W. Bush, B. Clinton, H. W. Bush, R. Reagan, J. Carter, G. Ford, and R. Nixon)

4. Can you name the states that are on the eastern coast of the United States? (Maine, New Hampshire, Massachusetts, Rhode Island, Connecticut, New York, New Jersey, Delaware, Maryland, Virginia, North Carolina, South Carolina, Georgia, and Florida)

5. Can you name five of the seven titles of the *Harry Potter* series? (*Harry Potter and the Sorcerer's Stone, Harry Potter and the Chamber of Secrets, Harry Potter and the Prisoner of Azkaban, Harry Potter and the Goblet of Fire, Harry Potter and the Order of the Phoenix, Harry Potter and the Half-Blood Prince,* and *Harry Potter and the Deathly Hallows*)

6. Can you make a drawing of the face of a penny with 80% accuracy? (Project an actual penny on an overhead, or have a picture ready.)

7. Do you know how to fill out a bank check? (Project a check on an overhead, or have a picture, and check for the accuracy of the four areas that need to be completed.)

8. Can you complete a long division problem with a three (or four) digit divisor in a 30-second time frame? (Select an example.)]

When Willingham did a similar activity, he found his students were overconfident about what they knew. They responded that they knew this and that; but when they were asked to answer the questions, their responses were not accurate or were incomplete. Let's check our responses to the Willingham-type test to see if your answers validate what he found with his students. Check the predictions against the actual, exact answers.

To compensate for what you think you know for actual exams and what you really need to know well, the researcher gave the students a solution. He told students they need to spend about 20% more time studying than they think they need. For example, if you think you need two hours to study for an exam, and you add 20%, you need to have two hours and 24 minutes available for studying. If you use his suggestion, you will find that during the extra time you will practice, repeat, and connect new ideas. Then, you will be more likely to have a deep understanding of the topic, and hopefully your test grades will reflect your extra work.

Critical Thinking Skills

Educating students to spit back information, lists, and descriptions from their working memory may make the grade on a test, but the long term benefits are questionable. Testing students from their working memory is easy to grade, but it is difficult to validate as learning. Education's challenge is to teach information, skills, and concepts that emanate from various parts of the brain's memory and can be used to resolve and react to the world in which we live. John Chaffee (2009) provides a strong look at motivating young learners beyond cursory knowledge in his book, *Thinking Critically*. This professor of philosophy at New York's LaGuardia College provides qualities of expert critical thinkers, which are capsulated in Table 7.1. Educators

Table 7.1   Characteristics of Expert Critical Thinkers Defined

o Open-minded students listen carefully and evaluate fairly.
o Knowledgeable thinkers offer opinions based on facts and are honest if they lack information.
o Mentally active people consciously confront challenges and problems.
o Curious thinkers explore situations to penetrate the depth of the issues.
o Independent thinkers are not afraid to offer opinions that differ from the group.
o Skilled discussants can present and discuss ideas in an orderly and intelligent manner.
o Insightful students are able to move beyond the obvious to the issue.
o Self-aware individuals are aware of their biases and speak of them to others.
o Creative thinkers can move beyond established patterns and produce innovative responses.
o Passionate students strive to see situations and issues with more understanding and clarity.

Source: Adapted from Chaffee, 2009, p. 44.

aspire to develop habits of thinking about cognitive abilities in their students. Students need help to understand how and why they need to engage their brains, so they can react with their minds.

WHAT CAN YOU TELL YOUR STUDENTS ABOUT BEING CRITICAL THINKERS?

Have you ever been startled by a friend's remark that was really on target and expressed with wisdom beyond what you thought was possible? Think about a time you even surprised yourself with the depth of knowledge you had or the considerate, knowing way you treated a situation. To understand what it is like to have expert critical thinking skills, author John Chaffee (2009) provides characteristics of young and older people when they show cognitive thinking capabilities.

[Provide a copy of Table 7.1 for each student. Leave space between each characteristic for writing.]

Look at the first description, "Open-minded students listen carefully and evaluate fairly." Can you give an example of being open minded?

[Be prepared with an example of each characteristic if students do not come up with one. Then, encourage their input. Record an example or two under each characteristic. Finally, ask students to evaluate their responses.]

Take a look at these characteristics. Put a check mark for each one you do. Look at the ones you would like to be able to do, and tell your partner or your small group what you could do to develop that critical thinking skill. Talk also about why that particular characteristic would be helpful for you to have.

THE BASICS—INFUSE TECHNOLOGY INTO THE SCHOOL SETTING

The study by Csikszentmihalyi (see Scherer, 2002) in the previous chapter specifically named technology as a motivational factor for older students. The lives of upper elementary students and teenagers are dramatically different than their parents ever imagined they would be when they were born. Today's high school students live in a technological world that is changing faster than the adults responsible for their education can grasp. Youngsters and young adults have never lived without technology. They are comfortable with incessant handheld technology and expect instant availability of information and perpetual contact with everyone they know. Adults responsible for decisions about their education must acknowledge this glaring truth and develop new literacies to fit the available media.

The personal computer has changed everything. It created a big disruption and exponential change to how the world reacts to information and to communication, according to Liz Kolb's (Kolb, Myers, Soloway, & Norris, 2009) webinar about cell phones as instructional tools. Innovative schools and districts are looking at cellular phones as the new computer. Interestingly, while there are millions of computers manufactured each year, production of cellular phones numbers in the billions. Almost everyone of school age has one or has access to one. It makes perfect sense to look at the advancements of cellular devices and to explore how they might enhance the curriculum with more time on task for students.

Digital Literacies

Digital literacies are defined by Dana Wilber (2008), assistant professor and author, who studies new literacies and adolescents. She describes teens who have social networking systems such as MySpace, Twitter, and Facebook. They additionally use blogs, wikis, podcasts, video casts and YouTube. They cannot imagine not having a camera available to them on their cell phone and the capability of shooting a picture to anyone, anytime, anyplace. Wilber insists that teachers must think differently about what is available in the classroom for teaching, and what can be accessed outside the school setting through digital literacies. Blogging, podcasting, visual text creation, and comics/manga can be a part of the way learning happens in a classroom; and through the process, teachers make connections to jargon common in every young person's world.

The brains of today's youth are challenged by their environment differently, their brains are wired differently, and they respond differently than any generation in the past. Neuroscientists widely accept that the human brain can only concentrate on one thing at a time. It cannot be assumed this situation has changed. However, parents report that their teens read and study a homework assignment, listen to music, and keep dialogues going with several friends through text messaging simultaneously. Are today's young adults able to concentrate on more than one situation at a time, or are they simply better than their adult parents or teachers at instantaneously switching from one area of concentration to another? Is their world better preparing them to multitask? Is their working memory ultimately going to be expanded from limitations that appeared in the past to be finite?

A term coined by Linda Stone and reported by Small and Vorgan (2008), *continuous partial attention,* may explain the neuro dilemma that is currently witnessed with youth. Teens and young adults are busy keeping tabs on a variety of stimuli—but not really attending to any one. Continuous partial attention is not multitasking. *Multitasking* means to have a purpose for each task and to divide attention on various important tasks to maximize the use of time and energy. When the mind is constantly searching for an opportunity to make a connection at any given moment, the task being attempted, such as a homework assignment, is done with partial mental thought. Chatting as messages flow, keeping tabs on perpetual buddy lists, searching for everything, everywhere is the essence of perpetual, partial attention (Small & Vorgan, 2008). Does working on a school assignment fit into this array of stimulation?

SERIOUS BRAIN MATTERS— STUDENTS REMEMBER MANY ASSIGNMENTS BUT ATTEND TO ONE

While many students, and adults alike, claim to be able to multitask, researchers prove that it is not possible for our human brains. Previously described, research explained that students are able to consciously decide to focus, attend, and study. Learners become very good at switching attention from one activity to another, but they only concentrate on one task at a time. A study by Daniel Weissman, leading lab researcher at the University of Michigan, was reported on National Public Radio by Jon Hamilton (2008). Project participants were required to respond to two or more complex tasks involving colored numbers. If the digits are green, for example, the task could be to select the larger number, while another color digit may require the subject to tell which number was printed with a larger font. As tasks became more complex, it was easy to confuse the person's thinking. Researchers observed brain function images during the process. They could observe how the brain responded, paused, and switched function when a different task appeared. Even when researchers challenged the participants to "go faster," the need to take a break before responding to the new task was observed (Hamilton, 2008). These observations give an insight into what the human brain does to deal with its limitation of being able to only concentrate on one thing at a time.

In middle and high school, students are required to handle many different assignments from numerous classes. The study would indicate the brain needs breaks between different classroom tasks. Students need to clear the details in working memory from one class experience to the next. A 5- to 10-minute passing period from one classroom to the next may or may not be enough time to switch concentration from one academic subject to the next.

Techno Brain Predictions

Rather than developing a form of attention deficit disorder, ADD, for technology, most technology-savvy people are improving their mental capacities. They are able to sift and sort large amounts of information quickly and accurately. Important information is selected and nonessential data is skipped. Internet users seem to develop the ability to rapidly focus attention, analyze information, and make quick decisions for what to use and what to ignore. Neuroscientists image and measure brain areas, such as the hippocampus, during this type of task. Young adults who use computer technology in socially and educationally acceptable ways are reported to have higher than average scores for self-esteem. The hippocampus, which is critical to maintaining short term memory, was actually observed to be larger in individuals who sport a healthy self-concept (Small & Vorgan, 2008). Again, a word of caution is needed for these conditions: A healthy self-esteem and a larger working memory area correlate one to the other; one does not necessarily cause the other. Using a computer in ways that society accepts is correlated with individuals who sport a healthy self-esteem, and individuals who have a good self-esteem are also observed to have a larger hippocampus. A larger-than-average hippocampus most likely is an advantage. The indication is that there are more connections and more dendrite growth, which would allow the individual to hold more information and complex thoughts in working memory. That is a good thing for learning. It cannot be said, however, that people who spend time on the computer in socially and educationally acceptable activities will grow a larger hippocampus. There is a correlation, but one does not cause the other.

Digital Natives and Novices

Teenagers and those in their early 20s are dubbed "digital natives," meaning they have never known a world without computers. Neuroscience assures us that daily exposure to high technology, computers, cell phones, and video games creates systems in the brain that are different from non-users of technology.

A Kaiser Family Foundation study conducted in 2005 (Small & Vorgan, 2008) used fMRI technology to determine what area of the brain functions during an Internet Google search for specific and accurate information on a variety of topics. Although the desired number of participants only totaled six, the researchers still had trouble finding enough participants who were novices at using the Internet. They eventually found three subjects in their 50s and 60s who were not computer users, but who agreed to participate in the study. During the baseline scanning session, images from the control group of computer savvy individuals yielded an active pathway in the left dorsolateral prefrontal cortex. *Dorsolateral* can be translated into the dorsal, top part, and lateral, side area, and can further be identified as the site of the basal ganglia. The novices showed minimal, if any, activation in the identified area. After five days of searching the Internet only one hour a day, images of the Internet-naive participants' brains showed activity on the same neural pathway used by the technology-savvy subjects. The highlighted area of the brain is activated when individuals make decisions and are involved with information that requires them to integrate complex information (Small & Vorgan, 2008). It is a striking result to discover "older brains" responding to new challenges after a minimal exposure. Also, it is interesting that brains of the new Internet users were reconfigured to respond using the same pattern of brain structures as the computer savvy control group. Neuroscience will be challenged in the coming years to understand brain development of the current and succeeding generations who are raised in a world that is developing and changing at unimaginable speeds due to digital technology.

WHAT CAN YOU TELL YOUR STUDENTS ABOUT ENGAGING THEM WITH INFORMATION ABOUT LEARNING AND TECHNOLOGY?

Today's adolescents, your generation, are called technological natives. *This means you have always had technology in your lives. Many of your teachers and parents, although they may use the computer now, have not had it available all their lives. You are asked to be patient with adults who are not as savvy as you are with the advantages of technology. How can we make good things happen for learning when classrooms are unequipped for students who are admittedly technology dependent? What do you know about how technology has made your life different from the way your parents or grandparents live? What information can you find to either support or discredit the use of technology for students in the classroom?*

[Give an assignment to bring information from the Internet. Create a panel discussion or assign work groups to present the information.]

Gaming Technology

The debate over gaming technology and classroom benefits is far from settled. A recent report from the University of California, Los Angeles, cites a decline in critical thinking and analytical skills among students who are frequent video game players ("Is Technology," 2009). But, the same study reports an increase in visual intelligence abilities and skills among students who engage in video gaming. Researcher Patricia Greenfield (2000) summarized her thoughts by supporting traditional classroom practices. She states there is no substitute for listening and engagement that happens through good instruction, and she further suggests encouraging the old standby, reading, as a good brain stimulating leisure activity.

Social Concerns and Classroom Responses

Many adults express caution about social misuse of technology and particularly the impact on youth, who are emotionally fragile. In numerous ways, social interactions have been replaced or altered by technology. Often, teens have some interpersonal inadequacies and may misinterpret social interactions when they appear as unemotional words on a screen. Face-to-face interactions allow a greater possibility that students will develop skills to rebound from ridicule and resolve social discrepancies. The impact of more technology interface and less personal interaction is a social issue that needs to be evaluated for each adolescent. Teachers can knowingly provide increased classroom student to student interactions to counteract the social dilemma technology creates outside the classroom. The need students have for more personal interactions can be met as teachers structure student work using research teams, partnering up, and other dynamic group designs to expand learning tasks.

TECHNOLOGY ASSIGNMENTS

It is time to join forces with secondary students. They like and are experts at technology. Their learning needs are more like adult needs than like those of children. They have curious, insatiable brains and social, interactive minds. Teaching for this generation of learners needs to be respectful of their learning characteristics, their needs for social interactions, and their progressive journey to develop as adults. Five sample teaching units, modifiable for any grade level and almost any subject, are suggested. They involve technology and use standards-based instruction. Curriculum and social needs can come together for students during standards-based technology assignments.

Techno Assignment: Research and Science Inquiry

What does a classroom activity look like that takes into account preteens or teens' curious minds and their preference for active engagement with technology? A language arts, math, and science assignment to embrace students' interest begins with a question and engagement activity. Students are asked, "What would your day be like without technology?" Initial reactions and responses are recorded on a class list. Use probing questions for more information. Then, students are asked to develop a working definition of technology. A sample definition could be provided and modified based upon input from the students.

Next, the class generates a list of all the technology they expect to use in a typical day. For a science application, the scientific inquiry method is used as students set up a hypothesis to predict how many times they will be inconvenienced without technology during a single day. Additionally, they are asked for a prediction of how much discomfort they will experience. Research questions are developed, and technical vocabulary is identified and defined. Next, students design an easy to use recording instrument with paper and pencil, which are examples of primitive technology. Many skills and techniques result from the study, such as charting, extrapolating numbers, developing formulas, and writing a report summary.

The assignment acknowledges an important aspect in adolescents' lives, infuses information about conducting scientific studies, creates problems for mathematical reasoning and statistics, hones in on report writing, and results in an interesting outcome. Captivating engagement and meeting curriculum standards can work together to motivate students in the upper grades through this project and other similar assignments.

Techno Assignment: The Internet as a Reference Resource

Instructors at the college level are finding that students write papers and use sources from the Internet. Scott Jaschik (2007) reports significant numbers of students who cite online encyclopedias, such as *Wikipedia,* in their papers. The standard of using primary sources or serious secondary sources still stands in university classes. While high school students might get general knowledge from sources such as *Wikipedia,* they are not acceptable as citable in a research paper. Steven Bell, associate librarian for research and instructional services at Temple University, is quoted in Jaschik's article:

> Students face "an ocean of information" today, much of it of poor quality, so a better approach would be to teach students how to "triangulate" a source like Wikipedia, so they could use other sources to tell whether a given entry could be trusted. "I think our goal should be to equip students with the critical thinking skills to judge." (p. 1)

The brain and the human mind working together are curious, and students are more than willing to creatively find and use shortcuts to complete school assignments. When information appears to be sufficient to complete an assignment using an Internet resource, students are quick to use it, regardless of its quality and source. Educators understand the reasoning students use to select the quickest and most easily available resources, but they cannot accept the practice. During the secondary years, it is a teacher's responsibility to set rigorous standards and help their students to discern a viable resource from a questionable one. The class and teacher working together can develop a list of qualifiers and work through a process of finding and citing an acceptable source. To show how the qualifiers work, these questions can be used to direct students to respond to the information they need about the sources of information they use.

1. Who is the author, and what qualifications does the author have to write this article or book?

2. Can I find the information for the applicable section (book, article, published piece, or personal interview) for the resource section of my report?

   a. Book: author names, publication date, name of the book, city of publisher, and name of publishing company

   b. Article: author names, publication date, name of the article, magazine or journal name, volume (number), and page numbers

   c. Published piece on the Internet: author names, publication date, name of the article, magazine or journal name, volume number, available website, and date of access

   d. Personal interview: names of interviewer and interviewee, date, topic, and where the interview took place

   e. Is there information that I will use in my report that needs to be verified by more than one resource?

Helping students know, during upper elementary years, that academic resource standards will be used for printed books, articles, papers, and also for interviews and Internet resources provides a mind-set for using the computer for research papers. An additional resource for teachers is the APA guidelines, which are available online (see The Writing Lab, 1995–2010).

Techno Assignment: Social Networking Sites

Signing up for a social networking site profile is relatively easy. Find out how many students have used memberships like Facebook or MySpace. What other blog-type memberships do students use? What are their advantages and disadvantages? Assign a class project to develop a "User's Manual" for Internet profiling, memberships, and blogging for someone who knows nothing about the Internet. Questions such as these can be selected by the teacher or developed by the class:

1. How much personal information should be posted?

2. What should be put on kids' pages?

3. For what age person is this type of computer use recommended?

4. What do parents need to know about computer public domain profiles?

5. How can a membership in a service, such as MySpace, be used advantageously?

6. What cautions need to be listed?

7. What is a current list of recommended profiles?

Obviously, this is an opportunity to get students to work in groups and to put their writing skills into action. Other outcomes from this project include the production of a manual with the best ideas of all that are submitted by the groups. Parents would find the insights interesting and may pay for a copy. The product could be an effective fund-raiser for some additional technology needed for the classroom.

Techno Assignment: Blogs

Have groups of students check out classroom blogs. How are other teachers and their students using blogs to augment class work and to communicate among students and with parents? Produce a classroom list of ideas, and involve the students in deciding what would be most useful for this particular class. Have technologically savvy students perform the tasks needed to set up a classroom blog, and see how creative this technology can be for teacher and students alike to augment the curriculum and the learning environment.

Techno Assignment: Choose Your Topic—Maximize Technology

A final suggestion for a techno assignment is designed for topics appropriate to any unit of study. Require that students use technology for every step of this assignment as they prepare a report to be presented to the class. Introduce the assignment by providing an example of how online services are ingeniously integrated into the "way things are done" for institutions and organizations. Two examples of interest to students are how colleges and universities handle online course registration, and how the Department of Motor Vehicles (California and others) allow driver license renewal online. Present the assignment with seven steps:

1. Select a topic relating to the unit of study.

2. Review available information, and list resources.

3. Write the report.

4. Decide how it will be presented.

5. Get feedback from at least three classmates.

6. Present your findings and the report.

7. Conduct a peer evaluation of the presentation's style and content.

Students are challenged to apply and use technology for each section of this assignment. They may even surprise themselves as they find new ways to use the tools from their daily lives for a productive classroom project.

Going Deeper Into Learning and Learning Struggles

Some students find school to be difficult, and they think of themselves as failing students. Often, school problems revolve around an inability to read well or to understand what is read. Chapter 8 addresses the issues and concerns students face when they are struggling readers and are unsuccessful when they need to read to learn. Subsequently, Chapter 9 continues with brain and mind responses to the cognitive processes of focusing for deep understanding and learning as research from neuroscience is applied to each area of the curriculum.

8

Older Students Who Struggle With Reading to Learn

Poor literacy skills among upper elementary, middle, and high school students have been a concern for decades. A reoccurring theme is that students must be able to automatically decode words and read with fluency to be able to comprehend what they read. In many ways, it is easier to teach children to read than it is to help students understand what they have read. However, skills that are needed to teach children to read are clearly identified and well understood. Complete reading programs and intervention programs are numerous, and student success from using direct, intensive instruction programs is thoroughly documented in reading education literature (Nevills & Wolfe, 2009). The reader is reminded to use the knowledge base provided in Chapter 5 for reading decoding with this chapter and its emphasis on reading comprehension for students who struggle with reading.

Literacy skills for comprehension are more difficult to teach according to what needs to happen in the brain for readers to comprehend text. What ways can teachers develop students' skills for remembering, integrating information, and producing meaningful responses? The earlier chapter dedicated to reading development gave strategies to engage students in understanding words, phrases, and sentences they hear or read. A deeper look at how students' brains are organized shows that students are also equipped with skills for analysis and synthesis, which are qualities of highly productive mind work. What is happening cognitively as learners engage with words they read and manipulate information to become expert literary consumers of society's knowledge? And, what is amiss when they fail to be successful with this reading task?

ADOLESCENT LITERACY TODAY

Among adolescents, poor literacy is not only an academic problem but rather one that impacts society as a whole. The National Governors' Association (2005) determined to make this issue its priority in a document, *Reading to Achieve: A Governor's Guide to Adolescent Literacy.* The publication explores how the national economy is affected by widespread adolescent illiteracy. Deficit reading and writing skills cost the nation's businesses, universities, and underprepared students as much as 16 billion dollars annually. It is estimated that almost 40% of high school graduates do not possess adequate reading and writing skills for the jobs they seek. Literacy deficits are increasing while literacy levels required for employment are rising (National Governors' Association, 2005). These statistics clearly illustrate the need for a new approach to literacy instruction. A commitment for the education system goes beyond helping children to learn to read between kindergarten and third grade but additionally demands that they are taught to "read to learn" in all the ensuing grades.

Insights Into Reading Disabilities

Some very serious research has gone into what the brain looks like for students who have reading disabilities. When a reading deficit is discovered, it is not the way the brain's structures have formed; rather, it is the connections among structures. Children with reading decoding problems do not access some word form identification structures along the language pathway in the brain. These structures are activated for successful readers. The cause of this disruption to the reading pathway could be a preschool or school environment in which instruction is provided, or the cause could also be an inherited one. Beyond simple word decoding connections among various other brain structures, memory and recall systems, and the ability to engage and call up information from multiple areas of the brain are required for reading with understanding. Not all readers develop the same skills even though they may receive the same instruction. Not all students have the same opportunities to develop into good readers.

An oral reading pathway develops as children become good word decoders and readers. In the book addressing reading development for preschoolers through third grade, *Building the Reading Brain* (Nevills & Wolfe, 2009), the reading pathway is carefully traced, and problems associated with roadblocks or derailment in this pathway are defined. It is a pathway that is essential to oral word identification and fluent reading. Reading teachers agree that struggling readers must have direct, intensive instruction in all the skills needed to develop the reading decoding pathway. When children struggle to read, they need direct instruction through intervention or replacement reading programs. These catch-up-and-succeed programs are specifically designed to provide more in depth instruction, practice, repetitions, and review for these struggling readers, which is beyond what their peers who are progressing at an age appropriate level need to be successful in word identification and reading production (Nevills & Wolfe, 2009).

SERIOUS BRAIN MATTERS—DIFFERENCES IN THE BRAIN'S WHITE MICROSTRUCTURES

While fMRIs have been used to help us determine a normal reader's activation pattern while decoding words, a new type of imaging techniques examines the myelination of axons along the same pathway. Two researchers, Niogi and McCandliss (2006), conducted a study using diffusion tensor imaging, DTI, which examines water diffusion along the axonal fibers. When the white matter of the brain is myelinated, water is obstructed. As in the study reported earlier by Keller and Just (2009), Niogi and McCandliss measured the variation in the diffusion of the water. From this information, they are able to realize individual differences in the brain's white matter. This particular study involved 31 children between the ages of 6.5 and 10.3 years of age who were carefully screened prior to the imaging session. The subjects were all right handed to eliminate variations in the study results that could be associated with the reversal of the hemisphere functions for left-handed children. All children were from moderate-income families, and their parents reported no psychological or other learning discrepancies. Eleven children with reading disabilities were also identified by standardized testing. The study revealed a difference in white matter microstructures in the area of the reading decoding pathway in the left temporal-parietal region. Good readers had greater amounts of white matter integrity than the children with a reading disability. Additionally, researchers found an independent relationship in working memory areas associated with the frontal lobes and posterior areas. A continuum of readings revealed greater white matter integrity among successful readers in the study population. A correlation is noted between white matter integrity and student scores on tests of cognitive ability. Students with more myelination, more white matter, showed higher scores on cognitive tests (Niogi & McCandliss, 2006).

Information from neurology cannot not translate directly into prescriptions for classroom practices. Rather, neurology's studies validate and explain behaviors we see in students as they learn through reading. Middle school students who have not mastered basic reading skills find curriculum printed materials very difficult to read and to remember. They have various behavioral responses, which cause problems during school and beyond. Science tells us that the brain can change and respond to the environment. Educators and parents need to advocate for exceptional intervention reading programs when a student experiences difficulties due to the brain's lack of development for successful reading. Neuroscience tells about improved pathways among the brain's structures and increased myelination of neurons for critical connections. Educational research helps us identify reading programs that yield successful readers. Students are locked into an education system within a society that values being able to read well. We must stop the system for students who are stumbling readers and yield to remedial programs that use the advantage of the learning brain and its ability to change through its plasticity. All able students must be taught to read and be capable of reading to learn.

Regular Classroom Placements for Readers Who Struggle or Are Reading Disabled

Students who are identified as having mild or moderate disabilities have a better chance of correcting reading disabilities when they remain in the regular classroom. Traditionally, students who are not achieving commensurate with their grade-alike peers are referred to special education after a reasonable attempt has been made for them to catch up. Special education services, specified in an Individualized Education Plan, an IEP, determine where students would be educated outside a regular education placement for their areas of need, who would provide the services, and what educational goals are planned. An IEP, infiltrated with extensive legal requirements, provides goals and performance-based objectives which attempt to specify what needs to be done in the classroom to develop a good learner or reader. Often, a variety of specialists are involved. Each one offers to remediate the learning difficulties according to specific testing and a responsive instructional plan. It can be difficult to coordinate the efforts and schedules of specialists, and it is hard to make up for the wealth of rich experiences that are missed when a student is relocated from the regular classroom for specialized reading services.

There are many examples of excellent special education programs, and large numbers of students have benefited and advanced in their reading abilities through the services provided in special education classes. However, too many students with mild reading disabilities have been removed from the regular education classroom for special education services and have not been able to catch up with the reading abilities of their grade-alike peers. It is well accepted that for a student to reach grade-level achievement from scores that rank two or more years behind, the student needs to make significantly more than one-year growth in one year's period of time. A single year's growth or less during one school year is unacceptable.

Current findings support the response to intervention (RTI) approach to correcting the disadvantages seen by struggling and disabled readers. The focus is for remediation to occur in the regular program as an add-on program with regular education teachers and with age and grade-alike peers. This approach makes perfect sense for a brain compatible way to learn. Reading is intensively important for success in all subject areas, and it can be remediated in a well-managed, regular education classroom. Students with reading deficits must be involved with rich classroom experiences to attain background information, interact with peers, have challenging conversations, and integrate all school subjects together through natural and actual experiences.

Schoolwide Literacy Efforts

Initiatives for whole school literacy are becoming more and more common for middle and high schools. These plans provide guidelines for the technical support teachers need to work with students who are below-average readers. The entire school staff focuses on the integrated roles that are needed between reading, writing, speaking, listening, and viewing during the many courses students must master that require adequate reading skills (Fisher & Frey, 2008). No longer are the problems students experience treated on a teacher to teacher basis. School plans identify that all students' learning needs are a responsibility of all the school's educators.

Identify and Address Nonlearners and Nonreaders

By the time they are in middle or high school, students have established their identities in and out of school. They know if they have a disposition to be successful in various academic, physical, and social pursuits. Litman and Greenleaf (2008), from WestEd's Strategic Literacy Initiative, insist that teachers can identify and help students who view themselves as incapable students and readers. Teachers can build relationships with students through the identities students accept as their successful selves. Building on what students see as their strengths is a way for teachers to encourage reluctant learners. Students in upper elementary grades and secondary schools possess curiosity, tolerance for ambiguous situations, and ways they concentrate to construct new learning. Basically, resource, reading, homeroom teachers, and tutors are encouraged to get involved with these students. They are capable of school success, but they need to be encouraged to try new ways and to develop different identities as successful learners.

WHAT CAN YOU TELL STUDENTS WHO IDENTIFY THEMSELVES AS NONLEARNERS AND NONREADERS?

Everyone learns during all waking hours. What is being learned is the point here. If you are sitting in chemistry class and thinking about how you will earn money to buy a car or what you want to do this weekend, you are learning new ways to support your out-of-school identity. You have many identities—based on where you are. There is an identity for you in your chemistry class, one for physical education, one as a family member, and who you are to your social network, for example. In school, you have some places where you are seen as a successful student and others where you accept the role of a nonlearner. Can you identify some of the different identities you have? Let's focus in on the places you feel that you are effective and successful. Where would that be? What about that environment makes you feel you can achieve? What personal skills do you have that help you in those situations?

Now, where do you struggle? Are there strengths that you can build upon to approach classes or situations where you struggle or fail? Let's negotiate a plan for you to change how you approach this class or these classes and determine what type of teaching strategies would help you the most.

Continue this discussion over a period of time. Use strategies that are compatible with how learners operate to *recognize* important, key learning, *reduce* learning into usable memory chunks, *record* the information in their working memory through practice, *remember* the information upon demand, and *recall* the information by writing, speaking, demonstrating, or making a product.

Reading Comprehension—a Difficult Skill to Teach

Students who are slow, laborious readers and need to develop the reading pathway are better understood and easier to remediate than students who are fluent readers but do not understand what they read. The operatives or key structures for a reading comprehension system are more difficult to pinpoint in the brain. Certainly, it cannot be delineated as precisely as the reading pathway. Comprehension and word associations are stored in a variety of places for a variety of reasons. All reading programs, basic or remedial in nature, provide instruction for reading comprehension, yet certain readers continue to struggle to understand what they read both orally and silently. How to prompt the brain to file and store information for easy access is less understood. Also, more brain structures are involved in many unpredictable ways. Successful reading comprehension depends on the brain's organizational plan as each learner stores information in unique and often obscure ways.

WHAT CAN YOU TELL STUDENTS WHO ARE UNSUCCESSFUL LEARNERS AND READERS?

There are essential skills you need to be a good reader. First, you need to be able to identify and say words that you meet during reading. You do this by reading silently and subvocalizing the words, or you may be asked to read out loud. During this process, you must know the sounds of words, understand the rules of phonics for pronouncing words, and you need to be able to keep a rhythm or pace of reading that is fluent.

Some students have not developed these skills. If students are unable to identify words and to read with a good pace, it is essential they have special help and intensive reading instruction to get up to an acceptable reading speed for their grade level. Another basic skill needed is to be able to understand and talk about what is read. As students progress through the grades, the textbooks and references have increasingly difficult sentence and paragraph structures, there are large demands to understand advanced vocabulary, and the reading selections are lengthy.

If you are able to understand a reading selection written at a level for fourth grade, but the texts you are expected to use are for ninth grade, you will have a difficult time in school. If you are able to identify words and read the texts at your grade level relatively easily, but you do not remember or understand what you have read, then you need more activities to help you work with the information and words in your textbooks. Strategies, such as an introduction to the reading selection, knowing about the author, making predictions about what you will read, and identifying vocabulary that you need to know, can help you begin to read. While you read, there are other activities that help you to pay attention and concentrate on what the author intends that you to know.

You do not have to continue as a struggling reader. Your teachers and the school system can provide extra programs, and they trust that you are capable of good reading. There is some hard work involved as we prepare your brain to recognize what you need to know, record important information in your brain, and allow you to remember and recall it while you are reading. But, we can do it.

THE COMPLEX NATURE OF READING COMPREHENSION

The era for simplicity in teaching reading comprehension has ended. No longer can teachers introduce a topic, review vocabulary, assign pages, and tell students to answer the questions at the end of the chapter. Our expectations for students are far too complex for this outdated style of teaching. Students must be introduced to many of the different types of activities publishers offer in reading programs to be fully aware and interactive with the content of a written selection.

Reading/Language Arts Standards for Reading Comprehension and Brain Learning—an Educational Standoff

Instruction needed for advanced reading skills is incongruent with the way the education system lists standards for reading/language arts frameworks. A highly specific list of required skills and concepts to direct reading skill development for all grade levels is needed and necessary. However, a list identifying reading standards for upper grades and beyond does not match with how a student can most effectively acquire reading competence. Teachers are tempted to teach skills according to a standards list as they are pressured to produce test results in these areas. The ability to think and respond with complex thoughts is not consistent with sequential, predictable, identifiable checklist type patterns.

Reading Literary and Informational Text

First, neurosmart teaching strategies can be applied to the kind of text students are expected to read and situations can be created that build student's brains for reading comprehension. Literary text includes *fiction, nonfiction, poetry,* and *prose.* A quick check of reading standards will identify the skills of integration, interpretation, critiquing, evaluating, and synthesizing. All of these mindful applications are possible through literary text. The other reading type is identified as informational text. In this genre, we find texts that are *expository, essay* (informational, argumentative, or persuasive), and *procedural.* Each type of material for students to read can be text or document format and can be used to integrate thoughts and information, to interpret for meaning, to critique and give opinion, or to evaluate and score (Foorman, 2007). Teachers can select from multiple types of reading for struggling readers. Realize that slow, laborious readers need to have texts that can be read and reread to build fluency. Also, rare, multisyllabic words should be minimal, and the majority of the words in the selection need to be those that are frequently encountered in the curriculum. Foorman provides an important insight as she encourages teachers to use science textbooks for repetitious reading, particularly during the upper elementary grades. Science texts provided for the elementary years have repetition of the core vocabulary which makes it an ideal choice for multiple readings (see Table 8.1).

Table 8.1   Types of Reading Materials and Skill Development

Literary Text	
	Fiction, nonfiction, poetry and prose
Skill Development	
	Integration, interpretation, critiquing, evaluating, and synthesizing
Informational Text	
	Expository, essay (informational, argumentative, or persuasive), and procedural
Skill Development	
	Integration of thoughts and information, interpretation and meaning, critique and opinion, or evaluation and assigning a score

Instruction for the Complex Nature of Comprehension During Reading

Selection of additional reading material may supplement, but not replace, the textbook for students who are struggling with reading comprehension. Even in high school, picture books are considered a viable choice to introduce a unit of study for any level of reader. For example, David A. Adler has an extensive picture book biography series. The books, which have been written during the last two decades, have brilliant pictures, moderate vocabulary at the fourth- or fifth-grade levels, and provide an accurate account of the historical time period. One specific book (Adler, 1992) features Harriet Tubman, the leader of the Underground Railroad, which helped slaves to escape and to gain freedom during the 1800s. A simplistic yet engaging book can be used to introduce a topic, which in this example is slavery before and during the Civil War. Teachers can select to use all or a portion of the introductory and preparation for reading activities that follow. Students can read the selected book individually, in small groups, or it can be read aloud by the teacher or a confident reader. Picture books can be used to provide background information while boosting interest in the unit to be studied.

Before Preparation to Read

Teaching strategies for reading a grade-level selection, book, or text starts with an examination of the cover and title page. Questioning and prompting stimulates the curious nature of the human brain:

What clues are provided for the reader from the cover, the table of contents, and the introduction of the book or selection?

What can be gleaned from knowing about the author? Does this writer have an interesting past or important position? Is there something in the writer's past that might color the written word, and does the reader need to be careful of biases or opinions?

How likely is it that the information will be accurate and worthy of being quoted?

What type of reading material is this?

What can we expect when the author selects this genre for writing?

What about the title invites you to read the selection?

Students who are carefully prepared with this type of engagement prior to reading the selection are more likely to pay attention and go through thinking processes that will help them to remember what they read.

Preparation for Reading

When the topic of the reading selection is foreign or unique to the readers, background information can be provided. Teachers can direct students to look through the table of contents and the chapter or topic titles. Making predictions by writing class or individual sentences is a powerful way of directing students' minds to the important aspects of the work they are about to read. A second strategy to prepare students for the reading selection is to take a walk through the selection page by page. Identify the pictures and figures. Students are directed to read the descriptions with the visuals in the book. While learners become acquainted with figures, charts, or pictures, they are asked to identify words they will need to know. A vocabulary list is generated, and the teacher can add important, predetermined words as well. Words are never approached as isolated words. They are the nexus, the core, the center, and they provide an interface between what is intended to be communicated and the way thoughts are presented. A knowledge base is built, refined, and modified during reading, according to Marilyn Jagar Adams (2009). Readers must know the meaning of the writing's vocabulary, so knowledge can be constructed, and the meaning of the text can be interpreted.

Brain-friendly strategies challenge students as they get ready to read. Word networks are stimulated and excited as the brain strives to locate information that is already familiar. Students are asked to make predictions to tell what they anticipate reading. Chemical interactions among the memory systems are stimulated, and potential for long term potentiation improves. Once the learner's brain is stimulated with prereading activities, which may include reading a picture book, working memory is activated. When students read something that links to what they have thought about and predicted before reading, that information is fortified and reviewed in the brain's association loops to ensure better remembering. Before reading, students are asked for one more prediction. They are asked if they think the piece will be *easy, about right,* or *hard* to read. This final step provides a valuable prereading assessment for the teacher.

Think about the value of this type of preparation prior to reading. It is a process that can be used for any reading assignment for any subject area. Teachers can provide students with a copy of Table 8.2 and encourage them to follow a similar process when they begin a new book or lengthy reading assignment on their own for any class.

Table 8.2 Instruction for the Complex Nature of Reading Comprehension

Prior to Reading	
	Examine the cover or title page
	Learn about the author
	Question the author's authority
	Review the table of contents
	Speculate on what will be covered
Preparation for Reading	
	Build background information (use picture books, visual aids, or media)
	Take a walk through the text
	Look at images, figures, and tables
	Make and write predictions
	Develop a vocabulary list
	Decide reading difficulty (easy, about right, or hard)
During Reading	
	Stop and monitor questions
	Visual aids (diagrams, tables, figures, timelines, mind mapping, translation into everyday language, or questioning and answering in a variety of formats)
	Thinking maps (for example, circle, bubble, and tree and bridge maps)
	Development discussions
Follow-Up to Reading	
	Review predictive questions
	Analyze vocabulary
	Learn from visual aids
	Identify key learnings
	Decide text difficulty level and why

Background Knowledge and Video Media

All readers do not have the same background knowledge and experience. Textbook vocabulary becomes more difficult, and concepts more advanced, as the grades progress. Teachers find there are an abundance of well-designed videos to help students with weaker reading skills or lack of domain knowledge. Not only do educational media motivate students to engage with the information due to the novelty of this form of instruction but it also fills in gaps of information that may be important to the selection that will be read. Adams (2009) states, "Unfortunately, evidence so far indicates that even while such educational media can be valuable for developing students' interest in a topic, their impact on the knowledge structures underlying language development and reading comprehension is minimal" (p. 25). This statement may be true when teachers expect students to learn simply because they are exposed to the information by watching a video. However, if students are prompted with questions and specific happenings or outcomes to look for during viewing, then they are more likely to become engaged with the information. After watching the media selection, students can expect to be accountable for information. Postvideo viewing activities require students to produce some type of product to demonstrate new learning or ideas that will relate to their reading.

Instructional Activities During Reading

Students who struggle with comprehension may actually struggle with attention and concentration. Their eyes may be automatically looking at each word and line on the page, but their minds may be thinking about something else. To combat this situation, teachers can employ a stop and monitor technique. Depending upon the age of the student and the severity of the attention problem, reading can be monitored by small bits. After a specified time, students stop reading and ask one or more self-monitoring questions. Students can be requested to give a written response to the selected question or an oral response to a peer.

What did I just read?

How would I explain this section to a classmate?

Is this making sense to me? If so, I will go on. If I am confused, I need to go back to read the section again or ask for help.

What do I predict I will read about next?

Was my prediction for this section correct, or did it cover something else?

What do I want to know next about this topic?

Did I learn anything new that cleared up a misconception I had before?

Use of Visual Aids

Another strategy is to divide the reading into segments with the teacher encouraging and prompting visual aids to deepen meaning. There are a variety of formats to use, such as diagrams, tables, figures, timelines, mind mapping, translation into everyday language, or questioning and answering in a variety of formats. Mapping activities are defined in *Student Successes With Thinking Maps,* edited by David Hyerle and colleagues (Hyerle, Alper, & Curtis, 2004). Graphic organizers developed in the 1980s have become obsolete. While they helped students to organize large amounts of information and aided scaffolding of material, they soon developed into static, blackline masters dominated by teacher thinking (Hyerle et al., 2004). Strategies that are more closely aligned with serious brain work are defined as *thinking maps.*

Five qualities of thinking maps include consistence, flexibility, development, integration, and reflection. These qualities are used to develop a visual aid that is dynamic in nature. Students select from a variety of formats, which include circle, bubble, tree, and bridge maps. The selection of the map format or formats and the symbols used remains relatively *consistent* throughout the process of development. *Flexibility* is prominent as the map grows and *develops* its shape with additional information the student adds. More than one format may be needed, and students are encouraged to combine different formats to *integrate* thinking processes and content knowledge (Hyerle, 2004). A completed map, enclosed in a rectangular box, is ready to be used for reflective thinking between study partners or a process group and serves as an assessment tool for the teacher (see Figure 8.1).

Teachers initially provide insights into what they are thinking and model the design for a visual aid, which may be a thinking map or one of the other formats previously listed. However, the most powerful learning comes when students advance to being able to determine the structure or format for recording information, concepts, or new understandings. Their choice is reflective of the way they organize information in their brains and the way information can most easily be accessed from their unique memory systems. Ten top ideas for uses of technology that are brain compatible are listed in Chapter 10. Three that are most appropriate to promote intensity of instruction through visual aids are ensure a good start, vocabulary enhancer, and curriculum-relevant visual technology.

Figure 8.1 Sample Thinking Map, Tree Model. (Notice the difference between the table—Table 8.2—and information presented as a thinking map.)

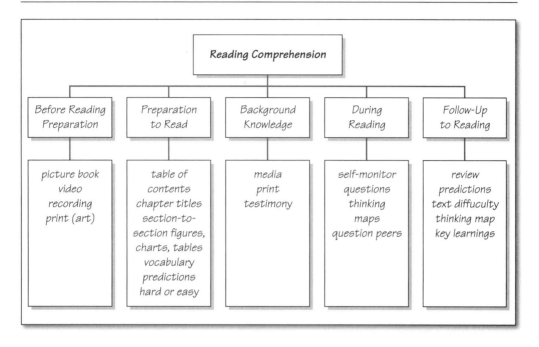

Follow-Up to Reading

The final part of this instructional sequence is for students to review their predictive questions, analyze vocabulary, learn from their visual aids, and identify key learnings. To begin, they look at their predictions at the onset of reading the selection and respond if their thinking was on target or needs to be modified. They talk about the level of text difficulty:

What made the selection easy, about right, or difficult to read?

What approaches to reading were successful for them?

Vocabulary identified at the onset of reading is reviewed:

Which words are now familiar and can be defined through individual student providing a definition in common language?

Are there words that need to be practiced more to be able to remember what they mean in subsequent reading assignments?

Included in the end of reading activities is a review of the visual aids that were developed during reading. First, look at the model that students selected.

How convenient or inconvenient was it to insert information?

Was it the best visual aid to use, or could students suggest one that would be better for this reading selection?

Note how valuable this end of the reading discussion can be for students to identify how they think to organize information and ultimately how it will be manipulated to be stored cognitively for recall. This discussion becomes quite dynamic when students are at an advanced level for working with visual aids and are able to select one based on individual preference. When teachers engage students in an intensive conversation about what they have read, it is obvious that students have more recall from long term memory and a depth of learning that is accomplished by using visual aids, such as thinking maps as a learning tool.

Finally, what can be listed as a key learning from the visual aid and reading? Small-group and whole-class discussions will ferret out the major and minor points from the key learning summary. A class chart can be made, or individuals may record the outcomes of this activity in their journals.

Yes, this type of activity takes a lot of classroom time. It demands that students thoughtfully work with the whole class, with small groups, and as individuals. Teachers find they spend time in careful, specific planning for lessons that require this type of intensity. They look at students for their unique learning needs and strengths. Students are placed in various groups at various times to meet immediate learning needs. Students who view themselves as nonlearners or nonreaders can build and establish new identities with careful, deliberate approaches to reading with this type of learning sequence in any subject area.

WHAT CAN YOU TELL YOUR STUDENTS ABOUT THE INTENSITY OF INSTRUCTION THAT IS NEEDED TO UNDERSTAND AND COMPREHEND TEXTBOOKS?

You need to know before we begin this unit that there will be a lot of starting and stopping. Understanding how your brain learns will help you to hang in with all these activities. Usually when students have difficulty understanding what they are reading, the cause is a lack of concentration. And, students may not concentrate because they do not know why they need to learn this. In other words, there is a lack of interest—you don't know why you need to know this. The purpose of expanded instruction and activities is to create curiosity about the reading selection and to stimulate background information you may already have. In almost all situations when students are prompted and the brain is excited with inquisitiveness, they find reading to be more pleasurable. Most textbook reading is purposeful, and students ultimately feel the information they learn and master will be helpful in some other class or situation in real life. Use this reading process for any text, book, or lengthy reading assignment.

[Provide a copy of Table 8.2 for the complex nature of reading comprehension.]

The table will prompt your thinking before, during, and after reading. If you expend effort to stay engaged with the work of reading, you will be rewarded with better reading abilities and more usable knowledge.

More Teaching Strategies for the Complex Nature of Reading Comprehension

The strategies presented for struggling readers and their normally progressing peers can be defined by terms educators know very well: focused lesson planning, modeling, directive, engaging instruction, collaborative learning, and differentiated learning, for example. Basically, the five or seven step lesson plan is validated for a daily or unit preplan. Teachers think, "This is what I plan to teach, these are activities I think need to happen, and here are the resources I think students will use to learn the learning objectives." But, teachers cannot count on holding to the static sequence of a written lesson plan for real student learning. It all depends on what the students need and how they respond cognitively and behaviorally to each day's lesson. So, while it is comfortable to move step by step through an instructional plan—if deep learning is to occur for all students recognizing all the various levels of learning needs they have, a sequence most likely will not be followed. Students may be well into independent individual or group practice, and the teacher may realize an important learning event is missing. A step back to model the missing concept or strategy will allow students to progress once again. Likewise, students during independent learning may uncover a significant concept the teacher did not anticipate. The entire class may benefit from the additional, unintended discovery.

It cannot be emphasized enough that whole group instruction has its place, sometimes, but not always. Classrooms with a high level of learning success have a variety of ways for student engagement. The ones who are doing the talking are also doing the most learning. Teachers can request students to respond not simply to answer a question but also to repeat the answer. If an answer is static, the teacher can motion for a group or the whole class to respond. Multiple responses to an open-ended question can be called out in a respectful manner that encourages attentive listening and active participation. Teachers can form dynamic small groups for intensive or remedial instruction. These truly are dynamic groups as neither the group members nor the teaching objective remain static. The teaching objective can be expanded for deeper, richer understanding. Students are assigned tasks for individual, partner, small-group, and whole-class work. These teaching choices are paramount to students learning different information, concepts, and skills throughout their school years. For important learning to happen, classroom learning activities must be dynamic, challenging, and inviting. Students need to feel success is possible. (Intensive teaching strategies to engage students and excite their minds can be found in Chapter 3 in a section titled "Learning Application: Engaging Students With Learning.")

Teaching practices matched with how the brain is built to learn are effective for students who struggle with reading. These teaching gems are scattered throughout the book, and other strategies for reading comprehension are provided in Chapter 5 while engaging adolescents and infusing technology is found in Chapter 7. Determining teaching strategies with the brain in mind expands learning intensity for students who are moving through the grades with academic success. Neurosmart teaching brings a depth of understanding for students that is not accessible through generally accepted teaching habits. But, for students who are nonreaders or unsuccessful with academic classes, matching how their brains work best with how they learn is time efficient and makes perfect cognitive sense.

9

Neurology for All Content Areas

Neurology and classroom applications for reading skills permeate this book, and include decoding, word recognition, comprehension, and fluency. Chapter 9 is unique as it addresses curriculum areas beyond reading/language arts. Brain attributes necessary for success in other subject areas are examined. For each subject, exciting insights from the new field of **neuroeducation** are explored. Classroom applications for the current discoveries from neuroscience along with resources are compiled in the next chapter.

NEUROLOGY INFLUENCES ALL SUBJECT AREAS

While it is accepted that the ability to read impacts all subjects in middle and high school, it is less accepted that neurology of learning is appropriate to infuse into instruction for any content area. Research and practical considerations from the field of neurology are discussed for each subject in secondary schools. Although secondary teachers may be inclined to look in this chapter for content sections that they teach, brain-related discoveries from one subject may be appropriate for other courses of study as well.

FOREIGN LANGUAGE

Why is foreign language taught in school learned differently from how the brain is programmed to initially learn language? The oral language pathway for a child's primary language develops as the child hears and plays with sounds and words. It is after the child is a fluent speaker that letter sounds, letter identification, and written words are learned. The reading pathway is constructed from the strongly established oral language route. Can this knowledge of learning affect how students are helped to acquire competency in a foreign or second language?

There is ample evidence that our foreign language curricula feature speaking and writing experiences simultaneously as foreign language is taught in high schools today. To help understand the demands upon the brain for speaking and writing tasks, it is important to identify the main differences between what is acceptable during speaking and the restrictions that accompany writing (see Table 9.1). It is seen that oral language is cut considerable slack in its format and structure. During conversation, the speaker is excused for uttering incomplete sentences or even random thoughts. Words are lost in time and space immediately after they are produced. For this reason, spoken language can be imprecise and peppered with colorful, elaborate words and phrases, even if they are not completely appropriate. Written language is hampered with an entirely different set of rules, rules that take years to learn through tedious and laborious study. It is simply not acceptable to write with the same words and structures we use for speaking.

Table 9.1   Main Points Differentiating Spoken and Written Language

Spoken Language	Written Language
Intonation patterns and pauses	Printed letters, punctuation, and correct spelling and grammar
Spontaneous	Carefully developed
Rich resources (gestures, imitations, and facial expression)	Rich resources (background information, vocabulary, and expressive and poignant words)
Colorful, elaborate words and phrases	Avoids overuse of adjectives
Imprecise, repetitive, seeded with premade expressions, incomplete thoughts	Complete sentences in logical order
Immediate, present with listener	Receiver not present
Lost after spoken	Lasting through print
Information without references	Source of information referenced

Source: Adapted from Ayllon, Smith, & Morrillo, 2006, p. 51.

An exception is a formal speech. Due to the stringent expectations placed upon a speaker, notes may be used, or the speech may need to be practiced many times prior to the formal presentation. It is as if a formal speech needs to meet requirements that are more common for writing. We teach foreign language as we teach reading and writing skills for English. Spoken language for conversation is sporadically infused throughout the study of foreign language, but it is not front-loaded the way the young brain responds initially to learning the primary language.

Teach Young Children a Second Language

Research is clear about the best way to learn a second language. It happens spontaneously by exposure during early childhood. Children between birth and age seven are able to learn more than one language quite naturally with the oral language pathway that constructs itself in the child's brain. This ability to learn any language begins to weaken early in life, even before the child begins to talk, according to Patricia Kuhl (see Neergaard, 2009) of the University of Washington. Although research generally suggests teaching a second language before a child enters puberty, it turns out earlier is better than later for foreign language exposure. Italian researchers wondered if there would be delayed speech for infants who heard two different languages during their first year. They tested 12-month-old **monolingual** and **bilingual** children and found no delay for those who were exposed to two languages. Surprisingly, these young bilingual children were able to learn two different sound patterns at the same time while monolingual babies learned one (Neergaard, 2009).

Reports of studies with young children identified bilingual youngsters as more capable of dealing with abstractions and possessing the ability to switch back and forth between tasks. Even rule changes did not deter them as it does with their monolingual peers (Foreman, 2002). What system or pathway is accessed in the brain when a preschooler is challenged to sort and learn two languages? We know speech production is generated from Broca's area, a small region in the left inferior frontal cortex. Wernicke's area, located further behind in the temporal and parietal juncture, is accessed for comprehension of spoken or written language. Researchers found that children learning a second language prior to adolescence used the same oral language pathway for both languages. Older students cannot learn a second language with the primary oral language pathway—as it has become hard wired. An older student's brain functions from an oral language pathway that is resistant to learning that appears incongruent with previous learning. To acquire a second language, they must develop another route and recruit additional brain areas to locate words already known in their native language.

Teaching Young Adults a Foreign Language

The development of the brain requires a different mode of teaching for secondary students than for young children learning a foreign language. We cannot expect adolescents to learn by being exposed to the new language solely by hearing and speaking it. Total immersion into an alien language will not lead to the student becoming bilingual unless written language skills are acutely developed simultaneously. The learner must be able to access what they already know from their native language and apply new learning in a separate, newly designed learning habit. It is hard work, and many are never satisfied with their ability to speak and communicate in the language they attempt to learn primarily during the high school years or later. The brain is just not accommodating enough. It becomes inflexible to change the primary language pathway that is well established since early childhood.

VISUAL AND PERFORMING ARTS

Schools need to raise test scores; consequently, students are often denied the chance to draw, sing, dance, and perform by acting during the regular school day. Visual and performing arts include both appreciation of others' performance or products as well as demonstration of individual and group skills. Neuroscience research includes current data about the effects of participation in arts training that will stimulate future investigation. The Dana Foundation with the Cognition Consortium held a symposium in 2008 of neuroscientists from seven United States universities to discuss education and the visual and performing arts. A summary of research from this group has impressive implications for educators.

1. An interest in a performing art leads to a high state of *motivation* that produces the *sustained attention* necessary to improve performance and the *training of attention* that leads to improvement in other domains of cognition.

2. Genetic studies have begun to yield candidate genes that may help explain individual differences in interest in the arts.

3. Specific links exist between high levels of music training and the ability to manipulate information in both working and long term memory: these links extend beyond the domain of music training.

4. In children, there appear to be specific links between the practice of music and skills in geometrical representation, though not in other forms of numerical representation.

5. Correlations exist between music training and both reading acquisition and sequence learning. One of the central predictors of early literacy, phonological awareness, is correlated with both music training and the development of a specific brain pathway.

6. Training in acting appears to lead to memory improvement through the learning of general skills for manipulating semantic information.

7. Adult self-reported interest in aesthetics is related to a temperamental factor of openness, which in turn is influenced by dopamine-related genes.

8. Learning to dance by effective observation is closely related to learning by physical practice, both in the level of achievement and in the neural substrates that support the organization of complex actions. Effective observational learning may transfer to other cognitive skills. (Gazzaniga, 2008, pp. 7–8)

The scientists adamantly warned of the need, as we saw earlier, to distinguish between correlation and causation in research study summaries and recommendations. Outcomes from neuroscience initially indicate a correlation—most likely that a certain type of brain activity happens at the same time a certain type of behavior occurs. If many studies cite the same result, the correlations tighten up, and a case for causal relationships develops. Many researchers whose work went into the above list cite correlations. Notice the use of the words *appear* and *may*, which are clues that results show correlation. We are cautioned against assuming too quickly that a particular teaching practice can cause an improved educational outcome.

New evidence about music training leads educators to believe instruction in music may have transferability to language and reasoning abilities. In a study by Winner and Schlaug (see Mauk, 2009) with 59 children between the ages of nine to fourteen, 41 children received music training over a 15-month period. At the end of the study, diffusion tensor imaging mapped the brain's connective white matter. Researchers observed strengthened connections among areas of the brain for auditory processing and motor skills in the group that had music lessons. They acknowledged the correlation between the improved skills and the amount of practice the students experienced (Mauk, 2009). Could these results be replicated for other visual and performing arts activities in addition to music? Possibly, music is not the causal variable; rather the same results could be obtained from other intensive activities in visual and performing arts that increase attention, rehearsal, and practice.

In another report (Tremmel, 2009), musicians were found to be superior to non-musicians in the ability to understand speech in noisy environments. In the study, Northwestern's Nina Kraus reports on the potential use of musical training to address auditory processing and communication disorders. It appears that musicians have better tuned circuitry for pitch, timing, and special elements of sounds. This study suggests music programs as a method to assist poor readers. Faulty interpretation of sounds can be at the phonological basis of early reading failure.

More definitive information from neuroscience's studies is needed before these results can be confidently applied to classroom programs.

SOCIAL STUDIES AND HISTORY

There are multiple dimensions to teaching a social studies or history curriculum. The National Council for Social Studies defines the teaching of social studies as an integrated course. Included within the school program are the disciplines of anthropology, archaeology, economics, geography, history, law, philosophy, political science, psychology, religion, and sociology. Additionally, the council includes related studies from the humanities, mathematics, and the natural sciences (see International Reading Association, 2006). What is an educator to do with this array of content for one course of study? Results from neurology that apply to social studies and history are inherently connected with visual and performing arts and the entire area of strong reading skills. In the previous chapter instructional activities and strategies to prepare students to read, engage during reading, and follow-up with discussion are provided (Table 8.1). Additionally, studies reported earlier about engagement with course content can be applied to social studies and history.

MATHEMATICS

The time has come for mathematics to receive the attention it deserves in the educational arena, particularly as it relates to how the human brain responds to numbers and their operations. Exciting new information is coming from neuroscience and cognitive psychology for the field of mathematics. One of the world's foremost mathematics researchers, Stanislas Dehaene, spends much of his career studying the specific intricacies between innately developed math abilities and those that must be taught to be learned. His studies involve animals, indigenous tribal people, and top mathematics students. He examines the folds and crevices of the cerebral cortex during various math procedures. Subjects are individuals with varying mathematical abilities. Different brain imaging technology is accessed. He aims to find out why math is easy for some children and adults and difficult for others (Dehaene, 1997; Holt, 2008).

According to Dehaene (1997), everyone is born with a mathematical instinct to equip humans for ancient, not current, living conditions. The naturally developed oral language pathway for children is clearly identified; now, it is known that there is also a naturally developed system for numbers. Math researchers label it an **approximate number system** (ANS). The operational number system appears to function primarily from the parietal lobes. It is evident and activated early in childhood and can even be observed during infant activities. ANS has been precisely studied in three-, four-, five-, and six-year-old children, as well as in adults, by these researchers from Johns Hopkins University. Halberda, Mazzocco, and Feigenson (2008) provide important information about age-related potential for processing approximate number relationships. This system differs from the exact counting procedures learned as children mature. ANS is imprecise. The Johns Hopkins University study uses a model to obtain measurements from a pairwise comparison called a Weber fraction. This process can determine the finest numerical ration that can be consistently discriminated at different ages. For example, when observing common objects, such as bunnies, crayons, flags, or umbrellas, children at three years of age can tell the difference between groups of two objects and three objects. Five-year-olds can consistently identify which is more or less between four and five objects. Adults have a higher accuracy of determining differences. Their ability generally levels out between groups of nine and ten items (Halberda et al., 2008).

More Support for the Approximate Number System

The Johns Hopkins researchers (Halberda et al., 2008) additionally studied 14-year-old boys and girls as they analyzed whether there were more blue or yellow flashing dots. They found the relationship between number sense and math ability in school to be independent of skills that typically are expected in intellectually challenging subjects, like mathematics. They also reported there is no relationship between the automatically developing ANS when compared to tests of intelligence, working memory capacity, visual-spatial skills, or verbal ability (Feigenson, 2006). ANS, an approximate relationship between numbers, appears to develop naturally in a "number-rich" childhood environment.

As researchers uncover more information about number systems that develop innately, educators may be able use this information to inform educational practice. This inherently developed system for numerical thinking is independent of language. Observers experience this automatically intact system for abstract numerical concepts by the behaviors of children (Cantion, Platt, & Brannon, 2009; Halberda et al., 2008). If this system does not mature according to age related expectations, students most likely will experience problems with math in school. The number sense prediction for success in mathematic calculations correlates to what we know about the necessity of learning phonological concepts prior to being able to decode words for reading.

During recent years, centers for mind and brain sciences around the world have made advances in unveiling the neural codes that underlie number representations.

During formal education, children are expected to understand how symbols represent numbers and to develop understanding of different counting and computational routines. To accomplish these expectations, the human brain's parietal system must undergo profound modifications, which neuroscientists do not fully understand. So, much as the oral language system is dramatically changed to accommodate reading decoding, and the approximate number system must undergo a partial recycling to support precise math procedures and methodology demanded by our society (see Table 9.2). The process of brain pathway recycling allows a student to be able to produce *exact numbers* required in school mathematics and the scientific and technical world (Piazza & Izard, 2009).

Table 9.2   Comparisons Between the Innately Developed Oral Language System and the Approximate Number System, ANS. (Each leads to specific learning that must be taught to meet societal demands.)

Reading and Language Arts	*Mathematics*
Oral language develops naturally in a language-rich environment.	An approximate number system develops naturally in an environment where children manipulate and observe objects.
Young children are able to speak and use the language system and rules.	Young children are able to determine imprecise responses to numbers-related problems.
Society requires its people to read with fluency and comprehend.	Society requires its people to identify numbers and provide precise answers to number problems.
Children must be taught to read.	Children must be taught to compute and manipulate numbers.

How Math Skills Develop

As neurology, cognitive science, and educators combine their expert knowledge, mathematics can be viewed with a series of developmental steps. Again, much like learning to read, the milestones are accomplished sometimes in an orderly fashion and often simultaneously. This very effort explains why it is so challenging to develop a curriculum for teaching mathematics. Program developers and textbook writers consistently move forward to teach new operations and spiral back to consolidate previously learned procedures. Many cognitive functions are needed for a student to become mathematically literate with the specificity required by today's society. Neurology may be able to help education understand how the brain works to accomplish this unnatural outcome. Naturally developed skills and their counterparts, skills that are developed by teaching, are listed. Understanding what should develop naturally gives educators a basis to test children to make certain they have a natural mathematical basis to build upon for the math that is taught in school.

- Naturally developed skills
  - Object-based attention
  - Object representations
  - Oral numerical representations and order
  - Object to oral number matching
  - Working and long term memory for numbers and groups of numbers
- Skills developed through teaching
  - Number-naming ability
  - Memorization of number facts
  - Computations performed with number representations
  - Sets of number representations and computation
  - Application of computations in an order of operations
  - Number operations applied to problem situations
  - Varied responses to applications
  - Substitution of numbers and/or object representations in multivariate applications

Entwined with the science of numbers is the development of other cognitive skills. They include executive function, reading and use of academic language, visual-spatial abilities, and memory attributes.

Necessary Math Skills for School

The implications from neurological studies are great, but it is too early to see direct application to what we do in school. There are many questions.

Children need to develop this innate system, but how can it be determined if a child's development for ANS is normally progressing or is delayed?

Researchers identify operation of the ANS system mainly happens in the parietal lobes. Is there a pathway that can be defined similar to the oral language pathway?

Is the ANS hemisphere specific? Do innately learned mathematics concepts and computations function in both hemispheres?

What can educators do to provide remediation for young children who are not developing as expected for this predictive number sense? And, what level of achievement can be expected at different age levels?

Educators eagerly await more information about the innate system for ANS. It is anticipated that neurology will provide more insights into the workings of the mind that develop naturally and into the needs of students as they learn the math defined by the school system and the technically based society.

SCIENCE

Recommendations for teaching science have changed. Reports from major national and international organizations encourage teachers to analyze how children and adolescents learn, and how they acquire background knowledge. This new approach views science as a dynamic process, one that requires students to know, use, and interpret scientific explanations they discover in the natural world.

Students, as future scientists, must be able to generate and evaluate scientific evidence and to enter into discourse about the scientific knowledge they discover. All the while, they learn they must be encouraged to mold new learning into meaningful concepts (McGinnis & Roberts-Harris, 2009). The National Science Foundation released a report (McGinnis & Roberts-Harris, 2009) that involved 8,310 students. The students were enrolled in introductory courses for biology, chemistry, or physics at randomly selected universities and colleges. Those who experienced intense month-long studies of science topics during their high school years gained a depth, rather than breath, of knowledge. Consequently, those who had deep understandings of topics were found to consistently earn higher grades in college science courses ("Structure," 2009). Depth of knowledge is achieved when instruction encourages students to be actively engaged, to repeat and practice, to associate new learning to what is previously known, and to develop a huge neural network of related information to represent the science topic studied.

Current science teaching practices are often stuck in a traditional follow-the-scientific method with steps, inquiry, and discover approaches. Textbook publishers, who are eager to meet course standards and framework requirements, provide guides, for example, to science reading with note taking. Students labor through workbook pages that ask them to *explain the difference, define the words, circle the letter,* or *follow these steps.* It is hard to imagine students getting excited and learning through a workbook that guides them through a science experiment or requires them to fill in answers to repetitive prompts. Likewise, classrooms across the nation require students to memorize human cell components, names for plant structures, and the number representations for order and size of each planet. The practice of *memorize and regurgitate* kills students' motivation for science. Now, memorization is not a bad thing to provide a basic foundation of scientific facts, but it cannot be the core of a science program. The type of classroom learning described here causes neuron networks to simply yawn and go on automatic pilot. Forced student attention could result from teaching based on memorization, but learning is not predictable.

Science With Brain Correct Instruction

When neuroscience grabs a hold of science instruction, there are some striking altercations. Berger (2009) enthusiastically writes, "we want techers to teach the beauty of science, the fun in it, the humor in it, and to bring examples of modern science into the classroom" (p. 1). Consider child development. First, we know children progress through elementary school, and, as students in secondary schools, enjoy longer attention spans, faster processing speeds, greater self-discipline to force extended concentration, and a wider breath of background knowledge. With enhanced brain power, students are able to acquire increasingly sophisticated views of science topics and to latch onto theories of science that are meaningful to them.

Next, as teachers become versed in findings from neuroscience, they change perceptions of how a learning classroom looks, sounds, and feels. Science classrooms look different as students become active physically and mentally to learn. Classrooms are equipped with materials for discovery, community resources are welcomed, and the business of learning can be extended beyond the physical classroom environment as needed.

A quiet orderly classroom is expected while the teacher is teaching to provide information, modeling is occurring, or technology usage is taught. This is an essential part of learning in science courses. Note, it is a matter of fact that self-led, self-structured inquiry is not the best method for all high school students, according to a study conducted by professor Robert Tai and researcher Philip Sadler (see "Structure," 2009). They encourage teachers to provide structured lessons coupled with continual guidance and support ("Structure," 2009). Then, during the longest part of the lesson, students are busy with social interactions or discourse needed to complete project-based problems. Students and teachers feel the intensity of learning through discovery, and they experience the drama of connecting new thoughts, skills, or concepts with something that is already known.

The third consideration for brain-based science teaching finds teachers inspecting what their students already know and expecting they will build a stronger knowledge base. To accomplish this feat, teachers must implant assessment, not for grades, but to assist learners where and when they need it. This formative assessment allows the teacher flexibility to pair and group students and to maximize students' combined knowledge base. Students placed in groups according to the diversity of their background information can learn with and from each other. Teachers armed with assessment information know how to make important instructional decisions, what to teach, how much time is needed, and when to move on to something new.

Science, Mathematics, and Gender

More males are successful with the technical fields of math, engineering, and science than are women. Although this idea is commonly accepted, it is not necessarily inherent, according to research results. Diane Halpern, from Claremont McKenna College, and her colleagues from many universities throughout the country (Halpern et al., 2008) studied issues related to this conundrum. They found that men and women could be equally successful at performing similar tasks and solving problems, but they use different parts of their brains to do so. The researchers reviewed a variety of brain imaging techniques to find male and female brain differences. Specifically, females have higher percentages of gray matter brain tissue, which suggests more density of neurons and faster blood flow among nerve cells. Men tend to have more white matter, indicating more efficient connections between nerve cells. White matter consists of axons coated with a fatty protein called myelin. Another difference identified while the subjects performed a task was that women tended to access both hemispheres of the brain symmetrically, while men tended to have and activate a higher percentage of gray matter specific to the left side of the brain (Halpern et al., 2008).

These observations do not suggest that structural or functional brain differences account for all the variation seen among men and women in the scientific fields. We know the human brain forms based upon genetics, hormone and protein influence, life and environmental experiences, learning opportunity, and emotional aspects. The lack of women in fields of math, science, and engineering is significant, but it is also diminishing. Events in women's lives may encourage or discourage the selection of a technical field for a career. But, the gaps in achievement and career participation are decreasing. One study analyzed results from the Scholastic Aptitude Test (SAT) in 1980 and again currently. As reported by Halpern and her colleagues (2008), the SAT was administered to subjects several years before the typical age to take the test. The participating 12- to 14-year-olds were intellectually talented. At the first testing, researchers reported that there were 13 times more boys than girls who achieved scores of at least 700 out of the possible 800. Current tests indicate the advantage of boys over girls has dropped to about three boys scoring in the top 0.1 percent to one girl.

Additionally, the number of women in scientific fields has increased. What are the multiple changes that have influenced higher test scores and promoted a larger number of women to choose these male dominated fields? Lise Eliot (2009) in her book *Pink Brains, Blue Brains* repetitively states that the structural and genetic differences in the male and female brains are too insignificant to result in the amount of differences we see among the genders in mathematical and scientific fields. The premise this neuroscientist and author uses is that society continues to mold boys who are more confident in and more likely to choose science and mathematical career fields. Girls are not made to feel that they can be successful with those career choices.

There may never be a simple answer to correct the difference realized between the numbers of men and women who work in science, math, and engineering fields. One response is for school programs to make attitude adjustments and education modifications to encourage more females to choose math and science careers.

HEALTH

The topics for health education appropriate for our study are those that can be consciously controlled: food choices, physical exercise, and sleep. Physical exercise is addressed in the next section of this chapter, and the importance of sleep and brain development can be found in Chapter 6 under the title "Sleep Issues." This section focuses on foods and eating.

Certainly, people are infatuated with eating and especially eating healthy foods, at least most of the time. *Eating on the Run* (Tribole, 2004), *Moms on the Move: Practical Solutions for Busy Lives (Family Meals in Minutes)* (Byrd, 2004), *Brain Food: Recipes for Success in School, Sports, and Life* (Caruana & Hammer, 2007), and a plethora of other titles bombard us through publications and other media. Researcher Gomez-Pinilla likens food to a pharmaceutical compound that affects the brain (see Wolpert, 2010). Society in general wants to eat right and knows it is best, but how much is known about foods and a healthy brain? Can this important information be provided for students throughout the grades?

More than 160 studies about food's affect on the brain were analyzed by a team of researchers headed by Gomez-Pinilla from the Department of Neurosurgery and Physiological Science at the University of California, Los Angeles (in Wolpert, 2010). Outcomes of the analysis explain how food directly affects the human brain. The team identified different foods and their impact on the synapses in the brain. Synapses work to connect neurons and allow learning and memory to develop. **Omega-3 fatty acids** positively affect the expression of the neurotransmitters as they chemically spill into the synapse. From previous information, it is realized that the chemicals in the synapse can affect learning potential and the speed and force of neurons as they fire, connect, and reinforce neural pathways. In addition to increasing learning and memory for normal brain function, the researchers found that omega-3 fatty acids also decrease the risk of mental disorders, including attention deficit disorders, dyslexia, dementia, depression, bipolar disorder, and schizophrenia.

Another study by this researcher (see Wolpert, 2008) provided the treatment group of students a capsule with omega-3 fatty acid. Additional nutrients, iron, zinc, folic acid, and vitamins A, B6, B12, and C were in the capsule. The subjects showed higher test scores on basic tests of achievement than students in the control group who did not receive the treatment. Researchers state they are not aware if getting the omega-3 fatty acids from food rather than from a capsule would yield the same or more beneficial results (Wolpert, 2008).

Surprisingly, the human brain can automatically, unconsciously discriminate between foods that have low and high fat content. Brain images from a study utilizing an EEG show brain behavior resulting from viewing food items. Researchers led by Ulrike Toepel (2009) in Great Britain distracted study participants by asking them to identify items as cooking utensils or food items. In actuality the researchers wanted to find out if the brain discriminated between the high (not a healthy choice) and low fat (a more healthy choice) content food items. They found distinctive patterns of brain activity in the temporoparietal regions during the first trial. The pattern of brain activity shifted to the prefrontal cortex during the second trial. This shift most likely indicates the second time participants experienced the task they shifted their focus. They were more concerned about if they should or should not eat the item (Toepel, 2009). This shift in thinking from the parietal and temporal areas to the decision-making frontal lobes indicates the brain is innately capable to discriminate between healthy and nonhealthy food items. It accomplishes this feat as effortlessly and quickly as it discriminates between lightness and darkness.

The Human Brain Demands to Be Fed First

When it comes to nutrients for the body, the most vital organs receive preferential treatment. Because the brain affects all other body parts, it gets first choice. Pediatrician William Sears and his wife (Sears & Sears, 2009), a registered nurse, are acutely aware of the importance nutrition has upon learning for their eight children. They are so focused on this area they provide a website, AskDrSears.com, to share what they have found. In addition to the effect of good food on the neurotransmitters in the synapse, they identify the impact of the food the body receives on the structure of neurons. A myelin sheath covers the neuron's axon. The transition of an electrical charge in the neuron and its action of dumping neurotransmitters into the synapse is speedy and more efficient when the axon is covered by a myelin sheath. And, the sheath is composed of fatty cells. Omega-3 fatty acids help with the development and continued health of the fatty glial cells that form the myelin sheath and coat the axons. Good nutrition with good fats speed transition of the signals between cells (Sears & Sears, 2009). There is strong supporting evidence from neuroscience that food choices have a direct impact on how well the brain works to learn.

PHYSICAL EDUCATION

There is no denying the benefit of exercise for a healthy body, but some are still unaware what exercise does for memory and learning. Researchers using sophisticated scanning tools and possessing an understanding of biochemistry are amazed at just how potent exercise is for better brain function. Neuroscientists have identified a specialized protein, **IGF-1** and use the term BDNF to represent a **brain-derived neurotrophic factor.** What this means for education is that every time muscles work, biceps or quads contract, they send out chemicals including the IGF-1 protein. This protein acts like a foreman directing the brain's neurotransmitter production. Neurotransmitters increase production of several chemicals and force the neurotrophic factor, BDNF. This molecule has the capacity to improve neuron branching and communicating in new and improved ways. Here, BDNF promotes the very process of learning as junctions between neurons are activated and change (Carmichael, 2007). Understanding the role of BDNF is expanded by other researchers. Ratey and Hagerman (2009) in their book, *Spark,* add that BDNF can improve mental function, promote **neurogenesis** (growth of new neurons), and protect existing neurons against cell death.

Chapter 3 identified a protein, PKM-zeta, as a potential chemical for long term potentiation, LTP. Now, another protein has been identified that also affects the learning process. Neuroscientists do not know how many proteins must be present for learning to occur. New discoveries continue to improve understanding of the exceedingly complex process for learning and memory to occur and to identify specific roles for the various proteins.

Exercise and Brain Structures

The body needs exercise, regardless of a person's age. Most likely, however, the effect of exercise is most important for brains that are still developing, according to Tomporowski, a professor of exercise science at the University of Georgia (see Carmichael, 2007). Until the age of 20 or later, parts of the frontal lobes are still underdeveloped. Third- and fifth-grade students' brains were viewed after exercise. The hippocampus for working memory is not the only brain area that is powered up after physical exercise. Executive function in the frontal lobes was also observed to be highly activated following physical exercise. Classroom outcomes included improved math, logical thinking, and reading (Carmichael, 2007). As previously emphasized, each skill performed by a student's brain involves many cognitive areas in addition to the hippocampus and the frontal lobes. Exercise may be considered one of the leading interventions for children who are slow or laborious learners. Physical education qualifies as an essential part of any school curriculum.

Research Correlates Physical Activity and Academic Success

Hardcore data confirming the value of physical exercise in school systems is available from two well-publicized programs. Naperville, Illinois, District 203 radically altered the perception of how physical education is provided in their elementary, middle, and high schools. Their program is based on fitness as a way of life. Students learn how to develop healthy habits to maintain personal goals for health, body performance, and to encourage a sense that exercise is fun. This program has been in place for more than 17 years, and not only have there been innumerable positive behavioral benefits but test scores are outstanding in academic areas as well. While District 203 continually ranks high when compared with other local and state schools, the international scores are noteworthy. An exam, the Trends in International Mathematics and Science Study (TIMSS), compares students' knowledge levels from different countries. Ninety-seven percent of Naperville district eighth graders participated in the competition. They finished first in the world in science, just ahead of Singapore. Their math rank was sixth behind only Singapore, Korea, Taiwan, Hong Kong, and Japan (Ratey & Hagerman, 2009). While other factors contributed to these successful rankings, the attribute that definitely stands out is physical activity.

Similar success has been recorded by the California Department of Education between standard scores of achievement and the FitnessGram. California's FitnessGram measures aerobic capacity, percentage of body fat, abdominal strength and endurance, trunk strength and flexibility, upper body strength, and overall flexibility. The outstanding results revealed that physically fit students consistently score higher on tests of academic achievement than their less fit peers, regardless of economic status (Ratey & Hagerman, 2009). More evidence to connect physical fitness and activity emulated from a massive review of over 850 studies by researchers from a variety of related fields. The resounding response was that school children should participate in an hour or more of moderate to vigorous physical activity a day (Ratey & Hagerman, 2009). It is undeniable that physical activity has positive authority over brain chemicals for enhancing memory, concentration, and classroom behavior.

NEUROEDUCATION, A NEW ADVENTURE

Whether the focus is on reading, math, science, health, physical education, or the performing arts, neuroscience has information for education. Neuroscience and education are well-deserved partners. The mysteries of the mind may never be fully understood. However, advances in neuroeducation, along with improved conversation between neuroscientists and teachers, will continue to define advanced ways to support students with their learning.

10

Resources, Connections, and Future Classrooms

Innovative and technologically savvy readers will be validated for their forward thinking and their responsiveness to the learning needs of our youth as they read this chapter. Followers of neurology and seekers of its impact on all aspects of the teaching curriculum will be inspired. Within this final chapter are a number of instructional activities, which inculcate brain appropriate learning for each content area. Additionally, publication and web-based resources are cited for the field of education as classrooms are defined for this and future generations of learners.

STUDENTS' ATTITUDES INFLUENCE
ALL SUBJECT MATTER CLASSES

Notable insights about student learning preferences can be ascertained by asking them their perceptions of the classes they like or dislike. Recently, upper elementary and middle school students were surveyed for their thoughts about school. Because this activity was conducted as a home survey, the comments are relatively unbiased. Additionally, there was no attempt to match comments with teachers or schools or to make a statistical analysis of this small informal survey. Selected answers are grouped into three categories: What students liked about their favorite class, what they did not like about their least favorite class, and what would make learning better for them. Interestingly, students did not have much to say about the third area. Could it be they do not understand themselves as learners?

Tell about your favorite class.

Science, it's really interesting and my teacher is funny and class is never boring because we almost never take notes and barely have any homework and I have a lot of friends in that class and the teacher has a lot of activities that involve walking around and getting out of our seats.

The teacher goes over the lesson with an overhead projector and gives kids a chance to answer questions. Then the kids do the worksheets on their own in class and then at home they do homework.

It is easy and logical.

Each day is pretty different, but we usually start with a language arts worksheet and then we go on from there. My teacher always has fun projects for us to do.

What is your least favorite academic class? Tell what you do not like about it.

Math, because its really boring taking notes all the time and she almost never makes it fun or even remotely interesting and none of us ever get the point of learning it but I always end up sitting by people that I know and aren't annoying or weird and almost never work in groups or partners and the teacher prefers if you ask her for help instead of other students and is kinda weird and out of it all the time like she never notices if we are talking to each other which is good but if we raise our hands she almost never sees them.

It seems to be the same routine every day. Read out loud, answer comprehension questions as a group, work individually on grammar and spelling, and take tests and quizzes at the end of the week.

The class is monotonous, difficult, the English language has many exceptions, especially in spelling.

She is always making us take long and very boring notes and always has us solve really hard problems and expects us to get the answer right.

We don't do a lot of science because my teacher talks a lot and math takes a long time. My teacher is pretty strict with what to do, so we need to definitely follow directions.

Tell how you learn best.

Make it interesting to my age group, e.g., working toward a reward or goal or treasure or earning points or stars that are posted visually. Acting things out, being creative.

I learn best when the room is quiet and I can actually try things instead of just reading about them.

The teacher explaining it to us and seeing it.

Questions on this focus activity were designed to find out what students think and feel about classroom activities that have been promoted through these chapters. A copy of the form is provided at the end of this chapter. It can be given as a paper-and pencil-activity, preferably completed at home and compiled anonymously. Another way to use this instrument is to conduct the survey orally with focus groups of four or five students. Answers for a focus group can be recorded as a group response, noting the number of times the same comment is given.

INFUSE TECHNOLOGY INTO CLASSROOMS

What technology is doing for classroom teaching cannot be overemphasized. It is dynamic, it is usable, and it is undeniably available. Every teacher at all levels of teaching, whether working with 3-year-olds at the youngest end or 20-year-olds or beyond, teachers find that technology greatly enhances teaching prospects and tremendously enhances the learning potential of students. Every opportunity is taken to confirm how the human brain responds to use of media. While the alluring call of technology can become reality in classrooms, it is a competent teacher who orchestrates the entire program and keeps students focused on the course content.

Use of Technology Tools

To maximize the use of technology for instructional purposes in any subject area, teachers determine what the students are able to do, what they need to learn, and then they decide which technologies will be the greatest enhancement to student achievement. To obtain the best learning outcomes for students, the teaching content is examined to determine what is nice to know, important to know, and essential to know. The next step is to choose a pedagogical approach that will meet what the students need to learn and covers the curriculum content. The third and final step in planning is to analyze what technology tools will enhance learning by stimulating the minds of the students to the extent that they cannot resist being engaged in learning.

Teaching Today's Students With Media

The use of technology in classrooms is receiving attention from the field of education, and it is acclaimed for supporting stronger learning. *Edutopia* ("Ten Top Tips," 2009), a relatively young and innovative publication, provides 10 top ideas for teaching with today's media rich resources. A summarized list from the publication's writing team identifies some powerful teaching strategies matched with Internet resources.

1. *Break Into the Digital World*—Integrate digital tools to conduct scavenger hunts, name games, and other introductory games. Voice Thread (voicethread.com) is an easy-to-use online resource that allows the user to access photographs and visuals with written as well as audible comments. Teachers prompt students to use the website by modeling its use with a projector or an interactive whiteboard. Secondary students use the website's features to develop their goals for the year with audio comments. The website enables each student to know the importance of their contributions to class topics as they make written or audio comments.

2. *Get Information With Ease*—Survey Monkey (surveymonkey.com) makes information gathering easy by providing a process to develop a customized survey and creating a spreadsheet with summary information. For example, it is used to find technology experts who are available as classroom resources. A survey of students identifies experts for graphic design, podcasting, animation, spreadsheet, or video editing. The survey also seeks those who have special media gear that they are able to share for special projects.

3. *Ensure a Good Start*—Begin the school year by providing organizational skills necessary for school success. Retain information for individual learners with the aid of iGoogle (google.com/ig). This virtual desktop keeps learning tools in one place and provides calendar, notepads, assignment sheets, and even a calculator. Add-ons to the original design are accessed anytime and anywhere.

4. *Global Interconnectivity*—Use an array of online and media tools to connect students internationally.

   Skype.com and a web camera is used for video conferencing.

   Taggalaxy.com provides access to photos for hundreds of topics called tags from anywhere in the world. Students find pictures from their community to share with epals worldwide.

   Epals.com provides an easy to use system to connect with classrooms throughout the globe. Students can have epals in any country by using the language translator, which is built in to the site. Collaborative learning projects include creative storytelling, reporting of natural disasters, having online conversations about global issues, or portraying the way we learn in our classroom.

Learner.org/jnorth connects seasonal migration projects to classrooms from northern and southern hemispheres. Students collaborate by tracking migration. They learn about monarch butterflies, whooping cranes, humming birds, or even about the sun's light at different global locations.

Rockourworld.ning.com connects students to other like-minded music lovers and creative thinkers to compose original music, make movies, and meet each other through video conferencing.

Sporcle.com supplies popular games and user created games that hit many curriculum areas: geography, language, science, history, and literature.

5. *Resources for Classroom Materials*—Post a request for needed materials on the website (donorschoose.org). Citizen philanthropists check this website to choose projects they wish to fund. Students follow up by letting donors know why the materials are needed and how the project developed. Donors furnish musical instruments, books, and classroom technology. Another source maintains items that will otherwise be trashed. SCRAP (scrapaction.org) is a school and community reuse project operating from Portland, Oregon. Freecycle (freecycle.org) also links classrooms with donation opportunities in the local community.

6. *Vocabulary Enhancer*—Turn text or a list of words into a cloud pattern with Wordle (wordle.net). The user manipulates the layout, font, highlighting, and color. This site is used to create a prereading activity, serve as a student independent writing tool, or generate a cumulative class word list for a lively class dialogue.

7. *Collaborative Group Work*—Set up workspaces for collaborative with Google Docs (google.com/educators/tools.html). Teachers assign students to use this website, and they follow what students are doing on projects by checking midstream during the assignment to offer comments or help. Students share notes and develop presentations together. Wikis offer the same advantages plus the benefit of video- or photo-enhanced publishing.

8. *Back Channels*—Use private chat rooms for individual classroom microblogging. Or, use twitter.com. All students in the class are involved as they watch a video or a student presentation and pose questions, express agreement, or give a dissenting view. Teachers set a high standard by teaching students to post relevant, respectful responses.

9. *Curriculum Relevant Visual Technology*—Access to actual works of art, documents, and publications is available through this Library of Congress website (loc.gov/teachers). Additionally, teachers access classroom materials, lesson plans, archived materials, news briefs, and professional development resources.

10. *Professional Resources*—Join social networks to meet professional needs through websites.

Digital Directions for Teachers (edweek.org/dd/) provides teachers with white papers on teacher proven digital practices, webinars, uses for mobile devises, and even job openings.

Classroom 2.0 (classroom 20.ning.org) is a social network for teachers to post questions and provide answers to other teachers' concerns.

Teachers Teaching Teachers (teachersteachingteachers.org) invites teachers to join a weekly teacher discussion with the combined sources of blogging, podcasting, and webcasting.

Social-bookmarking (delicious.com) supplies tools to organize, comment, and share resources with other like minded educators ("Ten Top Tips," 2009).

One final website resource is the *Neuroscience for Kids Newsletter* (nfknews@u.washington.edu). Brain Awareness Week (BAW) is scheduled in March of each year. Teachers are encouraged to participate in BAW by developing a brain fair or inviting a neuroscientist to the school or your class. The Society for Neuroscience has a list of neuroscientists who are interested in outreach projects to schools K–12. Check the list as neuroscientists are available in many areas (http://www.sfn.org/index.cfm?pagename=neuroscientistsTeacherPartners).

Technology and web connections are continually being added to teachers' lists of available resources. Educational practices and teaching strategies that transverse to the place where students are mindfully comfortable are continually are being added to incite students and excite their neural pathways in incredibly, inspiring ways.

INFUSING NEUROSCIENCE INTO CLASSROOM PRACTICE

Resources and neurologically infused classroom activities are the next focus based upon students with a proclivity for successful reading. Each subject area has one or more practical classroom activities based on how the young adult brain is designed to learn.

Foreign Language: In the Foreign Language Classroom

Teachers rely on active student engagement for foreign language instruction. Teachers talk, then students talk, repeat, and speak on their own. Writing activities fortify rules of the new language and help provide one more venue for the brain to use to make sense of how new words and clusters of words sound and look. That is the avenue for student success. Working memory has demanding needs to move words, thoughts, and concepts into long term declarative or procedural memory. Students must repeat, practice, rehearse, and associate the words of the new language they are learning. How would an activity based on how the brain learns in a foreign language classroom mimic the repetitions needed for the new language to be recorded in memory and capable of being reproduced?

Build on what students have as background knowledge in their native language through an activity called The Question for the Day. Give students a new prompt each day. Suggested prompts involve personal experiences, but they could also be from a previous unit of study. Provide the prompt in the foreign language.

Tell about a time you were a hero.

Where is the place you would most like to be?

My favorite relative is . . .

If I were in charge at my home, these would be my rules.

The best pet in the world is a . . .

My best time of the day is . . .

Here is something about me that no one knows . . .

I am saving my money for/to . . .

If I were principal of the school for a week, I would . . .

The best place I ever visited is . . .

If I were a teacher I would teach . . .

My choice of careers is to be a . . .

Students write their responses to the selected prompt in the foreign language using at least three sentences. They read their sentences to two or three other students and answer questions in their native language. They modify their sentences based on feedback from their peers. The activity could stop here, or students could work with a more advanced student as a tutor to edit the sentences. Words they need are given on a card or placed in their journal for future reference, and each word a student request to use is recorded on the board or on a class chart. Foreign words are listed with a definition in the native language. The teacher or advanced students may review papers with each person in the class to correct sentence structure and grammar. Students revise and finalize their papers. Once again, the teacher may opt for this to be the last step of the assignment.

A more intense strategy that could be used intermittently is to invite students to present their sentences to the entire class or in small groups by reading them out loud. Each listener writes one question or writes one summary statement in the foreign language after listening to each peer. Reading the paper several more times to rotating groups of students provides more practice. When the reading and listening activity is complete, students identify words that are new or difficult for the class to study. All student responses could be reproduced for the class to reread for oral language practice. It is easy to see that this activity can be short and simple or long and concentrated. Teachers decide how much intensity students require and how much practice is needed based on the importance of the topic and the vocabulary.

Continual exposure to the same vocabulary and sentences helps students to hear how the foreign language sounds, to see how words form together to make a complete thoughts, and to experience how words come together to paint a mental picture. Any good teaching and learning activity can be selected to increase learning potential. It needs to be approached in a variety of ways and over an extended period, exciting neural pathways in various parts of the brain over and over again.

Visual/Performing Arts: In the Visual/Performing Arts Classroom

Introducing drama through performance based learning contributes to any K–12 classroom according to teachers James Henderson Collins and Corby Kelly (see Bernard, 2008). These two entrepreneurs infuse the sounds and actions of theatrical performance as a part of a teaching lesson. By performing the course material, students become self-confident learners, experience emotions, and have fun (Bernard, 2008). Neuroscience validates the use of activities that are charged with emotions and feelings to increase the strength of learning (LeDoux, 2002).

A natural way to begin is to use known literary and historical figures. Students study the assigned or selected individual to develop a comprehensive and vibrant portrait of the person. They then take the role of the historical figure during improvisation to develop a deep understanding of the character and to bring history to life. A scenario is created based on the time period in a particular setting, and it is based on a real-life situation for students to reenact.

Another strategy builds group trust and confidence. It is called Improv Freeze. Two students begin to interact through an imagined scenario. At will, other students can call, "Freeze," and take the place of one of the actors or even change the scenario. Collins and Kelly (Bernard, 2008) may decide to invite local actors to interact with students. If a selected character had a specific disorder, personality flaw, or unique behaviors, a specialist can help students to develop a deeper understanding of how this character may act and sound.

A final strategy uses technology. Classrooms may have access to a non-HTML webpage (Wikispaces.com), which is available at no charge for classroom use. The advantage of using a web resource is for students' work to be widely visible to an audience expanded beyond the classroom or school. The confines of the classroom time and space are eliminated as comments and reflections from viewers from the global world of the Internet reach the classroom (Bernard, 2008).

There is nothing new about bringing music into the classroom to create a stimulating or calming environment. To expand the use of music beyond the role of creating a mood, teachers are also asking questions and leading students to form opinions about different music they hear. Students are encouraged to express the type of music they like, share music in the classroom, and engage in research about music composers. Music can be used in a variety of ways with many different classes. More research is needed to relate the use of music and learning outcomes. Presently, there is not enough information to determine the causal result of studying, playing, and listening to music on learning in specific subject areas.

Social Studies and History: In the Social Studies or History Classroom

A new approach to teaching social studies and history uses a collaborative learning model. Students are required to locate source documents, recognize and evaluate authors, synthesize materials, make connections between geographic regions or chronological eras, and present findings in written and spoken formats (International Reading Association, 2006). Here are some teaching innovations that reflect the requirements and are typical of student brain engaging techniques. Three are explored—personal involvement and reporting, social interest video games, and bringing the world into the classroom.

Beyond Traditional Reading/Reporting Strategies

To challenge, attract, and engage students' thinking about social studies, instruction needs to invite, excite, and engage students. Social interaction and civic engagement are critical to meeting lofty goals that are found in documents produced by national history and social studies councils and offices of education at state and federal levels. Student involvement can take many forms. They can experience situations or events by visiting an historical site, performing a simulation of an historical event, interviewing experts from the community, taking the role of a person and acting out an event (see the Visual/Performing Arts section above), participating in a debate, or conducting a community poll on a politically hot issue. Students need to be involved with situations or events, feel an emotional response, and then respond to what they learn from the experience. Traditional instructional techniques are employed after students have a personal experience.

After active engagement, a number of reporting techniques beyond and including a research report can be used. Innovative writing tools are available as instructional strategies.

History Frames and Story Maps—a thinking map can be used to look at key players, time and place of the event, problems, key events, outcomes, and other significant learning. (See more information about thinking maps in Chapter 8 under the title, Instruction for the Complex Nature of Comprehension During Reading.)

Carousel Brainstorm—terms, concepts, or key learning are placed on the top of a wall chart. Groups of students move from chart to chart and add comments, definitions, and examples.

Pattern Puzzles, Also Known as Mystery Pot—a sorting and manipulation activity which encourages skills of organization and sequencing. Topics, sentences, key concepts, or words written on cards are placed in a "pot." Students grab a card and then find peers who have a card that relates to or explains their card. They look for a hidden message and report it to the class.

3–2–1—a quick strategy to summarize and question. Have students list three things they have learned, tell about two extremely interesting things, and provide one unanswered question.

Clock Buddies—a system to create interaction among students during work activities is to assign study buddies for different time periods. For example, in elementary grades, it could be my 1:00 buddy; while in secondary school, it could be my 1:15 or 1:40 study partner.

Other unique and engaging strategies used for summarizing or reporting are found at a website created by Raymond Jones (2007), *Reading Quest* (http://www.reading quest.org/stat/home.html). Raymond maintains the website and provides instructions for the strategies. Many strategies have downloadable masters, charts, or maps.

Students may need to know what the expectations are for these and other less traditional methods of reporting. To align student work with expected standards and key concepts for each topic of study, teachers can furnish a rubric. With a scoring rubric, students can use a self-evaluate model to determine if their product meets the curriculum expectations. (An online rubric maker is located at http://rubistar.4teachers.org.)

Teens, Video Games, and Social Responsibilities

An interesting study by Princeton Survey Research Associates (Lenhart et al., 2008) was conducted as a random digit dial phone survey, which culminated in

2008. This Pew Internet Project is the first nationally representative report of teen video gaming and their involvement with civic activities. The study uncovered that 99% of boys and 94% of girls, who were surveyed, are video gamers. Many use online games to play with people they know in their offline lives. The report revealed that when games have civic overtones, they lead teens to have interest in and to take part in civic and political activities. Teens interviewed reported that activities encouraged by interactive online video games with social and civic themes include getting online information about current events and politics, giving or raising money for charity, staying informed about political issues, volunteering, persuading others on voting issues, and participation in protest marches. Understanding how young adults become involved with socially important activities can benefit classroom learning. Consider the sequence of having an experience first and analyzing the educational learning second; why not use a game assignment as part of the instructional plan?

Nontraditional Teaching With Technology

Technology can be used to provide access to preexisting background information students already have. It purveys an active, engaging learning technique, which can lead to globalized learning and understanding. For social studies, the computer, a video, telecommunications through cell phone usage, or a global positioning system (GPS) are all possibilities to create a classroom without walls or limitations.

Consider a history/social studies or mathematics class with the topic of life economies. Young adults are expected to take on huge responsibilities as they transition from high school to college or from high school to work. Skills for many adult activities are assumed to be understood; but often, students are not adequately prepared to figure out adult situations on their own. Independent young adults are expected to be able to manage a checkbook by writing checks, paying bills, and balancing the checkbook to a monthly statement. More advanced skills require the young adult to enter into a rental agreement, obtain a loan, complete an employment application, read and follow a company employee manual, prepare for a license to drive a car or be licensed to drive heavy truck or construction equipment, understand credit card interest and payment factors, obtain employment benefits, or run a household with a limited income. Experiences through simulations and games of real-life situations available through innovative technology and media can help to prepare students for challenges beyond high school before they have these real-life challenges.

Giving a student preference survey to determine students' unique needs prior to embarking on technology-intense lessons can curtail unexpected detriments to learning. At Key Largo School in Florida, teachers consider how well technology will work for their students before they select technology-intense lesson assignments. They search and question to determine if students work better alone or in groups and how information can be most effectively received. Students in secondary school usually have individual learning inclinations that result from earlier classroom and study experiences. They may have a partiality to receive information from the auditory, visual, or another sensory system. Teachers at this Florida school look also at how the noise, movement and background sounds generated by using technology might affect student learning (Curtis, 2003). It is easy to get excited about technology for its innovativeness, and it becomes a vital classroom resource when it is selected for its benefits to student learning.

Mathematics: In the Mathematics Classroom

For math teachers to fully engage students, the instructional climate can be rich with numerical prompts, representations, procedures, and challenges. Students do need to spend time to memorize numerical facts, and the time spent on these activities may be hastened by computer technology. Learning math facts well enough to have them stored in long term declarative memory is also a good way to prime the brain for other things that need to be automatically remembered in daily life—phone numbers, addresses, prices of items, identification numbers, and passwords, to name a few. Until students have memorized and can recall number facts for operations (adding, subtracting, multiplying, and dividing), teachers provide prompts either by displaying charts in the classroom or by providing individual prompt cards. Step-by-step procedures can also be posted. It is critical that students practice and rehearse mathematical procedures that need to move from working memory to long term procedural memory to be available to use at will with automaticity. Teaching strategies are suggested to help students memorize math operations and procedures and to become teachers of their peers.

FIRST INDEX CARD STRATEGY

Memorization With the Brain in Mind

- *Teaching outcome:* Students will obtain automaticity with math facts, remember known math facts, and employ procedures automatically by using long term declarative and procedural memory.
- *Application to daily life:* Memorization, especially of numbers, will help students manage phone numbers, e-mail addresses, the cost of items, identification numbers, and passwords.
- *Classroom activities:* Mad math minute (practice of number facts or operations), sporadic review (provide a number problem answer to line up for recess), flashcard review, math game boards, and computer programs all provide neurosmart classroom activities.

- *Classroom prompts:* Bulletin boards or charts are available to list procedures, steps, rules, operations, or answers until facts or process can be automatically recalled from memory.
- *Sample:* Students like to be challenged. They like to solve mysteries, complete puzzles, or compete for prizes. Math class can be exciting by lacing repetitious drill with contests and unexpected dilemmas. Imagine students entering a classroom in the upper elementary grades with answer cards on their desks. Everyone has a different answer, and the answers are from their current study unit. Students are asked to write as many different problems for the answer that they can think of during three minutes. They sign their names and pass their card to another student. The next student has two more minutes to add problems. The cards are collected. The teacher chooses problems the students have developed for their math practice that day. Teachers also have students type the best problem they thought of into mathematic practice software to produce a worksheet to be used with the entire class.

SECOND INDEX CARD STRATEGY

Practice Math With a Purpose

- *Teaching outcome:* Students learn how look for key math concepts, think about teaching strategies, and learn through teaching others.
- *Application to daily life:* Students are respected for their unique classroom contributions. They learn to work with others to problem solve. They learn to help others as peer tutors.
- *Classroom activity:* Students are challenged to analyze, understand, and prepare to teach the concepts from a new chapter. Assign groups of three or four students to preview an entire new math chapter. The group is responsible to find out what needs to be learned and to make a teaching plan. Technology use is encouraged if it is available. Require each group to answer the following questions:

  o What math procedures need to be learned?
  o Why are these procedures important to students?
  o What regularly used and innovative, exciting teaching practices could be used to teach the lessons?

Students in each group make a teaching proposal and present their ideas to the class in presentations lasting no more than three minutes. Each student evaluates the ideas by assigning points for each presentation. The point system is to give a 5 for a teaching proposal that they think would work very well; 3 points means it is an average plan, and 1 point is given for plans that are incomplete or confusing. Points are tallied. The group with the most points works with the teacher to teach the math unit and is awarded bonus teaching points.

The practice of involving students as teachers dramatically improves their rate of learning. This technique is also used as an instructional strategy in the section on health.

Science: In the Science Classroom

Science classes traditionally include laboratory assignments, which are successful strategies to maximize student learning. Students are engaged in forming predictions, following a procedure, discovering outcomes, and publishing their findings. This process is a strong educational practice that contributes to long-lasting learning and matches how the students' brains are equipped to learn. The strong educational practice of clinical involvement science is expanded beyond the classroom walls with the use of technology.

Teaching Science With Technology and Media

Informal science media has become more available and accessible. Media allows students to experience lessons in biology, physics, and other subjects, and it extends their ability to envision themselves as scientists. Science classes are allowing students to work and communicate through various media, which includes movies, television, web-based games, e-mail, text messages, and blogs. Innovative teachers challenge students to watch selected television programs and to take notes on science-related information. Students are asked to research and present the information they identified more completely. Teachers also encourage students to be on the lookout for scientific misconceptions. Students are challenged to identify and validate that the scientific information presented on the show was indeed correct or probable.

The use of available technology for science instruction is an area that has not been validated by researchers. There are no research claims to support the use of technology and media in educational settings. The clearest benefit of the use of instructional media comes from teacher reports. Science is a subject in which students may not see themselves as being capable of successful learning. However, teachers observe and report that science instruction with technology motivates and engages students in science with positive learning outcomes (Cavanagh, 2009).

Male Dominance in Scientific Fields

It was addressed earlier that there are substantially more males working in the fields of science, engineering, and mathematics than females. The apparent and critical need for more young adults to select math and science professions could be partially resolved by recruiting more women into these fields. A current study (Center on Education Policy, 2010, pp. 13, 16–17) reports that high school males and females throughout the United States score a mere difference of one to four percentage points for proficiency in math. Females are as likely as males to achieve the higher scores, which are reported to show very little variance among the states.

The fact remains that there are limited numbers of females in scientific fields. This discrepancy may best be explained by career decisions children make. Primarily, choices for a profession are determined by success with academic subjects. Other deterrents females face when they consider work in math and science fields include how teachers and mentors interact with youngsters, the impact of hormones at various ages, remediation practices for female students, how adult peer review impacts achievement in technical fields, how men and women use their brains differently, and what life responsibilities women have that affect their career choices. Gender differences are significant and are complex to understand, but the way science is taught can make a difference for both genders.

Teaching With Media and Student Success

Using media in science instruction is one relatively attainable educational choice to encourage engagement for both genders and all different types of learners. Media as an instructional approach appeals to students' visual, auditory, and often motor senses and invites them to attend and concentrate, creating mind storms. Scientific facts, information, concepts, and theories are more likely to be validated and stored in memory. Through media experiences, students, especially female young adults, are more likely to see themselves as capable in the various science fields, which are considered by many to be the most unattainable courses for success.

Health: In the Health Classroom

An instructional strategy that is consistently effective is the act of teaching itself. It is often said that teachers get better and better educated about their course contents as they practice and repeat information during lesson delivery. It is easy to see that children taking on the role of teaching can reinforce their learning and strengthen the neural networks that make up their memories. This strategy of teaching to learn is particularly effective when it is applied to health education. Three different student levels, elementary grades, middle grades, and high school can employ this teaching strategy.

In the elementary grades, *students as teachers* has many applications, and one in particular is provided. Children are given a health vocabulary word or a food item. A list of healthy foods could include blueberries, wild salmon, nuts and seeds, avocados, beans, pomegranate juice, freshly brewed tea, and dark chocolate (Sorgen, 2006). Classroom resources are provided—pictures, food charts, books, videos, computer access, clipped pictures, or physical objects. Children plan to tell the rest of the class about the item they selected or were assigned. After the child teaches about the word or item, the student can ask a question or two. Just like a teacher, students can check to see if the class learned what the *student as teacher* taught. For more advanced learning, a class summary chart can be provided with labels of the selected words or items. Children complete information on the class chart about their assigned word by writing, dictating, or drawing.

Middle grade students have influence upon their parents and family. Generally, parents are acutely aware of the classes their youngsters are taking and topics they are studying. A *student as teacher* assignment takes full advantage of the good conversations that can take place between parents and their young adults.

Knowing about brain foods is important for school success, and food selection is controlled mainly at home and by the family. This topic provides an appropriate topic for a health unit. Good teaching units from the health curriculum often begin with a pretest. In this case, the pretest is given at home to the family or with the adult who shops and prepares the meals. The pretests are brought back to school, and the answers are analyzed and summarized. Students identify the areas that need to be addressed for their families' education. They select or are assigned group projects to research food concepts and to plan a presentation for their peers. An important aspect of the assignment is to provide the class with not only resources for information but also with teaching strategies, materials, and prompts that can be shared at home. After field testing the lessons with their classmates, students present the information in the form of a lesson to their families. To complete the assignment, a posttest is given at home, and results are again tabulated by the class. Students can self-evaluate their effectiveness as teachers by giving themselves a grade on how well they taught the unit to their families.

High school students have different learning needs that can be addressed by teaching others. Teachers begin by providing an introduction to a "healthy eating and the brain" unit from the standard curriculum. In this case, students use an organizer, What I Know, What I Want to Know, and What I Learned, K-W-L. Items identified as what students want to learn are then organized, sorted, and matched with the unit objectives developed by the teacher. Individuals or groups of students select the areas they want to study and prepare. Students prepare to teach their topic to the class with teacher assistance. Resources, including access to technology, are available. If students are unaware of how to access research using an Internet search engine, that process can be modeled. *Students as teachers* present information to their peers. An important aspect of this process is feedback from other students on their lessons. Comments can be given orally or on a feedback form. A chart of excellent teaching strategies used by these students as teachers can be developed and continue to be maintained. To finalize the unit, students provide an individual or a class list of what they learned.

Students as teachers is a powerful teaching strategy that infuses all the technical aspects of how learning occurs. If mental actions lead to permanent learning and response automaticity, how much can be expected from the next area of the curriculum that requires physical activities?

Physical Education: Physical Activity's Impact on the Classroom

Most people accept as fact that physical exercise and movement are important for bodily health. It is well known that a regular program of exercise will strengthen muscles, control body weight, energize the body, and stave off depression. What more could we want from an intensive and consistent habit of physical exercise? The answer is a lot more. What has not been so well understood is the impact exercise has on the chemical aspects of the brain and ultimately on learning. Understanding the importance of physical activities is so important that John J. Ratey, a medical doctor and professor of psychiatry, and Eric Hagerman (2009), an editor of science publications, dedicated an entire book to the topic. *Spark: The Revolutionary New Science of Exercise and the Brain,* while not written specifically for educators, provides information that will revolutionize how society views exercise and learning.

Exercise increases levels of **serotonin, norepinephrine,** and **dopamine.** Serotonin and norepinephrine decrease the affects of stress. Beyond that simple statement, neurologists have revealed that stress erodes connections between billions of nerve cells and actually shrinks some areas of the brain. Exercise is a medical response to depression and emotional confusion as it releases neurochemicals to augment the brain's infrastructures. Serotonin regulates the signals at the brain stem to police activities at every junction within the emotional center of the brain. Its counterpart, norepinephrine, produces a chemical response to arouse alertness and attention to the senses and to modulate anxiety response. A third neurotransmitter, which is commonly known, is dopamine. Dopamine is often referred to as the pleasure chemical. It is released from the thalamus and creates a feeling of euphoria. By definition, it also is critical to attention, motivation, and cognition.

Exercise has not been embraced as an essential part of the school curriculum. But, it should be. It does not simply raise the level of good neurotransmitters; it adjusts them to create the ideal situation for learning. Translated into school business, this means that after physical exercise children and young adults are in an ideal state to engage and concentrate for learning.

The message is strong and clear: Keep physical education as a part of the school curriculum. Learning how to play a game, watching the P.E. teacher draw a diagram of how a game is manifested, learning rules, or even learning about how physical activity improves brain function are not physical activities and cannot take the place of the designated P.E. time. Children and older students periodically must be physically active. Active movement does not have to be limited to the time designated for a course called physical education—it can happen anytime students need to have their brains powered up. Simply put, when children are nodding off and falling off their chairs, stop. Engage in some sort of physical activity appropriate for the age level of the students. Experience the elevated levels of interest, engagement, and remembering that will follow. The evidence is overwhelming—physical activity and brain stimulation for learning are interconnected.

All Academic Areas Amalgamate in a Well-Designed Brain

School, the community, and home can provide the ideal climate for young children to design and build a brain that allows them to read with ease. As children mature through the school years, they can attain high levels of achievement all academic areas as they read to learn. But, reading is not enough for school success. Engagement in learning, concentration on information, and practice, practice, practice all lead to long term remembering of essential learning. Fortunately, teachers can find innovative and engaging strategies for all subject areas in books, such as Antonacci and O'Callaghan's (2010) *Developing Content Area Literacy: 40 Strategies for Middle and Secondary Classrooms*. Teachers with explicit knowledge encompassing how students use their reading brain to learn are equipped to select brain effective practices for students.

A well-designed and well-connected brain allows students to not only access information they need but also to redesign, create, and develop ideas. They learn to problem solve, deal with ambiguities, work with others who do not learn and think as they do, and see and accept change. Through the use of current and future technologies, today's students are empowered to produce outcomes that decision makers in the field of education are only beginning to conceive. It is society's responsibility and duty to encourage young people to construct brains that expand and develop beyond what current adult generations know and understand. Information can be used from experience, educational and neurological research, and current resources and technology to help today's students build a brain that is ready to take on challenges and opportunities in the world as it develops and expands within their lifetime.

FOCUS INTERVIEW QUESTIONS

First name: _____

Grade: _____ Male or Female: _____ Date: _____

1. On a scale of 1–10, with I meaning *not at all,* and 10 meaning *very much,* how well do you like school? _____

2. Using the same 1–10 scale, with 1 meaning *not good at all,* and 10 meaning *very good,* tell how well you *do* at school. _____

   How many academic classes do you have? _____

3. What is your favorite academic class?

   Tell what the teacher does to make the class meaningful in each area:

   • How the class is organized:

   • How students are involved with running the classroom:

   • How information is provided—circle all the responses that are true of the class:

lecture	problem solving	reading
computer research	guest speakers	videos
group work	partners	other

   If you circled other, please explain.

   • How you learn—circle all responses that are true. I learn best by

reading on my own	listening to someone tell me
problem solving	going on the Internet
talking it over with a study group or partner	taking notes during class
doing research	Other

If you circled *other*, please explain.

Tell me anything else you can about why this class is your favorite one.

4. What is your least favorite academic class?

Tell what you do not like in each area.

- How the class is organized:

- How students are involved with running the classroom:

- How information is provided—circle all the responses that are true of the class.

lecture	problem solving	reading
computer research	guest speakers	videos
group work	partners	other

If you circled *other*, please explain.

- How you learn—what would make this class better?

Tell me anything else you can about why this class is your least favorite one.

5. Tell how you learn best.

Glossary

adult learning theory. A description of effective means for adults to learn, which include input and choice for learning, meaningful application, and active engagement.

amygdala. A structure in the limbic system that reacts to the emotional context of sensory input.

angular gyrus. A brain structure located at the junction of the occipital, parietal, and temporal lobes. It is here that the letters of written words are translated into the sounds of spoken language.

approximate number system (ANS). An imprecise number system operating from the parietal lobes. It develops naturally during childhood and allows youngsters to learn number concepts in preparation for formal mathematics taught in school.

arachnoid layer. A middle protective membrane between the skull of the brain and the cerebral cortex. *Arachnoid* is Greek for its resemblance to a spider's web.

astrocytes. A specialized type of glial cell in the brain that administers to neurons by cleaning up debris formed of dead or ineffective neurons.

automaticity. A brain response to a person's need to conduct a procedural activity to allow the activity to happen without conscious thought.

axon. A single appendage with multiple terminals that responds to an electrical charge from its neuron to spew chemicals into a gap for uptake by dendrites from other neurons.

basal ganglia. Subcortical nuclei located under the motor cortex that modulate stimuli, regulate actions for movement, and also control the flow of information into working memory. Groups of nuclei are called *ganglion*.

bilingual. Being able to speak two languages with competence.

brain. The cerebrum, consisting of the cerebral cortex or forebrain, the brainstem and the surrounding limbic system or midbrain, and the cerebellum or hindbrain.

brain-derived neurotrophic factor (BDNF). A protein that acts to increase interaction in the synapses between neurons. Researchers report that every time muscles work, a bicep or quad contracts, it sends out chemicals including the IGF-1 protein, as a brain derived neurotropic factor.

canonical neurons. A specific type of neuron that activates parts of the observer's brain by observing an object.

central nervous system (CNS). Structural parts of the brain with central and peripheral parts. The peripheral nervous system (PNS) is the branching spinal and cranial nerves that take messages from the brain to the rest of the body while the CNS is the brain and the spinal cord.

cerebral cortex. The deeply folded outer layer of the cerebral hemispheres that is responsible for perception, awareness of emotion, planning, executive function, and conscious thought. Also called the neocortex.

corpus callosum. A large bundle of myelinated fibers (axons) that connects the left and right hemispheres of the brain.

cranium. A bony structure that encases and protects the brain from abrasions and jarring. It is also called the skull.

declarative memory. Explicit memory to allow storage of information in an organized manner so it can be subsequently recalled by speaking or writing.

dendrites. Extensions from the cell body of a neuron that seek messages from other neurons by receiving chemical substance (neurotransmitters) from an axon.

dopamine. One of the better known neurotransmitters that influences brain reactions for cognition, attention, motivation, and pleasure. Because it contributes to euphoric feelings, it can influence addiction.

dorsolateral prefrontal cortex. An area that is composed of the dorsal (top) part and lateral (side) area and can further be identified as the site of the basal ganglia.

dura mater. An outer layer of membranes that protects the brain and is located between the cranium and the soft tissues of the brain. Dura mater is Latin for hard mother.

epigenetics. The study of changes in DNA located within a neuron's nucleus. Manipulation by scientists or natural changes in the nucleus during learning do not permanently alter the genetic construction determined by heredity.

excitatory postsynaptic potential (EPSP). A stellar activation process among neurons that becomes the essence of what happens when learning occurs.

forebrain. The largest part of the brain, which consists of the cerebral hemispheres for conscious thought, the lower part with the limbic system initially processes sensory information and responses to emotional aspects of input from the environment.

frontal lobes. The left and right hemisphere areas above the eyes, and covering the area back to the ears, of the neocortex. This area is responsible for problem solving, future planning, dealing with abstraction, and other issues that require the highest level of thinking. It is often referred to as the chief executive of the thinking brain.

ganglion. A congregation of neurons joined to do the same or a related job. For word form areas, the neurons may relate to meaning of a word or phrase (the plural form, which is often used to name parts of the brain, is *ganglia*).

genetic material. Genes and chromosomes that exist in cell bodies to direct the activities and connections of the cells.

glucose. This simple form of sugar works with oxygen to provide energy to neurons, so they can fire and communicate with each other. It is supplied to brain cells through the blood stream.

Golgi stain. A process developed by Camillo Golgi for dyeing approximately 10% of the neurons in a small area. By staining some neurons, neuroscientists can identify and compare neurons.

gray matter. Substance in the brain that is more gray in color. In the living brain, the gray portion is mainly the cell bodies and dendrites of neurons. While brains of the deceased are mainly gray in color, living brains are also white (myelin-coated axons) and pink (caused by blood and food supply to the cells).

gyrus. Convoluted folds rising above the surface of the cerebral cortex (plural form is gyri).

hemispheres. Two halves of the brain, a left and a right. Structures in one side are duplicated in the other side. For example, there is a right and a left hemisphere frontal cortex. The two hemispheres are divided by a ridge and connected by a thick band of fibers, the corpus callosum.

hindbrain. The bottom part of the brain that connects with the spinal cord and regulates unconscious processes, such as breathing.

hippocampus. Small left and right hemisphere structures located in the innermost area of the brain responsible for the survival but also involved with working memory. New potential learning activates the hippocampus until the learning is dropped from memory or moved to another area of the brain for permanent recall.

histones. Small, basic proteins most commonly found in association with the DNA of genetic makeup.

hypothalamus. Key brain nuclei located above the hippocampus to regulate body functions in response to emotional sensory input.

IGF-1 protein. A chemical found in the synapse between neurons that is stimulated by muscular activity. This protein improves the brain-derived neurotrophic factor (BDNF), improving speed and effectiveness of neural transmissions.

inhibitory neurons. Nerve cells that screen out most of the unimportant signals from the sensory systems when they reach the thalamus.

inhibitory postsynaptic potential (IPSP). A weak response among neurons may shut down neuron action, and there is no improvement or permanence of the neuron firing pathway.

learning cycle. A four-step process to describe how learners are initiated to new information, concepts, or skills and how they reflect, use, and consolidate something new into their way of doing.

learning potentiation. The ability to remember information or a process as a result of rehearsal, practice, or repetitions that cause masses of neurons to become unstable and fire with intensive action and speed.

limbic system. A primitive part of the brain, which contains structures that respond to emotional input and can respond chemically to those responses at an unconscious level.

long term memory. A system in the human brain to allow identification of the location, access, and recall of significant learning and events.

long term potentiation (LTP). The chemical possibility that information or actions will be remembered. The potential chemical is further identified as the function of the protein PKM-zeta.

medulla. A structure in the primitive part of the brain, the limbic system, that helps with the automatic processing of normal body functions.

microstructures. Neuron and glial cells functioning at the electrical and chemical level during connections among brain systems, which are foundational to learning.

midbrain. Structures in the interior part of the brain, often considered the mammalian brain, that respond to input from the environment that could be a danger or opportunity. Included in this area are the thalamus, amygdala, hippocampus, and hypothalamus.

mind. The directed actions and behaviors that result from the working of the physical structure, the brain. Human actions and reactions are a result of the brain's functions—but apart from it.

mirror neurons. A specific type of neuron present in the hippocampus that allows a person to activate brain areas while watching another person, as if the observer is performing the action.

monolingual. Being able to speak one language with competence.

motor cortex. This may be called the *motor strip*—the motor cortex sends messages to other parts of the body for movements that result from conscious thought.

myelination. A maturation process in structures and areas of the human brain where one type of glial cell wraps itself around axons and results in speedy transmission of neuron connections.

nerve fibers. Appendages from neurons that allow these cells to connect and communicate to make neural networks for memory and remembering.

neurons. Nerve cells, microstructures in the brain that contain a nucleus, a single axon, and large numbers of dendrites to interact and connect with each other and form neural networks.

neuroanatomy. A study of the structures of the central nervous system (the brain and the spinal cord) and the peripheral nervous system (the nerves in the cranium and spinal cord), which carries information throughout the body.

neuroeducation. A new field of study combining the work of neuroscience, cognitive psychology, and education.

neurogenesis. The birth of new neurons in the brain. Neuroscientists have observed neuron generation in the hippocampus.

neuroimaging. Scientists use a variety of devices to look at the brain and gather information about it. The reports generated include graphs, images of tissue, identification of different areas of activation, or brain images showing a running sequence of how the brain acts during different thinking tasks. There are many different ways we can get information about the brain, its structures, systems, and functions through scanning and imaging.

neurophysiology. A study of the ways the brain's structures work together as a complex unit. This particular type of study examines brain activity when a specific task needs to be processed and for learning to occur.

neuroplasticity. The human brain's potential to build cognitive networks during childhood and beyond for lifetime learning potential.

neurotransmitters. Protein molecules that allow movement of information among the neurons. Molecules are released into the synaptic gap from a neuron when it becomes unbalanced. They are collected by a receptor on another neuron to allow molecular information to move from one neuron to the next.

nondeclarative memory. Memory consisting of habits and skills that have been practiced to the point that they can be performed automatically without conscious thought (procedural) or with a prompt (priming).

norepinephrine. A neurotransmitter that signals the sympathetic nervous system to improve alertness, attention, and mood.

occipital lobes. Areas of the brain located at the back of the cerebrum to receive and associate visual input with stored memory for visages.

oligodendrocytes. Glia cells in the brain that wrap around a neuron's axon to form a myelin sheath. When an axon has been myelinated by these cells, the speed of signals transmitted between neurons is enhanced.

omega-3 fatty acids. These proteins are brain chemicals. They come from foods containing these acids. When the proteins spill into the synapse, neurotransmitters are positively impacted, and there is more long term learning potentiation. Additionally, glial cells, which are fatty acids that coat a neuron's axon, may be positively impacted by intake of foods with omega-3 fatty acids.

oral language system. A system located in the parietal, occipital, and temporal lobes to receive auditory input and interpret it for spoken language and other communication sounds.

OTX 2 protein. This substance is sent when the visual processing system has completed its development. The retina of the eye sends the protein to other parts of the brain as a signal that visual input is coming that needs to be interpreted and stored.

parietal lobes. Areas of the cerebrum located in the cerebral cortex toward the back and in front of the occipital lobes. Their function involves language interpretation and sensing the status of the human body.

phoneme. The smallest sound of speech that corresponds to a particular letter or letters of an alphabetic writing system.

pia mater. A soft layer of membranes between the skull and the tissues of the brain. It is the third and last layer and is a Latin term meaning soft mother.

pineal gland. An endocrine gland located under the back end of the corpus callosum, which spews melatonin to respond to and adjust the circadian rhythm of the human body.

PKM-zeta protein. A protein that has been identified as the potential chemical for long term potentiation, LTP, for memory.

pons. Structures of the hindbrain that function to respond automatically to the needs of the body from input from the environment.

prefrontal lobes. These structures located at the foremost part of the cerebral cortex for executive function are considered to be the most recently evolved part of the brain.

reading system. A pathway of neural connections in the brain adapted from the oral language system to accommodate the process of reading.

sensory cortex. These areas in the somatosensory area of the brain function to receive and identify a combination of parietal (touch), occipital (sight), and temporal (hearing) input.

sensory memory. A system that is identified by name but is unidentifiable in location in the brain. The operation of this system occurs at various places in the brain depending upon the sense that receives input. Most input is ignored and is not remembered.

serotonin. A neurotransmitter to regulate the signals at the brain stem and to police activities at every junction within the emotional center of the brain. It squelches overactive or out of control responses in many of the brain's systems.

somatosensory cortex. An area of the brain located in the foremost part of the parietal lobes to interpret sensory input. See Sensory Cortex.

sulcus. Shallow valleys located between gyri in the cerebral cortex (plural is *sulci*).

synapse. An infinitesimally small space between neurons where chemical neurotransmitters are exchanged to stimulate more neurons to become electrically charged.

technology. Any tool, invention, process, or method that allows people to progress a knowledge base beyond what individuals are able to do on their own. For the purposes of this book, the term *technology* equates to computers, media, handheld devices, and telecommunication applications.

temporal lobes. Areas of the cerebral cortex located above the ears to receive auditory input and interact with the parietal and occipital lobes for interpretation of sensory input.

thalamus. A central area of the midbrain to receive and filter input from the sensory cortex for danger prior to sending it back to the cerebral cortex for interpretation.

vermis. The curvy, winding, lacey area existing between the two hemispheres and occupying the zone adjacent to the cerebellum.

vestibular system. A sense that perceives body movement and location in time and space in reference to gravity and motion. It helps to maintain coordinated and smooth movement.

visual system. A pathway used by the cerebral cortex to receive images and associate them with memory of stored shapes for interpretation and identification.

white matter. Substance consisting of myelinated axons located below the exposed outer layer of the cerebral cortex.

working memory. A system of the learning process that holds and actively concentrates on a limited amount of information as it attempts to stimulate enough neuron activity to link it to what is already known.

References and
Further Reading

Adams, M. J. (2009). The challenge of advanced texts: The interdependence of reading and learning. In E. H. Hiebert (Ed.), *Reading more, reading better: Are American students reading enough of the right stuff?* New York: Guilford. Retrieved July 29, 2010, from http://www.childrenofthecode.org/library/MJA-Challengeof AdvancedTexts.pdf.

Adler, D. A., & Byrd, S. (Illustrator). (1992). *A picture book of Harriet Tubman.* New York: Scholastic, Inc.

Allen, J. (2009, March 19–21). *Real kids, real books, real reading, real results.* Presentation given at the Illinois Reading Council Conference, Reading! Engage! Excite! Ignite! Springfield, IL.

Allstate Insurance Company. (2007). *Why do most 16-year-olds drive like they're missing a part of their brain?* Northbrook, IL: Author.

American Psychological Association. (2009, May 21). Tying education to future goals may boost grades more than helping with homework. *ScienceDaily.* Retrieved July 21, 2010, from http://www.sciencedaily.com/releases/2009/05/090519434711.htm.

Antonacci, P. A., & O'Callaghan, C. M. (2010). *Developing content area literacy: 40 strategies for middle and secondary classrooms.* Thousand Oaks, CA: Sage.

Ayllon, C., Smith, P., & Morrillo, A. (2006). *Spanish composition through literature* (5th ed.). Upper Saddle River, NJ: Pearson/Prentice Hall.

Barnett, R. C. (2006, June 28). *Single-sex schools: A biological imperative.* Presentation given at the Co-Education Conference, Wellington College, UK.

Barnett, R., & Rivers, C. (2008, November 23). Differences should not drive a curriculum. *The Boston Globe.* Retrieved July 23, 2010, from http://www.boston.com/bostonglobe/editorial_opinion/oped/articles/2008/11/23/differences_should_not_drive_a_curriculum/.

Bell, N. (1991). *Visualizing and verbalizing for language comprehension and thinking.* San Luis Obispo, CA: Gander.

Berger, E. (2009, April 9). In science class, students are learning to hate science. *Houston Chronicle.* Retrieved July 21, 2010, from http://www.chron.com/disp/story.mpl/metropolitan/6367232.html.

Bernard, S. (2008). How to use performance-based learning in the classroom. *Edutopia, the best of cool schools project learning.* San Francisco: The George Lucas Educational Foundation.

Berninger V. W., & Richards, T. L. (2002). *Brain literacy for Educators and Psychologists.* San Diego, CA: Academic Press.

Blankenburg, F., Taskin, B., Ruben, J., Moosmann, M., Ritter, P., Curio, G., et al. (2003, March 21). Imperceptible stimuli and sensory processing impediment. *Science, 299*(5614), 1864.

Bonnet, M. H., & Arand, D. L. (1995). We are chronically sleep deprived. *Sleep, 18,* 908–911.

Braiker, B. (2007). *Your igloo or mine? Web sites like Club Penguin have introduced social networking to children.* Retrieved July 21, 2010, from http://www.clubpenguin.com/parents/downloads/your-igloo-mine.pdf.

Buster, S. (2008). *Training with the brain in mind: A study of brain-compatible strategies and their relationship to elementary grades K–6 teacher professional development.* Ann Arbor, MI: ProQuest.

Byrd, J. (2004). Moms on the move: Practical solutions for busy lives (family meals in minutes). Uhrichsville, OH: Barbour.

Calamai, P. (2006). Committed to memory. *Brain in the News, 13*(11), 1–2.

Campbell, I. G., & Feinberg, I. (2009). Longitudinal trajectories of non-rapid eye movement delta and theta EEG as indicators of adolescent brain maturation. *Proceedings of the National Academy of Science, 106,* 5177–5180.

Cantion, J. F., Platt, M. L., & Brannon, E. M. (2009). Beyond the number domain. *Trends Cognitive Science, 13*(2), 83–91.

Carey, B. (2008, December 5). H. M., an unforgettable amnesiac, dies at 82. *New York Times.* Retrieved July 21, 2010, from http://www.nytimes.com/2008/12/05/us/05hm.html?scp=1&sq=H.%20M.,%20an%20unforgettable%20amnesiac,%20dies%20at%2082.%20&st=cse.

Carmichael, M. (2007). Stronger, faster, smarter. *Newsweek, 149*(13), 38–46.

Carter, R. (1998). *Mapping the mind.* Berkeley: University of California Press.

Caruana, V., & Hammer, C. G. (2007). *Brain food: Recipes for success in school, sports, and life.* Lanham, MD: M. Evans.

Cavanagh, S. (2009, January 28). Informal experiences can go a long way in teaching science. *Education Week.* Retrieved July 21, 2010, from http://www.edweek.org/login.html?source=http://www.edweek.org/ew/articles/2009/01/28/19informal.h28.html&destination=http://www.edweek.org/ew/articles/2009/01/28/19informal.h28.html&levelId=2100.

Center on Educational Policy. (2010, March 17). *State test score trends through 2007–08, part 5: Are there differences in achievement between boys and girls?* Retrieved July 21, 2010, from http://www.cep-dc.org/index.cfm?fuseaction=document_ext.showDocumentByID&nodeID=1&DocumentID=304.

Chaffee, J. (2009). *Thinking critically.* New York: Houghton Mifflin.

Claxton, C. S., & Murell, P. H. (1987). *Learning styles: Implications for improving educational practices.* Washington, DC: ERIC Clearning House for Higher Education.

Cloud, J. (2007, March 30). Parents relax. *Time in Partnership with CNN.* Retrieved July 21, 2010, from http://www.time.com/time/printout/0,8816,1604945,00.html.

Collins, J. L., & Gunning, T. G. (Eds.). (2010). *Building struggling students' higher level literacy, practical ideas, powerful solutions.* Newark, NJ: International Reading Association.

Curtis, D. (2003, September 24). From brain-based research to powerful learning: innovative teaching techniques in the classroom. *Edutopia.* Retrieved July 21, 2010, from http://www.edutopia.org/brain-based-research-powerful-learning.

Dahl, R. E. (2004). Adolescent brain development: A period of vulnerabilities and opportunities. *Annuals of the New York Academy of Science, 1021,* 1–22.

Dehaene, S. (1997). *The number sense, how the mind creates mathematics.* Oxford, UK: Oxford University Press.

Dehaene, S. (2009). *The science and evolution of a human invention, reading in the brain.* New York: The Penguin Group.

Desaulniers, M. (2008, August 11). How exercise improves learning: Spark: The revolutionary new science of exercise. *Suite101.Com.* Retrieved July 21, 2010, from http://mindbodyfitness.suite101.com/article.cfm/how_exercise_benefits_the_brain.

Diamond, M., & Hopson, J. (1998). *Magic trees of the mind: How to nurture your child's intelligence, creativity, and healthy emotions from birth through adolescence.* New York: Penguin.

Diaz, C. R., Pelletier C. M., & Provenzo, E. F., Jr. (2006). *Touch the future . . . TEACH!* Boston: Pearson Education & Allyn and Bacon.

Doidge, N. (2007). *The brain that changes itself: Stories of personal triumph from the frontiers of brain science.* New York: Penguin.

Dweck, C. (2007). Students who believe intelligence can be developed perform better than those who believe intelligence is fixed. *Society for Research in Child Development, 78*(1), 246–263.

Eliot, L. (1999). *What's going on in there?* New York: Bantam Books.

Eliot, L. (2009). *Pink brains, blue brains: How small differences grow into troublesome gaps—and what we can do about it.* New York: Houghton Mifflin Harcourt.

Epstein, R. (2007). The myth of the teen brain. *Scientific American Mind, 18*(2), 56–63.

Even, M. J. (1987). Why adults learn in different ways. *Lifelong Learning: An Omnibus of Practice and Research, 10*(8), 22–27.

Fallone, G. (2010). Sleep and children's physical health: Biological factors that affect sleep, societal factors, effects of insufficient sleep. *Educational encyclopedia.* Retrieved July 24, 2010, from http://education .stateuniversity.com/pages/2422/Sleep-Children-s-Physical-Health.html#ixzz0uWTCmtBd.

Feigenson, L. (2006). Continuity of format and computation in short-term memory development. In L. Oakes & P. Bauer (Eds.), *Short- and long-term memory in early childhood: Taking the first steps toward remembering* (pp. 51–73). Oxford, UK: Oxford University Press.

Fewer, K. (n.d.). *Adolescence: an anthropological inquiry, Schegal and Barry.* Retrieved July 21, 2010, from http://www.stthomasu.ca/~parkhill/rite101/ireps/adoles.htm.

Fischer, K. (2004). The myths and promises of the learning brain. *HGSE News.* Retrieved July 21, 2010, from http://www.gse.harvard.edu/news/features/fischer12012004.html.

Fisher, D., & Frey, N. (2008). Instructional moves that support adolescent learners who have histories of failure. In K. A. Hinchman & H. K. Sheridan-Thomas (Eds.), *Best practices in adolescent literacy instruction* (pp. 261–274). New York: The Guilford Press.

Fitch, K. G. (2010). New voices: Get students to read (and think) like content specialists. *ASCD express, 5*(511). Retrieved July 21, 2010, from http://www.ascd.org/ascd_express/vol5/511_newvoices.aspx.

Foorman, B. (2007, May 13). Text difficulty and assessment: The role of text in comprehending written language. Presentation given at the International Reading Association meeting, Toronto, ON, Canada. Retrieved July 21, 2010, from http://www.fcrr.org/staffpresentations/Foorman/IRA_Hiebert%20symposiumA_Toronto_May_13_2007.pdf.

Foreman, J. (2002). The evidence speaks well of bilingualism's effect on kids. *The Brain in the News, 9*(19), 2.

Gallistel, C. R., & Gelman, R. (2000). Non-verbal numerical cognition: From reals to integers. *Trends in Cognitive Sciences, 4,* 59–65.

Gazzaniga. M. (2008). Arts and cognition: Findings hint at relationships. In J. Nevins & D. Gordon (Eds.), *The 2008 progress report on brain research* (pp. 7–11). New York: The Dana Press.

Giedd, J. (2004). Structural magnetic resonance imaging of the adolescent brain. *New York Academy of Science, 1021,* 77–85. Retrieved July 21, 2010, from http://intramural.nimh.nih.gov/research/pubs/giedd05.pdf.

Greenfield, S. (2000). *Brain story.* London: BBC Worldwide Limited.

Gurian, M. (2001). *Boys and girls learn differently! A guide for teachers and parents.* San Francisco: Jossey-Bass.

Halberda, J., Mazzocco, M. M., & Feigenson, L. (2008, October 2). Individual differences in non-verbal number acuity correlate with maths achievement. *Nature, 455,* 665–669. Retrieved July 21, 2010, from http://www.psy.jhu.edu/~halberda/publications/HalberdaEtAl2008,Nature.pdf.

Halpern, D. F., Benbow, C. P., Heary, D. C., Gur, R. C., Shibley Hyde, J., & Gernsbacher, M. A. (2008). Sex, math and scientific achievement: Why do men dominate the fields of science, engineering and mathematics? *Scientific American Mind, 18*(6), 44–51.

Hamilton, J. (2008, October 2). Think you're multitasking? Think again. *Morning Edition, National Public Radio, Inc* [Radio broadcast]. Retrieved July 21, 2010, from http://www.npr.org/templates/story/story.php?storyId= 95256794.

Hensch, T. (2008, September). Trigger for brain plasticity identified. *ChildrensNews.* Retrieved July 27, 2010, from http://www.childrenshospital.org/chnews/09-01-08/research_0908.html.

Hernandez, N. (2008, October 28). Learning about learning: Brain research may produce results in the classroom. *The Washington Post,* HE1.

Hesman, T. (2006, January 3). Trouble and the teen brain: Research shows mental health problems begin in adolescence, a fact with broad implications for just about everyone. *The Santa Rosa, California, Press Democrat,* Life and Health, 1–2.

Hickman Brynie, F. H. (1998). *101 questions your brain has asked about itself but couldn't answer . . . until now.* Brookfield, CT: Millbrook Press.

Hilts, P. J. (2009). Stolen memory: With Henry's tragedy . . . came new knowledge. *Brain in the News, 16*(1), 4.

Hinchman, K. A., & Sheridan-Thomas, H. K. (2008). *Best practices in adolescent literacy instruction.* New York: The Guilford Press.

Holt, J. (2008, March 3). Numbers guy, are our brains wired for math? *The New Yorker.* Retrieved July 21, 2010, from http://www.newyorker.com/reporting/2008/03/03/080303fa_fact_holt?printable=true.

Hyerle, D. (2004). Thinking maps as a transformational language for learning. In D. Hyerle, L. Alper, & S. Curtis, (Eds.), *Student successes with thinking maps* (pp. 1–16). Thousand Oaks, CA: Corwin.

Hyerle, D., Alper, L., & Curtis, S. (2004). *Student successes with thinking maps.* Thousand Oaks, CA: Corwin.

Iacoboni, M. (2008). *Mirroring people: The new science of how we connect with others.* New York: Farrar, Straus and Giroux.

International Reading Association. (2006). *Standards for middle and high school literacy coaches.* Retrieved July 21, 2010, from http://www.reading.org/downloads/resources/597coaching_standards.pdf.

Is technology producing a decline in critical thinking and analysis? (2009, January 29). *ScienceDaily.* Retrieved July 21, 2010, from http://www.sciencedaily.com /releases/2009/01/090128092341.htm.

Jaschik, S. (2007, January 26). A stand against Wikipedia. *Inside Higher Ed.* Retrieved July 21, 2010, from http://www.insidehighered.com/news/2007/01/26/wiki.

Jensen, F. (2007, November). *A briefing on the adolescent brain.* Presentation given at the annual meeting of the Society of Neuroscience, San Diego, CA.

Jones, R. (2007). Reading strategies for social studies. *Reading Quest.* Retrieved July 29, 2010, from http://www.readingquest.org/strat/home.html.

Joshi, R. M., Treiman, R, Carreker, S., & Moats, L. C. (2009). How words cast their spell: Spelling is an integral part of learning the language, not a matter of memorization. *American Educator, 32*(4), 6–16, 42.

Juel, C., & Deffes, R. (2004). Making words stick: What research says about reading. *Educational Leadership, 61,* 30–34.

Keller, T. A., & Just, M. A. (2009, December 10). Altering cortical connectivity: Remediation-induced changes in the white matter of poor readers. *Neuron.* Retrieved July 21, 2010, from http://www.psy.cmu.edu/news/news_ 2009_12_10.pdf.

Kolb, L., Myers, R., Soloway, E., & Norris, C. (2009). Cell phones as instructional tools. Retrieved July 23, 2009, from http://event.on24.com.

LeDoux, J. (2002). *Synaptic self: How our brains become who we are.* New York: Viking, the Penguin Group.

Lenhart, A., Kahne, J., Middaugh, E., Macgill, A. R., Evans, C., & Vitak, J. (2008). Teens, video games and civic engagement. *Pew/Internet & American Life Project.* Retrieved July 21, 2010, from http://www.pewinternet.org/Reports/2008/Teens-Video-Games-and-Civics.aspx.

Levine, A. (2008). Unmasking memory genes: Molecules that expose our genes may also revive our recollections and our ability to learn. *Scientific American Mind, 19*(3), 48–51.

Litman, C., & Greenleaf, C. (2008). Traveling together over difficult ground: Negotiating success with a profoundly inexperienced reader in an introduction to chemistry class. In K. A. Hinchman & H. K. Sheridan-Thomas (Eds.), *Best practices in adolescent literacy instruction* (pp. 275–296). New York: The Guilford Press.

Lyon, G. R., & Krasnegor, N. A. (2001). *Attention, memory, and executive function.* Baltimore, MD: Paul H. Brookes.

Mauk, B. (2009). Music training changes brain networks. *The Brain in the News, 16*(5), 1–2.

McCollough, A. W., & Vogel, E. K. (2008). Your inner spam filter: What makes you so smart? Might be your lizard brain. *Scientific American Mind, 19*(3), 74–77.

McGinnis, J. R., & Roberts-Harris, D. (2009). A new vision for teaching science. *Scientific American Mind, 20*(5), 62–67.

McKhann, G. (2008). Once more into the scanner. *Brain in the News, 15*(11), 3.

McNab, F., & Klingberg, T. (2008, October 10). Prefrontal cortex and basal ganglia control access to working memory. *Nature Neuroscience.* Retrieved July 21, 2010, from http://www.nature.com/neuro/journal/v11/n1/full/nn2024.html.

Morrison, G. S. (2006). *Teaching in America.* Boston: Pearson Education & Allyn and Bacon.

Moskowitz, C. (2008, September 8). Humans have astonishing memories, study finds. *LiveScience.* Retrieved July 27, 2010, from http://www.livescience.com/health/080908-detailed-memory.html.

The National Governors' Association Center for Best Practices. (2005). *Reading to achieve: A governor's guide to adolescent literacy.* Retrieved July 25, 2010, from http://carnegie.org/fileadmin/Media/Publications/PDF/0510GOVGUIDELITERACY.PDF.

Neergaard, L. (2009). Unraveling how children become bilingual so easily. *Brain in the News, 16*(8), 6.

Nevills, P., & Wolfe, P. (2009). *Building the reading brain* (2nd ed.). Thousand Oaks, CA: Corwin.

Niogi, S. N., & McCandliss, B. D. (2006). Left lateralized white matter microstructure accounts for individual differences in reading ability and disability. *Neuropsychologia, 44*(11), 2178–2188.

Nolte, J. (2002). *The human brain: An introduction to its functional anatomy* (5th ed.). St. Louis, MO: Mosby.

Orlich, D. C., Harder, R. J., Callahan, R. C., Trevisan, M. S., & Brown, A. H. (2007). *Teaching strategies: A guide to effective instruction.* Boston: Houghton Mifflin.

Ormrod, J. E. (2008). *Educational psychology: Developing learners.* Boston: Pearson Education & Merrill/Prentice Hall.

Parker-Hope, T. (2009). The 3 R's? A fourth is crucial, too: Recess. *New York Times.* Retrieved July 21, 2010, from http://www.nytimes.com/2009/02/24/health/24well.html?

Patoine, B. (2008). Teen brain's ability to learn can have a flip side. *Brain Work, the Neuroscience Newsletter, 17*(6), 1–2.

Pence, K. L., & Justice, L. M. (2008). *Language development from theory to practice.* Upper Saddle River, NJ: Pearson Education & Merrill/Prentice Hall.

Piazza, M, & Izard, V. (2009). How humans count: Numerosity and the parietal cortex. *Neuroscientist, 15*(3), 261–273.

Pinker, S. (1997). *How the mind works.* New York: W. W. Norton.

Poldrack, R. A., & Rodriguez, P. (2003). Sequence learning: What's the hippocampus to do? *Neuron.* Retrieved July 21, 2010, from http://www.poldracklab.org/Publications/pdfs/Neuron%202003%20Poldrack.pdf/view.

Poldrack, R. A., & Rodriguez, P. (2004). How do memory systems interact? Evidence from human classification and learning. *Neurobiology of Learning and Memory, 82,* 324–332.

Price, L. F. (2005). The biology of risk taking. *Educational Leadership, 62*(7), 22–26.

Ratey, J. J., & Hagerman, E. (2009). *Spark: The revolutionary new science of exercise and the brain.* New York: Little, Brown and Company.

Sabbagh, L. (2006). The teen brain hard at work: No, really! *Scientific American Mind, 17*(4), 20–25.

Scherer, M. (2002). Do students care about learning? A conversation with Mihaly Csikszentmihalyi. *Educational Leadership, 60*(1), 12–17.

Schlosser, A. (2008). *Keep boys and girls together in the classroom to optimize learning, research suggests. Science Daily.* Retrieved July 29, 2010, from http://www.sciencedaily.com/releases/2008/04/080411150856.htm.

Schwartz, J., & Begley, S. (2003). *The mind & the brain: Neuroplasticity and the power of mental force.* New York: HarperCollins.

Sears, W., & Sears, M. (2009, September 29). Family nutrition: Brain foods. *AskDrSears.Com.* Retrieved July 29, 2010, from http://www.askdrsears.com/html/4/T040400.asp.

Shaywitz, S. (2003). *Overcoming dyslexia: A new and complete science-based program for reading problems at any level.* New York: Alfred A. Knopf.

Sloan, W. (2010, March 18). Analyzing the issues, gender in the classroom. *ASCD Express.* Retrieved July 21, 2010, from http://www.ascd.org/ascd_express/vol5/512_sloan.aspx.

Small, G., & Vorgan, G. (2008). Meet your ibrain: How the technologies that have become a part of our daily lives are changing the way we think. *Scientific American Mind, 19*(5), 42–49.

Society for Neuroscience. (2007, November 7). Mirror, mirror in the brain: Mirror neurons, self-understanding and autism research. *ScienceDaily* Retrieved March 4, 2009, from http://www.sciencedaily.com/releases/2007/11/071106123725.htm.

Sorgen, C. (2006). Add these "superfoods" to your daily diet, and you will increase your odds of maintaining a healthy brain for the rest of your life. *WebMD.* Retrieved July 21, 2010, from http://www.webmd.com/diet/guide/eat-smart-healthier-brain?

Stickgold, R., & Wehrwein, P. (2009). Sleep now, remember later: Researchers are exploring the mysterious and important links between memory and slumber. *Newsweek.* Retrieved July 21, 2010, from www.newswek.com/id/194650/output/print.

Structure more effective in high school science classes, study reveals. (2009, March 25). *ScienceDaily.* Retrieved July 21, 2010, from http://www.sciencedaily.com/releases/2009/03/090326114415.htm.

Sukel, K. (2008). Brain responds quickly to faces. *The Neuroscience Newsletter, 18*(5), 1, 4.

Sylwester, R. (2005). *How to explain a brain: An educator's handbook of brain terms and cognitive processes.* Thousand Oaks, CA: Corwin.

Ten top tips for teaching with new media. (2009). *Edutopia.* Retrieved July 21, 2010, from http://www.edutopia.org/node/6660/done?sid=160515.

Thompson, A. (2009, May 18). Child brains organized differently than adult brains. *Live Science.* Retrieved July 21, 2010, from http://www.livescience.com/health/090518-child-brain.html.

Thompson, A. (2009). Children's brains are organized differently than adults' brains. *Brain in the News, 16*(6), 1–2.

Toepel, U. (2009, February 16). The brain's fatty food radar. *British Psychological Society Research Digest Blog.* Retrieved July 21, 2010, from http://bps-research-digest.blogspot.com/2009/02/brains-fatty-food-radar.html.

Tomlinson, C. A. (2002). Invitations to learn. *Educational Leadership, 60*(1), 7–10.

Tomlinson, C. A., & McTighe, J. (2006). *Integrating differentiated instruction and understanding by design.* Alexandria, VA: Association for Supervision and Curriculum Development.

Tremmel, P. V. (2009). Taking up music so you can hear. *The Brain in the News, 16*(9), 8.

Tribole, E. (2004). *Eating on the run.* Champaign, IL: Human Kinetics.

Trotter, A. (2009, January 9). Mobile devices seen as key to 21st-century learning. *Education Week's Digital Directions, 2*(4). Retrieved July 21, 2010, fromhttp://www.edweek.org/dd/articles/2009/01/09/04mobile.h02.html?qs=cellphones.

Valeo, T. (2007). Sturdier brain networks may help children resist peer pressure. *Brain in the News, 14*(9), 8.

Wallis, C. (2004). What makes teens tick. *Time, 163*(19), 56–65.

WestEd. (2009). Science and mathematics education solutions. *WestEd.org.* Retrieved July 23, 2010, from http://www.wested.org/cs/we/view/serv/84.

Whitlock, J. R., Heyman, A. J., Shuler, M. G., & Bear, M. F. (2006). Learning produces long term potentiation in the hippocampus. *Science, 313*(5790), 1093–1097.

Whitmire, R. (2010, March 12). Whitmire: New data on how far boys are falling behind. *Washington Post.* Retrieved July 21, 2010, from http://voices.washingtonpost.com/answer-sheet/guest-bloggers/whitmire-new-evidence-on-how-f.html.

Wilber, D. J. (2008). iLife: Understanding and connecting to the digital literacies of adolescents. In K. A. Hinchman & H. K. Sheridan-Thomas (Eds.), *Best practices in adolescent literacy instruction* (pp. 57–77). New York: The Guilford Press.

Willingham, D. T. (2008–2009). What will improve a student's memory? *American Educator, 44,* 17–25.

Willingham, D. T. (2009). What will improve a student's memory? *American Educator, 32*(4), 17–25.

Wise, B. (2008). High Schools at the tipping point. *Educational Leadership, 65*(8), 8–13.

Wolf, M. (2007). *Proust and the squid.* New York: HarperCollins.

Wolfe, P. (2001). Brain matters: Translating research into classroom practice. Alexandria, VA: Association for Supervision and Curriculum Development.

Wolpert, S. (2008, July 9). Scientists learn how what you eat affects your brain—and those of your kids. *UCLA Newsroom.* Retrieved July 21, 2010, from http://newsroom.ucla.edu/portal/ucla/scientists-learn-how-food-affects-52668.aspx.

Woolfolk, A. (2008). *Educational psychology: Active learning edition.* Boston: Pearson Educational and Allyn & Bacon.

The Writing Lab, The OWL at Purdue, & Purdue University. (1995–2010). General APA guidelines. *OWL: Purdue online writing lab.* Retrieved July 25, 2010, from http://owl.english.purdue.edu/owl/resource/560/01/.

Yurgelun-Todd. D. (2002). Inside the teenage brain. *Frontline.* Retrieved July 21, 2010, from http://www.pbs.org/wgbh/pages/frontline/shows/teenbrain/interviews/todd.html.

Index